12286

JF
51
.Z5

Zink, Harold

Government in wartime
Europe.

ISSUED TO

DATE DUE

JF
51
.Z5

12286

Zink, Harold
Government in War-
time Europe.

Government in Wartime Europe

GOVERNMENT IN
WARTIME EUROPE

Edited by

HAROLD ZINK
DePauw University

and

TAYLOR COLE
Duke University

REYNAL & HITCHCOCK : NEW YORK

PRINTED IN THE UNITED STATES OF AMERICA
BY THE CORNWALL PRESS, CORNWALL, N. Y.

IN MEMORIAM
ROBERT C. BROOKS
1874-1941

*Distinguished Scholar, Able Teacher,
Beloved Colleague*

Preface

THE European Affairs sessions of the 1940 meeting of the American Political Science Association were devoted to a survey of the effects of the war on the political institutions of the several European countries. The contents of this book are the outgrowth of the papers and discussion which were presented in that connection, but, needless to say, there has been a great deal of expansion, additional attention to organization, and general revision in bringing the material up-to-date. As they now stand, the various sections of this book were planned and prepared for the use of students in university courses dealing with European governments, comparative government, current European politics, and related subjects, as well as for laymen who seek to inform themselves as to what has taken place behind the war scene.

This collection of studies does not claim to bring to the reader every official document relating to government and politics which has appeared in Europe since the outbreak of hostilities. The quantity of such material would make such a book formidable to begin with; furthermore, the censorship prevailing in many countries has not permitted all documents to reach the United States. However, the editors believe that the several sections of this book have been prepared by men who are as competent both from a scholarly standpoint and from familiarity with current European affairs as any in the United States. Despite the difficulties necessarily attendant upon the preparation of such studies, the editors feel that reasonable coverage has been achieved and that a high degree of objectiveness has been maintained.

In general, the greatest changes have taken place in the governments of France, Norway, and the Balkan states; indeed the rapidly changing scene has made it difficult if not impossible to present more than a general picture of these governments. It is a tribute to the strength of democratic traditions in England that healthy criticism can be made of her institutions, both inside and outside her frontiers. On the other hand, the facade presented by the rigid censorship in the totalitarian states does not permit either a detailed examination of the functioning of their institutions or a complete discussion of the inherent weaknesses that are present.

We wish to express our appreciation to Professor W. Brooke Graves, 1940 program chairman of the American Political Science Association, and to Professor Grayson Kirk of Columbia University for his careful reading of galley proofs and his many helpful suggestions.

H. Z.
T. C.

May, 1941

Contents

CHAPTER

    I. The Government of England in Wartime . .   I
       BY EUGENE PARKER CHASE, Lafayette College

    II. Policy and Administration in Wartime England 43
       BY W. HARDY WICKWAR, Rockford College

    III. The Effects of the War on the Government of Germany 74
       BY FRITZ MORSTEIN MARX, Queens College

    IV. Wartime Theories and Policies of the Third Reich 101
       BY TAYLOR COLE, Duke University

    V. The Impact of the War on Soviet Political and Economic Institutions 120
       BY JOHN N. HAZARD, Institute of Current Affairs and Columbia University

    VI. The Impact of the Second World War on Italian Fascism 145
       BY WILLIAM EBENSTEIN, University of Wisconsin

    VII. French Government under Pétain 171
       BY J. G. HEINBERG, University of Missouri

CHAPTER

VIII. The Impact of World War II on the Balkans   188
    BY JOSEPH S. ROUCEK, Hofstra College

IX. The Effects of the War on the Governments
      of Norway and Sweden. 205
    BY A. G. RONHOVDE, Rutgers University

Notes 221

Index 241

Government in Wartime Europe

CHAPTER I

The Government of England in Wartime

BY EUGENE PARKER CHASE

Lafayette College

D URING the war which began in September, 1939, the English government has pursued two aims—to wage war and to preserve for England the type of popular free government known as the parliamentary system. Its success in the attainment of these aims, during the first eighteen months of the war, suggests an analysis which will be devoted in part to institutions and in part to policies.

The war was planned, by the Chamberlain government, in almost conscious imitation of the war of 1914. This was natural, since the elder statesmen of 1939 had been the middle-aged men of 1914, and the habit of all governments is to imitate. In some respects the early history of the war might have been more satisfactory, and the rulers of England might have faced the new war with a greater sense of reality, had not the other war occurred so short a time before. Critically-minded observers must remember, however, that the government of Mr. Chamberlain, in spite of its huge parliamentary majority, rested upon a delicate and easily disturbed balance of domestic political forces. A government pledged, like Mr. Chamberlain's, to conserve old social and economic values, must try to obviate any considerable change. Changes are more nearly inevitable in wartime than in peace. To move slowly, and to disturb as little as possible, were the natural and proper aims of the government that found itself pressed to extreme measures in September, 1939. This policy of Mr. Chamberlain's government, combined with the failure of Germany to attack England as soon as war began, proved to be conditions that facilitated the maintenance of parliamentary government in England and made possible the preservation of pre-war economic and political systems, with modifications which have destroyed some of their accidents but not their essence.[1]

On the side of the direct domestic preparation for war the touch was sure and safe, if a trifle old-fashioned. Many things that had proved necessary in the last war would be done at— or even before—the start of the new war. The Committee of Imperial Defense, and the government departments, had filled their pigeon-holes with a mass of draft statutes, Orders in Council, and regulations. As soon as the war was imminent, these draft statutes, orders, and regulations were pulled out and enacted, approved, and made.[2]

Let us look first at the preparations to refight 1914 but to do it better.

The Armed Forces

There was no doubt, hesitation, or delay as to methods of recruiting the armed forces. The Military Service Act, 1939, which became law on May 25, had provided for three years of enforced enlistment of British subjects of the ages of 20 to 21 resident in Great Britain. Residents of Northern Ireland were excluded because of Eire's disapproval. The National Service (Armed Forces) Act, 1939, passed on September 3, repealed this act (but only for the duration of the war, which conscription is to survive) and allowed conscription of men between 18 and 41. Under the National Service Act men are

called up by age-groups, being required to register themselves
on a particular day and to report for service, unless exempted,
about two months later. By February 22, 1941, the age-groups
from 18 to 36 had registered under the act. Extensive and
numerous exemptions are provided for. There is an official
schedule of reserved occupations, and all men included within
it are automatically exempted. This schedule was at first very
inclusive, indeed, and was not narrowed until the autumn of
1940. Subsequently modifications have removed certain occupations from the schedule altogether, and have limited the
exemption for other scheduled occupations to men over a
certain age, which in most cases is 30. The act does not authorize conscription for non-military purposes.

Both the Military Service Act and the National Service Act
include arrangements for conscientious objectors, which are
more forthright and more easily administered than those in
force during the war of 1914. Men registering as conscientious
objectors are put on a special register, so that each case may
be heard by a local tribunal, subject to appeal to a central
tribunal. The tribunal has three options: to remove men from
the special register, to assign them to non-combatant work,
or to exempt them from military service altogether. Though
the number of men registering as conscientious objectors has
increased greatly since the war of 1914, it has been as low as
one-half of one percent in some age-groups, and has not
seemed a threat to a political system organized on the basis of
compulsion. These circumstances, combined with the comparative lack of urgency in the need for army recruits, have
made it possible for the government to achieve a distinct success in the handling of a problem which is of considerable
political importance.

Under other acts passed in either May or September of
1939, reserve and auxiliary forces were called into the service

of the crown or found their periods of enlistment extended. The Reserve and Auxiliary Forces Act, 1939, enacted on May 25 for three years, permits the government to call out reserve and auxiliary forces at its discretion, and without public proclamation. The Royal Marines Act, 1939, of September 5, permits the government to extend the period for the enlistment of marines. The Military and Air Forces (Prolongation of Service) Act, 1939, of September 5, and the Armed Forces (Conditions of Service) Act, 1939, of September 1, extend the period of enlistment for the designated services for the duration of the emergency, and give the authorities control over the use of enlisted men in all the services.

The necessary control over the population preliminary to any general compulsion for military or civil purposes was provided in the National Registration Act, 1939, of September 5. This act established a national register for the duration of the emergency, and authorized the issuance of registration cards. The register was made on September 29. It is used as a check for military registration, for the issuance of food ration books, and potentially "to meet all the contingencies of war conditions." [3] It was supplemented by special registration of aliens under the Aliens Order, 1939.[4] By an order of February, 1941, under the Defense Acts, special registers of men required to engage in fire-fighting may be established under the authority of the Regional Commissioners.

EMERGENCY POWERS DEFENSE ACTS

Within the non-military field control of the whole business of everyday life was taken by the Emergency Powers (Defense) Act, 1939, passed in all its stages on August 24. This act provides, fundamentally, for the government of Englishmen by administrative order rather than by statute. Under it,

the King in Council makes such regulations as he thinks necessary or expedient for securing the public safety, the defense
of the realm, the maintenance of public order, the provision
of supplies and services necessary to the community, and the
efficient prosecution of "any war in which His Majesty may
be engaged."

During the war of 1914 the domestic affairs of Englishmen
had been regulated under the Defense of the Realm Act, popu-
larly known as DORA. Under this act officials had exercised
regulatory and inquisitional powers, thought in those days to
be characteristic of continental rather than of English methods
of government. Objections rose out of opposition not to the
purposes which the act was intended to secure, but to the unreasonable nature of the regulations and the arbitrary character of their administration. Political and legal commentators,
after the war, argued that the popular disapproval of wartime
had been largely justified. But "government by order" had
become a commonplace since the last war, and the government in 1939 assumed as a matter of course that it could not
administer the country, in wartime, without quasi-dictatorial
powers.

The Emergency Powers (Defense) Act of 1939 is best described, by those who lived under or have studied the Defense
of the Realm Act, as a "bigger and better" DORA. The act
of 1939 goes much further than that of 1914. Almost every
power that the courts, between 1914 and 1919, had found
that DORA had failed to give, the act of 1939 specifically
bestowed.[5] In addition to providing for the regulation of almost every aspect of daily life, the act extends to the punishment of persons or to their detention at the discretion of the
Secretary of State.[6]

This power has been used to detain indefinitely not only
Sir Oswald Mosley and a number of other leaders of the Brit-

ish Union of Fascists, but even one member of parliament, Captain Archibald Ramsay. It allows the control of any property in the name of the Crown, and the acquisition of any property other than land.

The Act did not authorize the imposition of compulsory service whether military or industrial, nor the trial of persons not subject to military law by any other than the regular courts. During the year, these two lacunae were filled. The Emergency Powers (Defense) Act, 1940, passed in all stages on May 22, empowers the making of regulations "for requiring persons to place themselves, their services and their property at the disposal of His Majesty as appears to be necessary or expedient for securing the public safety" and the other purposes of the act of 1939. This act permits industrial conscription and the military conscription of conscientious objectors and other groups omitted in the National Service Act. It appears to give the government no powers over property which the government did not already possess. The Emergency Powers (Defense) (No. 2) Act, 1940, passed on August 1, permits the establishment of special courts, though not of courts-martial, for the trial of persons not under military law. It provides for the creation of new offenses, which may be punishable even by death.[7] The Treachery Act, 1940, passed during a fear of imminent invasion in the spring of 1940, provides the death penalty for acts of espionage and sabotage done with intent to help the enemy. Under the three Defense Acts the King in Council may apparently do anything but acquire the ownership of land, borrow money, or levy taxes.[8]

From the technical point of view it is noteworthy that the Defense Acts provide for the making of orders, which may provide for the making of regulations (under the orders), which may in turn provide for the making of regulations under the regulations—delegated legislation extending to the third degree. Orders under the Acts may, of course, modify Acts of Parliament. Regulations under the Acts must be laid before Parliament, which might reject them but may not amend them. So far is the principle of delegated legislation extended that even the administrative control of the orders and regulations tends to be no more than formal. Many of the less important orders are not published even as a matter of record.

The first Defense Act was passed at the instance of the government by Parliament specially recalled from recess for that purpose on August 24, 1939, and such opposition as may have existed was neither organized nor vocal. The second Defense Act was passed enthusiastically under critical conditions in May, 1940. The third Defense Act, passed on August 1, 1940, was resisted strenuously by a considerable and varied minority of the House of Commons, and greatly amended before it was passed. Orders under the Acts have never received formal parliamentary disapproval. But a public campaign of protest was waged in the autumn of 1939 against some of the orders that were most restrictive of individual liberties. The matter was raised in Parliament, and the Home Secretary yielded to the protests and modified some of the orders.[9] Sporadic complaints of unreasonable application of the orders have been made, but in general, until the suppression of the *Daily Worker* in January, 1941, the government exercised such consideration for susceptibilities as to avoid all grounds for complaint. It is not pretended by the government that the rule of law in the historic senses in which the phrase was used by Dicey is maintained. The most acute analyst of the emergency legislation points out that the two traditional safeguards of the liberties of the subject are lacking—a careful limitation of the special powers granted, and internal checks to secure that the limitations are effective.[10] Under the Defense Acts neither of these safeguards exists. But Jennings maintains that a more fundamental basis of the rule of law continues to exist and is sufficient—the supervision of Parliament. Whatever the validity of this *ad hoc* argument, it is strikingly true that parliamentary scrutiny and intervention have served to keep within very reasonable limits the use of the unprecedented powers which the government has exercised.[11]

CIVIL DEFENSE AND EVACUATION

The expectation that war, if it should come, would be opened by heavy and constant air attacks on Great Britain caused the passage of the Air-Raid Precautions Act, 1937, supplemented on July 13, 1939, by the Civil Defense Act, 1939. These acts, supplemented after the war began by orders issued under the Emergency Powers (Defense) Act, authorize the Minister of Home Security to approve and enforce schemes submitted by local authorities for air-raid protection. The initiative is to come from the local authorities, but the minister possesses the power to step in if the local authorities do not perform their functions properly. Under these acts provision was made for air-raid shelters and for the creation of a force of air-raid wardens and helpers. This force, which has consisted both of full-time and of part-time workers, some on a volunteer and others on a paid basis, has given general satisfaction.[12] The provision of air-raid shelters, however, was the subject of a wrangle between the ministry and local authorities both as to the division of cost and in some cases as to the nature of construction. Plans for deep shelters were rejected by the ministry on the ground that such shelters were unnecessary and ineffective. After some weeks of air raids, in the autumn of 1940, the London tubes were opened as shelters, and plans for a future provision of deep shelters were made. Sir John Anderson, whose name was to become attached to the inadequate shelter officially recommended, became minister charged with responsibility for civil defense in 1938 and remained in that position until October, 1940. He was succeeded by Mr. Herbert Morrison, who had been a believer in deep shelters but who found himself unable to supply them immediately.[13]

For the administration of Air Raid Precautions, local government councils were asked to appoint Emergency Committees, to act instead of the council when, under conditions of attack, the council might be unable to function. At first, in pursuance of supposed government suggestion, these Emergency Committees began in some instances to exercise as quasi-dictators the entire peacetime functions of their councils. Another provision for the expected emergency was the division of the entire country into regions, each of which was put in charge of a regional commissioner. The expectation was that in time of emergency and of difficult communications these commissioners would exercise the authority of the central departments in their areas. Had the expected attack come at the beginning of the war, Emergency Committees and Regional Commissioners might have shared all power between them. But in the period of quiet that lasted so long, the ordinary local authorities continued or resumed their normal activities. Under defense regulations of August, 1940, the Regional Commissioners began to assume a general power to coordinate local defense activities.

As a further defense against attack from the air, comprehensive plans for evacuation had been made—particularly of government agencies and of school children. For the evacuation of children, the country was divided into three types of area—evacuation, neutral, and reception. Under slight legal

compulsion householders in reception areas were to be obliged
to receive children, school teachers, and in some cases mothers
from evacuation areas. On the first week end of September,
1939, the evacuation began. It was successful as far as it went,
but many children did not go at all, and during the quiet early
days of the war the return tide set in, to become a flood during the Christmas holidays. Another voluntary evacuation was
begun in September, 1940, but even that did not enlist the
support of all parents, so that 80,000 London school children
were still at home at the end of January, 1941.

To provide against prospective severance of communications and other difficulties of wartime administration, many
members of staffs of government departments and agencies,
and also such institutions as the constituent parts of London
University were also evacuated.[14]

Ample provision had been made for the accommodation
of civil servants, and for the staffs of the armed forces by the
commandeering of hotels and of school buildings, both public
and private. Hospitals were required to free a large proportion of their beds to leave space for military casualties. When
intensive warfare did not follow the declaration of war, many
commandeered premises went unused, but the original tenants
remained excluded. The problem of school children was the
most serious.

Other dislocations were less, though productive of inconvenience and economic loss. England was mobilized for war,
but her people and her economic life seemed immobilized.
A witty member of Parliament spoke of the *Sitzkrieg*, and
serious publications demanded the invention of new games
to alleviate the boredom of the blackout. For the first six or
eight months of the war, most Englishmen of responsible
position spent most of their time in the wrong places doing
the wrong things.[15]

Direction of Military Activities

After civil defense, the two great problems of government peculiar to wartime were the direction of military activities and the control of production and supply.

On the military side, the war of 1939 was not intended to be directed, nor has it been directed, either by Parliament or by the Cabinet. During the years 1916 to 1918, from which so many precedents were borrowed in 1939, the problem of who should direct the war was fought out by Mr. Lloyd George. Mr. Lloyd George, as prime minister, vindicated the principle of civilian control, but discovered that civilian control could not be exercised by even a small war cabinet; it must be exercised by the prime minister himself. Mr. Lloyd George's "War Cabinet" was actually a cabinet directing civilian affairs, and so was Mr. Chamberlain's war cabinet of 1939 and Mr. Churchill's of 1940. The direction of the war was in the hands of the prime minister.

This arrangement had not been arrived at without difficulty. Some years ago a demand had arisen for the coordination of the three independent service departments: the Admiralty, the War Office, and the Air Ministry. A Minister for the Coordination of Defense had been appointed, and given cabinet rank. But whether because of the strength of vested interests or the weakness of the minister himself, the service departments still went their several ways. When the war began in 1939, the Minister for the Coordination of Defense then in office was continued. On his retirement in April, 1940, he was not replaced, but Mr. Winston Churchill was appointed as "coordinator and senior service minister" to preside over the Ministerial Committee on Military Coordination. When Mr. Churchill became prime minister, he assumed also the title of Minister of Defense.[16] No service minister sits in his War

Cabinet, and the service departments have been entrusted to ministers who perhaps carry less weight than many of their colleagues.

The present arrangement for the direction of a war is the consummation of plans made a generation ago when the Committee of Imperial Defense was established. Agreeing that civilian control of wars was essential and that the cabinet was incompetent to exercise it, the Balfour and Asquith ministries of the early years of the century set up and continued the Committee of Imperial Defense, of which the Prime Minister is chairman and whose members are the heads of the fighting departments, the chiefs of staff of the fighting services, and other ministers at the discretion of the chairman. In times of peace, and particularly under Mr. Baldwin and Mr. Chamberlain, the committee had been comparatively inactive. In wartime it serves as the center of the direction of the war, a place in which the prime minister (who takes complete responsibility) can receive both civilian and military advice.[17] The one serious discussion in Parliament of the conduct of the war was the debate on the failure of the Norwegian adventure—an attack on the government for its political aims rather than for its military and naval failure.

PRODUCTION AND SUPPLY

In direct contrast to the way in which the military control of the war is centralized in the heart of the government, the control of economic affairs has been entrusted to a variety of authorities, both private and public, with little coordination among them.

It is a common, though not universal, assumption that modern war requires a high degree of government control over private business, that war is essentially socialistic at least in its immediate result. This result was avoided in England as far as possible, for the majority of those in power have been averse to socialization. But control of distribution, and in some cases of manufacture, was provided for in the earliest defense regulations. And in Defense Regulation No. 55 the government assumed "as much control over industry as the most 'advanced' socialist has ever sought." [18] Power was taken to prohibit certain types of transactions, to impose maximum prices, to license transactions, to requisition goods. Under the Regulations financial control extends to the issue of securities and dealing in them, to the control of currency, capital issues, gold, loans, and savings banks.[19] No change has occurred in the management of the ordinary business. But the control of each industry, or each unit, was put in the hands of a committee, and the committee was composed predominantly of managers chosen from the industry. The cartelization of British industry had progressed greatly since 1931; wartime control came close to granting the cartels complete power and independence. Even the supply of necessities for direct war purposes had to be largely the product of the voluntary efforts of the private producer.[20]

The result was a lack of enterprise in production and a sluggishness in supply.[21]

The Ministry of Supply, created in the summer of 1939, was filled by Dr. Leslie Burgin, a long-time protégé of Mr. Chamberlain. The Minister of Labor, who on the outbreak of the war became also Minister of National Service, was Mr. Ernest Brown, who likewise owed his position to his political availability and personal acceptability to the prime minister. The complaint heard early in the war, that economic affairs were not being organized as a whole, was answered by the appointment, on October 9, 1939, of Lord Stamp as Adviser on Economic Co-ordination to the Gov-

ernment—a part-time post, since Lord Stamp was to continue
as chairman of the L. M. S. railway. On October 13 Sir John
Gilmour, an experienced and successful office-holder, was appointed to the newly created Ministry of Shipping.[22] Within
this ministerial framework, in which so little change was made
at the beginning of the war, the production and supply of
necessities for war purposes was almost entirely the product
of the voluntary efforts of the private producer, a continuation of peacetime arrangements. Dr. Burgin and Mr. Brown
perhaps deserved some of the contemptuous criticism which
they received; nevertheless, the chief fault was not theirs but
the system's.

A change in the organization of production began in the
summer of 1940. Among the causes producing a reorganization in governmental methods was the discovery, disseminated
to the public by men returning from the Norwegian expedition, that the army was underequipped. The Churchill government, on coming into power, adopted the policy that supply,
for war purposes at least, must be organized in the national
interest—though the problem of organization remained as difficult as ever.

In the Churchill government as first constituted Mr. Ernest
Bevin became Minister of Labor and National Service, and
Mr. Herbert Morrison Minister of Supply. These two successful and respected leaders of the Labor party had ability,
initiative, and prestige. Lord Beaverbrook was made Minister
of Aircraft Production and brought energy into the most
important single field of production, gradually making up
for the laxity of previous heads of the air ministry, though
sometimes interfering with the efforts of other production
departments almost as important as his own. There remained,
however, a minimum of coordination of economic effort.
United direction was still attempted by sets of committees

and councils. The official organization during the summer and autumn of 1940 provided a committee in charge of each field of production effort. A Production Council, whose chairman was the Minister without Portfolio, Mr. Arthur Greenwood, was responsible for organization for war purposes, and for priorities. An Economic Policy Committee, under the same chairmanship, was (though only in theory) a general planning agency. A Food Policy Committee was presided over by the Lord Privy Seal, Mr. Attlee. These three committees were coordinated by the "Lord President's Committee," of which Mr. Chamberlain was chairman until his retirement. This committee was composed of the chairmen of the lesser committees, together with other members of the Cabinet.[23]

In spite of the improvement under the Churchill government, dissatisfaction continued. The ministerial changes on Mr. Chamberlain's retirement in October merely put Sir John Anderson in Mr. Chamberlain's place, shifted Mr. Morrison to Home Secretary, and put Sir Andrew Duncan into the post of Minister of Supply. Production remained inadequate and "planning" nonexistent. Several factors, at the end of 1940, brought the situation to a crisis. The war from the air had been held in check and plans could be made for the future. The government announced, in November, its need of a million more workers in war industries by August 1, 1941.[24] The government had full powers of industrial conscription under the Defense Acts and Regulations. But the Minister of National Service announced in December that "we are a democracy and we are determined to rely in the main on a great voluntary response." In preferring not to impose compulsion, the government was influenced by the fact that labor conditions were not good. Wages had not kept pace with the rise in the cost of living, with the result that the standard of living was appreciably depressed for many workers. Industry might be better organized. The government's arrangements for control were ineffective.[25] A deadlock lasted for weeks.

On January 6, 1941, a reorganization of production machinery was announced by the government. The previous committees were replaced by an Import Executive and a Production Executive. The former is presided over by the Minister of Supply, the second by the Minister of Labor. Each is a committee composed of five members of the Cabinet. The prime minister coordinates both Executives with the War Cabinet. The existing "Lord President's Committee" continues as a directing committee for the Import Executive, the Production Executive, and the committees on civil defense, home policy, and food policy.

On January 16 was published a report of the Select Committee of the House of Commons on National Expenditures urging immediate reduction in the hours of munitions workers, which had been extended almost indefinitely during the summer, and urging the three-shift system with a maximum weekly average of 60 hours. The Committee urged the use of compulsory powers to recruit and to train additional labor. On January 22, the government announced its acceptance of a plan for mobilization of labor by compulsory registration of age groups. A brilliant defense by the prime minister on January 23 secured parliamentary approval of the new departure.[26]

THE WAR CABINET

The formation of a War Cabinet was announced by Mr. Chamberlain on September 3, 1939, the day on which the war formally began. The War Cabinet was a presumed imitation of the similar institution created in 1916, and its existence, like that of the War Cabinet of 1916-1918, has been more for the value of the name than in its performance of a special political function. For Mr. Chamberlain always determined policy, with the help of his chosen advisers of the moment, and Mr. Churchill was to do the same. Nevertheless, the constitution of the War Cabinet and the ministerial changes in the large body of other ministers have been of importance in relation both to the nature of the government's policies and the efficiency with which they have been carried out. They have a much greater significance than mere changes in personnel would suggest.

Mr. Chamberlain's War Cabinet began its life with nine members. It included the Prime Minister, the Chancellor of the Exchequer, the Foreign Secretary, the Minister for the Coordination of Defense, the three "defense" ministers, the Lord Privy Seal, and a Minister without Portfolio. In April, 1940, it lost one member, the Minister for Coordination of Defense.

Mr. Churchill in forming his ministry in May, 1940, established a War Cabinet of five: the Prime Minister, who was also Minister of Defense; the Lord President of the Council, Mr. Chamberlain, whose presence was politically necessary; the Foreign Secretary, Lord Halifax; the Lord Privy Seal, Mr. Clement Attlee; and a Minister without Portfolio, Mr. Arthur Greenwood. The Prime Minister himself was not at that time the leader of a party. The Lord President was leader of the Conservative Party; the Lord Privy Seal was leader of the Labor Party. The Foreign Secretary was another trusted Conservative; the Minister without Portfolio was another leader of the Labor party. The Cabinet was therefore politically balanced. Moreover, with Mr. Attlee leading the House of Commons and Mr. Greenwood presiding over important coordinating committees, the War Cabinet, in this first form, was a true super-cabinet.

The first change in the nature of Mr. Churchill's War Cabinet arose from the addition of Lord Beaverbrook, the Minister of Aircraft Production, in August. Other changes on Mr. Chamberlain's retirement in October destroyed the original nature of the Churchill War Cabinet altogether. It was increased to a membership of eight. Included was the Chancellor of the Exchequer, Sir Kingsley Wood, who was the nominee of Mr. Chamberlain and who represented Mr. Chamberlain's point of view. Additional members were a Conservative, Sir John Anderson, as Lord President of the Council, and a Labor Party member, Mr. Ernest Bevin, as Minister of Labor. This expanded War Cabinet continued to contain Mr. Churchill's chief advisors, but ceased to have administrative unity.[27]

New Ministries and Ministerial Changes

Within the ranks of ministerial heads of departments a constant but usually gradual change has occurred.

Shortly before or after the beginning of the war, a number of new ministries were created. The Ministry of Supply was set up by the Ministry of Supply Act, 1939, passed July 13. This ministry was to organize the supply of goods for war purposes, though it has never occupied the field, serving partly as a general purchasing agent and more generally as a service department for the army. On the outbreak of the war a Ministry of Home Security was established and entrusted to the Home Secretary. Its duties are the supervision of Air Raid Precautions and the control of all agencies of civil defense. A Ministry of Food was established at the same time, to buy and sell food, to control the imports and domestic production of food, and to regulate the supply whether by directions to merchants or by rationing to consumers. A Ministry of Economic Warfare was created, to perform the functions of the Ministry of Blockade of the previous war. The Minister of Labor was made also Minister of National Service, with control over conscription, whether military or industrial. On October 13, 1939, a Ministry of Shipping was created, which was merged in May, 1941, with the Ministry of Transport into a Ministry of Wartime Communications.

Peculiar and in a sense unique amongst the wartime ministries is the Ministry of Information. As at first constituted, this ministry was in charge of disseminating information and of the censorship of the press, cable, and wireless. Before long, the duty of censorship was withdrawn and redistributed among other departments. The British Broadcasting Corporation, previously responsible in some measure to the Postmaster General, was put under the direct control of the Ministry of Information, which has come more and more to dictate its policies and censor its broadcasts, though the B. B. C. still possesses a small discretion in non-political matters.

At the outbreak of the war, Mr. Chamberlain continued in office most of the members of his previous cabinet, the greater number of whom had been chosen by him for their support of his ideas and his methods. He brought into the government, however, Mr. Winston Churchill as First Lord of the Admiralty and Mr. Anthony Eden as Colonial Secretary—two men commanding much support in the country at large. Mr. Chamberlain offered to the Labor and Liberal parties a share in office, asking them to help him form a coalition government. This offer was rejected largely because the leaders of those parties thought they would be more effective in opposition than as minority members of a large ministry. Mr. Chamberlain's only other important appointment, when the war began, was to make Sir John Anderson Secretary for

Home Affairs and Home Security.[28] Only two other major changes occurred in Mr. Chamberlain's ministry. In January, 1940, Mr. Leslie Hore-Belisha, the Secretary for War, left the cabinet. He had been made Secretary for War in 1937 in order to reorganize the army, and had apparently exhausted his usefulness to the prime minister. When Mr. Oliver Stanley replaced Mr. Hore-Belisha, Sir Andrew Rae Duncan, a successful business man, took Mr. Stanley's place as President of the Board of Trade.

In May, 1940, a parliamentary attack on the government for its failure in Norway produced such a situation that Mr. Chamberlain was obliged to secure further support if he was to continue in office. Since the Labor party refused to enter a cabinet over which he presided, he withdrew from the office of prime minister but continued in the cabinet as Lord President of the Council, retaining his leadership of the Conservative party. The new prime minister necessarily had to be a Conservative, because of the enormous Conservative majority in the House of Commons. Mr. Winston Churchill, who had for so many years opposed Mr. Chamberlain's international policy, and who was highly regarded for his energy and ability to command confidence, took the office of prime minister. The Labor and Liberal parties cordially supported him, and their leaders joined his ministry.

Besides Mr. Churchill and Mr. Chamberlain themselves the most important minister carried over from the Chamberlain government was Lord Halifax, who continued as Foreign Secretary and remained a member of the War Cabinet. Mr. Clement Attlee and Mr. Arthur Greenwood were placed in the War Cabinet as leaders of the Parliamentary Labor party. Outside the War Cabinet the most significant ministerial appointments were Mr. A. V. Alexander (Labor) as First Lord of the Admiralty, Sir Archibald Sinclair (leader of the Parliamentary Liberal party) as Minister of Air, Mr. Anthony Eden as Secretary for War, Lord Beaverbrook as Minister of Aircraft Production, Mr. Ernest Bevin (Labor) as Minister of Labor and National Service, Mr. Herbert Morrison (Labor) as Minister of Supply, and two ardent Conservative imperialists, long-time associates of Mr. Churchill, Lord Lloyd as Secretary for the Colonies, and Mr. L. M. S. Amery as Secretary for India. Mr. Hugh Dalton (Labor) as Minister of Economic Warfare, Lord Woolton (a successful organizer in civil life) as Minister of Food, and Mr. Alfred Duff Cooper (Conservative) as Minister of Information were appointments successfully calculated to add energy and courage to the performance of vital duties. For the rest, a number of ministers were continued in office, a number were demoted, and a few were dropped. Sir Samuel Hoare was sent to Madrid in a diplomatic capacity, Sir John Simon was made Lord Chancellor, and Sir Kingsley Wood retained the vital position of Chancellor of the Exchequer. The personnel of the ministry was by no means completely changed. All varieties of thought in the Conservative party were still represented. But the direction of policy from the top was revolutionized.[29]

The new ministry proved a strikingly successful instrument of government during the summer of 1940.[80] In October, 1940, Mr. Neville Chamberlain resigned on account of ill health, dying shortly afterwards. Sir John Anderson was given his place as Lord President. Mr. Herbert Morrison took Sir John's place as Minister of Home Affairs and Home Security, and Sir Andrew Duncan became Minister of Supply. Each of these changes was considered an improvement. In December, Lord Halifax was made Ambassador to the United States, and his place as Foreign Secretary was taken by Mr. Eden. Mr. Eden's place at the War Office was filled by Captain H. D. Margesson, promoted from a long and successful career as Chief Whip.

Changes in lesser offices, inevitable at any time, have been frequent during the Churchill government. The total number of ministerial members of the House of Lords and House of Commons now amounts to about 150, a wartime increase much greater than that of the war of 1914.

The twin aims of political and personal acceptability and administrative efficiency have been secured in the Churchill government with a high degree of success. The ministry has become more trusted, more intelligent, and more competent. The loose and shifting organization characteristic of the English cabinet system has continued to prove itself consistent both with flexibility in policy and with good administration.

The Civil Service

Much of the success of British administration has traditionally been ascribed to the ability of its permanent officials, organized in a permanent civil service. In wartime the administrative machine expands, and new officials are needed in all ranks. No planning can determine in advance in what numbers or with what equipment they must come. The peacetime civil service, only slightly depleted by military requirements, is the basis of the civil service of wartime. A great many temporary additions have been made.

The civil service during the present war has been the subject of much severe criticism. Part of the criticism has been the usual complaint of lethargy, "bureaucracy," and lack of imagination. This complaint arises during or after every war; it came earlier than usual in this instance. There is no doubt, however, that the morale and initiative of the civil service suffered greatly when Sir Warren Fisher, for many years its very competent head, was replaced by Sir Horace Wilson. And a change of direction from the conciliatory policies of Mr. Chamberlain's government to an activist policy took time. Most of the legitimate criticism of the civil service seems to have arisen, however, from the methods used for temporary appointments.

At the beginning of the war the government decided that no recruits to the civil service should be selected in the usual way, that is, by examination. Instead of admitting the normal quota as permanent appointees, all appointments during the war were to be temporary. For temporary appointments no examinations were required, so that it was left largely to the discretion of the minister to decide who should be appointed to his department, particularly in the higher positions. The usual complaints of favoritism and incompetence followed, sometimes with justification. However, the Ministry of Labor keeps a Central Register of men and women with scientific, technical, and professional qualifications, from which appointees with special qualifications are supposed to be chosen.[31]

REGIONAL ADMINISTRATION

The difficulties of the civil service, however, are only one of the problems of administration of civil affairs which the war has made acute. The problem of coordination of local and central authorities assumes a different aspect in war from its appearance in peace. Before the war, particularist sentiments and local interests combined to defeat proposals for the reorganization of local administration. During the war, the need of close cooperation and mutual support between local and central authorities was felt by both. Regional administration, which had been the ideal of reformers, has come in some considerable degree to exist.

Regional organization came into existence for civil defense purposes, and at first very tentatively. Great Britain was divided into twelve regions, ten in England, one in Wales, and one (subdivided into five sub-regions) in Scotland. Each region has a regional commissioner, whose original duty was conceived to be the direction of civil defense in his region, if circumstances should arise such that the region should be cut off from Whitehall. The first regional commissioners appointed [32] were such men of distinction and experience as Sir Warren Fisher, who had been head of the civil service and permanent undersecretary of the Treasury, and Mr. Harold Butler, who had been director of the International Labor Office. Their administrative responsibility is to the Home Secretary as Minister of Home Security.[33]

During the early months of the war, when the problems of home defense were not pressing, the regional commissioners built up an elaborate and intricate organization. In each region was created "a microcosm of the central government" with a regional commissioner, a deputy regional commissioner, responsible officers representing all the main civil departments, and an adequate technical staff.[34] In their original capacity the regional commissioners were agents of the department of Home Affairs, with supervision over ARP, the police, and the fire brigades. But the regions were also used as units for an area organization of other departments, in regard to whose areas the regional commissioner was to act in an advisory capacity. Area organizations were established in the regions for such ministries as Supply, Transport, and Food. Aliens Advisory Committees and Civilian Advice Bureaus established by the National Council of Social Service were organized on the same regional basis.

At first the regional commissioners were entrusted with very little legal authority except to build up an organization that would become of use in an emergency. They created what have been called "shadow governments".[35] In May, 1940, however, a Defense Regulation conferred on the regional commissioners executive authority in places designated by regulations as "defense areas." In these areas the regional commissioners had delegated to them the power to issue directions or orders necessary for defense in their regions. These orders must if possible be submitted to the Minister of Home Security and receive his approval. On August 19, 1940, the whole of Great Britain was made a defense area, and all the regional commissioners became vested with this power.

The regional commissioners have been compared to Cromwell's Major Generals.[36] If so, the Home Secretary is their Cromwell. But not only must the Home Secretary approve the regional regulations made by them, he also serves as the chief link between them and the government. Previous to the establishment of the regional organization, many powers could be exercised by local government councils only after the approval of the central government department had been secured. Nowadays many of these requests for authority are routed through the regional commissioner's office. This practice adds to the complexity of local administration, but it gives a single agent of the government general supervision over the affairs of a whole area. For civil defense purposes, the regional organization showed its value in a particularly high degree in London and in Coventry after destructive air raids covering areas larger than those of ordinary local government districts.[37]

Parliament in Wartime [38]

What of the control of political affairs—the traditional duty of Parliament? If England were to remain, during the war, in any sense a self-governing country, Parliament could hardly be dispensed with. Yet when the executive had been entrusted with quasi-dictatorial powers, should Parliament be allowed to interfere with their exercise?

The problem of Parliament in this war was like the same problem in the war of 1914—the first war in modern English history in which the executive had been granted vast discretionary powers. On the whole, the war of 1914 had weakened the position of Parliament. And since the formation of the first National government in 1931 the position of Parliament had grown weaker still. For a generation before 1939 the central conflict in English government was a struggle between Parliament on the one hand and the ministers on the other—ministers seeking to avoid responsibility to Parliament and Parliament trying to assert control. In this struggle ministers had latterly won the advantage. In view of such circumstances, the emergency of 1939 might well have served to give the final blow to the actual exercise of parliamentary control over the government. Parliament might have become as ineffective, if not as pusillanimous, as its counterparts in many continental countries.

Furthermore, methods of political control unknown in times of peace were ventured upon, so that the political advantages which the government enjoyed at the beginning of the war should not be disturbed. The Labor and Liberal parties refused to join the ministry and continued in opposition in Parliament. But they agreed, without enthusiasm, to a "party truce" for by-elections for the duration of the war. Whenever any seat in the House of Commons fell vacant, the party previously holding the seat was to select a new member, unopposed by either of the other major parties. Conservatives, members of the Labor party, and Liberals have consequently succeeded to seats vacated by their fellow party-members. Such opposition as has appeared in a few cases has consisted of communists, fascists, or pacifists, and has been totally ineffective. The "party truce" was of obvious advantage to the Conservative government which had a huge majority of the House of Commons supporting it, since under this arrangement its majority was secure. At the same time neither minority party could benefit appreciably by fighting by-elections. From the point of view of the Conservative, the Labor, and the Liberal parties alike, the party truce saved trouble and did little harm.[39]

The party truce applied only to by-elections. The opposition parties had expected, ever since 1935, that in the general election to come they would regain a representation in the House of Commons more proportionate to their strength in the country.[40] The life of the 1935 Parliament was due to end legally on November 25, 1940. Following the precedents of 1916 to 1918, Parliament extended its own life for one year, by passing the Prolongation of Parliament Act. The Labor and Liberal parties, which supported this bill, thereby for the time being gave up any attempt to receive increased support from their followers in the country.

The result of these arrangements might have been the complete abdication by Parliament of its duty to criticize, to direct, and to control the government. And indeed the House of Lords, so useful in the war of 1914, has passed into practical uselessness. But the House of Commons, to everyone's surprise and its own delight, resumed, at the outbreak of the war, its almost forgotten role of critic and performed it more skillfully than for many years. Whatever institutions may have suffered from the war, the House of Commons has indubitably gained.

THE HOUSE OF LORDS

The House of Lords presents, it would seem, the interesting spectacle of an institution which has been permitted to keep a position, until some sudden emergency dislodges it. The House of Lords had suffered from the barren part which it played in the controversies over the Budget and Home Rule. But during the war of 1914 it provided a forum for liberalism and dissent. It commanded respect because it heard the views of all parties alike.[41] During the present war, when a spirit of tolerance has characterized the House of Commons, the House of Lords has been almost consistently intolerant in the opinions expressed, and its debates have been scanty and uninformative.[42]

THE HOUSE OF COMMONS

The House of Commons, on the contrary, has served as a place for full and open discussion of national problems from every point of view. The reasons are interesting. The government which had finally carried Britain into war had been so reluctant to undertake it, that Mr. Chamberlain had moved to a position where he stood as a symbol of national unity. For many months no parliamentary criticism touched Mr. Chamberlain himself. His popularity in the House remained as great as ever. In the country it reached new heights. Since fundamental parliamentary and national unity existed, lively criticism of every detail of governmental action seemed reasonable and patriotic. The party truce was so complete that even members of the Conservative party could feel safe in criticizing their leaders. Moreover, in the early months of the war there was leisure. During the first few weeks of the war the

House of Commons had so proved its usefulness that its war-time position was secure.

The war inevitably caused certain changes in the manner of conducting business of the House of Commons. In ordinary times the House meets five days a week during the greater part of the year, with holidays at Christmas, Easter, and Whitsun, and a long recess in the summer. Called back unexpectedly from its summer holiday on August 24, 1939, it has met more or less continuously ever since. The recesses have been shorter and more irregular than usual, and the summer recess of 1940, in particular, hardly existed.

Ordinarily, the time of the House is divided between government business, when the government controls the time, and private members' business, when motions and bills may be introduced by private members. From the beginning of the war the government has taken the entire time of the House for government business. Though the generous grants of power in the Defense Acts made legislation less necessary than usual, the House up to the autumn of 1940 was kept fairly busy with the amount of legislation before it. During the first part of the war many acts were necessary to modify peacetime arrangements. More than the usual proportion of time has been allotted to finance, since several supplementary budgets were brought forward. New legislation in the ordinary sense has been rare, but some permanent measures of general social benefit have been passed. After one year of war, the legislative program of the government seemed to be exhausted, and only the War Damages Bill required serious legislative consideration during the winter of 1940-1941.

From the first, the House adopted the practice of meeting three days a week and of rising early. Proposals to move Parliament to the country were made but not seriously entertained. Since the beginning of the air attacks on London,

however, the precise days and hours for House of Commons
sessions have not been publicly announced, though it is known
that the House generally meets during daylight hours.

The ordinary peacetime procedure of the House of Commons provides an elaborate framework for daily procedure.
The war has simplified this greatly. The question hour, so
useful as a check on administration and as a method of securing information, has been preserved—indeed many private
members have wished it extended. Opposition to legislative
proposals has been less than in normal times. Even while the
Labor and Liberal parties were in opposition, they seldom
protracted the debates on government proposals, and since
the formation of the Churchill coalition, legislative opposition has been very scant. As a consequence the number of
divisions (formal votes) declined, and divisions at present
are unusually rare. With what, then, does the House occupy
itself?

At the beginning of the war the prime minister formed
the habit of making reports at intervals of every week or so
on the progress of the war. These reports were often debated.
Mr. Churchill as prime minister continued the custom, though
less frequently and often with the understanding that his
speech should not lead to a debate. Late in 1940 he dispensed
with anything in the nature of a report of progress, on the
ground that it gave information to the enemy. The natural
curiosity of members of the House as to the conduct of the
war continued, however, with the result that an increasing
number of secret sessions of the House have been held. In
these secret sessions it is understood that ministers allow some
discussion of actual military events. During September, October and November, 1940, seven of the twenty-four sessions
were held in secret.[43]

Public sessions have now come to be meetings where the

question hour is followed by a general discussion taking place on a motion for adjournment. On such a motion discussion is free, and does not need to result in a decision, but by "the usual channels" (i.e., consultation between whips) the general subject to be discussed on any day is determined in advance. In this way the House of Commons passes in review, largely at its own discretion, the general conduct of affairs by the government. The ideal of many of the more radical reformers of parliamentary procedure seems nearly attained. The government performs the functions of administration, according to a general plan approved by Parliament, and Parliament from time to time comments and criticizes.[44]

At first the usual arrangements of government and opposition were continued into the war. The Chamberlain government was a party government, and the Labor opposition led by Mr. Attlee and the Liberals led by Sir Archibald Sinclair performed their customary duties of criticism and opposition. On many matters, to be sure, the opposition supported the government's proposals: this was true of all emergency legislation. In many cases the effort of the opposition was not to oppose the government's plans so much as to urge the government on to increased activity and efficiency. On social and economic questions, as far as these obtruded into wartime, the Labor party took its habitual party stand.

With the formation of the Churchill government, which included the leaders of both oppositions, there was no opposition at all for the first time in the history of the parliamentary system as we know it. Only the Independent Labor party and the Communist party did not formally support the government, and they numbered a total of four members. The Speaker suspended, by his own authority, the handsomely paid office of leader of the opposition which had been held by Mr. Attlee. Mr. H. B. Lees-Smith, a Labor privy counsellor who was not included in the government, assumed the formal duties of leader of the opposition in asking questions as to the order of business. This unprecedented and potentially dangerous situation was tentatively remedied by the growth of a number of private oppositions, nonpartisan in character. Groups of members, regardless of party, think alike on questions and tend to work together. Some of them are "ginger groups"; some of them are groups with a particular philosophy. Most nearly approaching a political opposition is a small group of men representing the left wing of the Labor party and the extreme left of the Liberals who are particularly interested in questions involving the liberties of the subject.[45]

Early in the war the House made the usual decision that service in the armed forces was compatible with membership in the House. A number of members are therefore irregular in attendance on that account. Since about one hundred and fifty members hold ministerial appointments of some sort, attendance in the House is diminished on that account also. There has, however, been a much more considerable decrease in average attendance than can be explained by those factors alone.

THE PARLIAMENTARY HISTORY OF THE WAR

The parliamentary history of the war falls into rather clearly defined stages, determined by the interaction of political and military factors. For the first nine months things appeared to be going well at home and abroad. During this period the House of Commons thoroughly justified its existence. Its questions prevented bureaucratic tyranny; its discussions on evacuation, food supply, education, and propaganda forced changes in government policy; its attack on the Defense Regulations modified them. Furthermore, the House exercised a judgment in regard to ministers, which was impossible so long as the party system defended its own. Actual changes in the ministry were very rare during this period. But reputations were made and lost, and when a comprehensive change of government occurred in the spring, men who had proved their incapacity could be demoted and those who had proved their ability could be advanced.

During this first period of the war, however, the House, like the country, lacked sufficient information about the general state of affairs in Europe to exercise any broad political judgments. The keenest emotion caused by the failure of the Norwegian expedition was intense surprise, for the newspapers, the weeklies, and the B. B. C. had echoed the quip that Hitler had missed the bus, and the Prime Minister had stated categorically that the German invasion of Norway was a serious error in judgment. When Mr. Chamberlain rose, on May 7, 1940, to report the progress of the war, he was surprised to discover that members of Parliament had first-hand information which he himself appeared to lack—that members knew the British expedition to Norway had been ill-planned, ill-managed, and ill-equipped, a governmental rather than a strategic failure. The government mustered all its resources. Mr. Churchill, whose popularity was undiminished and who as First Lord of the Admiralty was at least technically responsible for the expedition, formally assumed the responsibility. Mr. Chamberlain publicly called on his friends to come to his aid. With their help, Mr. Chamberlain won the division of May 8, 1940, but realized that he must reconstruct his government and get the opposition into it so that they could oppose no longer. Labor continued to refuse to serve under Mr. Chamberlain. Yet a coalition was necessary, if the government was to be carried on with the Conservative party still dominant. "When half-gods go, the gods arrive." Mr. Winston Churchill, a Conservative yet not too dependent on party, a man of vigor, eager for responsibility, and a man who had demanded a strong policy towards Germany even during Munich, was available and was called upon. He formed a coalition government, the "truly national" government since it included members of all three great parties. His government was an immediate parliamentary success, and his popularity in the country soon surpassed that of any prime minister since David Lloyd George.[46]

The Labor party under Churchill in 1940 was singularly like official Labor under Lloyd George in 1916—a willing captive at the chariot wheel of one whom it had always mistrusted. But the change of government of May, 1940, was a victory for the House of Commons—the first such victory over a ministry in power and anxious to continue, since 1886.[47]

The second period of the parliamentary history of the war began with Mr. Churchill's formation of a government and lasted through the autumn. During this period Mr. Churchill won his great reputation as national leader. At first he was looked upon with suspicion by many Conservatives who trusted him less than they trusted Mr. Chamberlain. But when France withdrew from the war and then again when the attack from the air began, his position became unshakable.

As soon as Mr. Churchill assumed the reins of government, the House of Commons was asked to pass a new lot of emergency legislation, and was then expected to drop into a position of subordination. The prime minister, like his great prototype of 1916-1918, never appeared in the House except to make a statement, and it was often understood that the statement should not be discussed. Mr. Attlee, the new Bonar Law—like his predecessor able, hardworking, and self-effacing—was to lead the House and protect the prime minister from annoyance. The "truly national" government, as stated above, included members of all parties but the I. L. P. and the Communist party. A period of extraordinary harmony between House and government ensued. The harmony was stimulated doubtless by fear of invasion, but it was real nevertheless. And yet, again, no sooner had the government done its best to avoid criticism than criticism reared its head. In the last days of July the House spent many hours showing its disapproval of the exceptional powers sought in the new Emergency Powers (Defense) (No. 2) Bill, 1940, and in a defense order calculated to restrict the press; and it discussed disapprovingly the supplementary budget which it thought not extreme enough. Furthermore, taught by the lesson of Norway, the House insisted on debating general policy, though the government was able to get the discussions carried on in secret sessions. The House had come to have the most complete confidence in the prime minister, and its criticism was friendly, but it still was critical.

The third period in the parliamentary history of the war began in the late autumn of 1940. After two months of bombing from the air, resisted successfully, the English people (and their Parliament) were convinced that they had survived not only the immediate attack but any possible attack. And the House of Commons began to feel that it should reassume its functions of criticism and control. Its criticism grew less friendly to the government, though never to the prime minister himself. The particular attack on the government was at its most vulnerable point—its failure to organize production.[48]

The House of Commons and the Ministry

One of the most important of all duties of the House of Commons is to scrutinize and control ministers. The war of

1939 began with a ministry in control, most of whose members were of second-rate ability, and the establishment of a so-called War Cabinet made no essential change in the determination of policy, which continued to be in the hands of Mr. Chamberlain and his confidants. As the need of new administrative departments developed, Mr. Chamberlain, like Mr. Lloyd George in the earlier war, experimented with the introduction of business men or other men of very limited parliamentary experience into positions of high importance. But no long-time supporter of Mr. Chamberlain was removed from office, and appointments quite obviously served partisan as well as national ends. When Mr. Churchill became prime minister, he introduced into office members of the Labor and Liberal oppositions, and some Conservatives, like Lord Lloyd and Mr. Amery, who had been too reactionary to serve with Mr. Chamberlain. But Mr. Churchill retained almost all of the men who owed their position to party requirements. Gradual shifts from office to office have been made, so that the level of competence is distinctly higher than it was. But even after the changes that accompanied Mr. Chamberlain's resignation in October, the important ministers of today are mostly sound Conservatives or men taken over from private business.

But if the House of Commons has had nothing to do with determining what political views a minister shall hold, it has often made itself the judge of his competence. During the war a striking series of changes in office has resulted from House of Commons criticism. The House was responsible for the eventual demotions of Mr. Ernest Brown, Dr. Burgin, Sir John (Lord) Reith, Sir John (Lord) Simon, Sir Samuel Hoare, and at long last Sir John Anderson. It refused to protect Mr. Hore-Belisha, whom it distrusted.[49]

THE HOUSE AND THE FUTURE

The final, and perhaps in the long run the most important, duty of the House of Commons is to prepare for future governments and future policies which shall be different from those of the present. This it does without difficulty in ordinary times because of the close relationship between the members of the House and the country, so that views expressed in the House are discussed in the country and win support or opposition, and views expressed outside Parliament are discussed within its walls. Tentative proposals for future change are thus brought under public scrutiny while they are still tentative. In the same way future exponents of policy and future ministers have to win their way forward from the most distant of the back benches, or from the obscurity of private life. For all this activity the House of Commons serves as a point of focus, and the interaction between the House and the country produces that peculiarly high degree of integration between leaders and followers which is characteristic of the English parliamentary system. When the House (or the government it supports) is out of touch with feeling in the country, a general election, or by-elections, or criticism in the press will instruct it. When the country gets out of touch with the House, speeches in the House, or by ministers and other members on public platforms, will influence thinking in the country.

In wartime, as we have seen, many of the conditions necessary for the normal working of this system are lacking. When the government commands the support of almost all members of the House, the House will spend very little time expressing any but majority ideas. Such opposition as exists, or may come to exist, must be outside Parliament. And, outside Parliament, ideas may crystallize without having to undergo serious scrutiny, and opposition leaders may come to maturity without being forced to learn the technique of the parliamentary system.

The political aftermath of both the Boer War and the war of 1914 showed the British voter and the House of Commons welcoming with enthusiasm, very shortly after the termination of these wars, new prime ministers who had been critical while the wars were in progress. In both cases the country had turned, in a political reaction, to a government which had refused to bear responsibility for the war itself. In both cases the new leaders chosen were men of parliamentary experience. But if the same reaction should occur after a successful conclusion of the present war, the leaders of the new government might have to be sought among the Conservative back benchers who are out of sympathy with the present government, or outside Parliament in the ranks of those who are too far to the left to be represented by the Labor party.

Underneath the very real national unity of wartime England lies a political situation of the utmost intricacy. When the war began, the political pattern was one which had been crystallizing for some years. By far the largest group in Parliament, and one of the most important in the country, was the group which accepted Mr. Neville Chamberlain as their leader because he expressed their ideas. The domestic policy of this group was conservative in a strict sense: it desired to keep things as they were, with no change at all. Its foreign policy was one of conciliation, with a much greater fear of communism than of fascism, a considerable admiration of the Italian régime, and a desire to keep on good terms with the Third Reich. From a parliamentary point of view, this group comprised the majority of the Conservative party, and controlled its organization.

One extreme wing of the Conservative party consisted of a

smaller group, who might be called old-fashioned imperialists —strongly conservative or even reactionary at home and in regard to India, and afraid of Germany as a threat to the British empire. Their admiration for Italian fascism had led many of them to approve Italy's policy in Africa and Spain. On the other extreme wing of the Conservative party was the group which under normal political conditions would have belonged to the Liberal or Labor party—men strongly anti-fascist in foreign policy who believed in democracy and reform and who were not untinged with socialism in their domestic policy.

The two oppositions, Liberal and Labor, had come, after Munich, to a close approximation of policy both at home and abroad. Most members of these parties were such strong opponents of fascism abroad that their domestic policy of reform was subordinated to their foreign policy. A minority of both parties considered domestic reform more essential than a "strong" foreign policy.

On the right was a group of fascist sympathizers, not organized in a political party, but associated together with the vague intention of bringing a fascist system to birth in England. On the left was the Independent Labor party, a small fragment of the once large group that had worked for a thoroughgoing socialist England. Farther still to the left were the Communists, orthodox in their views, and very few in number, but represented by one member of the House of Commons.

The immediate effect of the declaration of war was to rally the great majority of all groups to a common cause. On one issue, though on one alone, they agreed. But if action were to be taken on any other issue, each separate group would want it to be taken in fulfilment of its own special program. On September 3, 1939, English politics became like a pond suddenly covered by ice. There is unity and uniformity and lack of movement on the surface, and the surface will bear weight. What goes on beneath the surface cannot be seen and does not matter for the present. If the ice should melt soon, it is reasonable to suppose that the contents of the pond would be found unchanged. If the surface unity is prolonged, unseen forces working hidden beneath may produce unpredictable results.

RECONSTRUCTION

During the war of 1914 and particularly during its later and more difficult stages the Lloyd George government laid plans for post-war reconstruction. Not only did it create a Ministry of Reconstruction to plan for the future, but it secured the passage, during the war, of a number of reform statutes. It extended education by the Fisher Act, democratized the House of Commons by the Representation of the People Act, tried seriously to reconcile Ireland, and laid plans for giving more self-government to India. So far, the governments during the present war have committed themselves to no domestic reforms, though education, Parliamentary reform, Ireland, and India again present problems whose solution would make a better future and perhaps a stronger present.[50] There are signs, however, that the Churchill government like the Lloyd George government may presently take time for reconstruction.

The government has made two tentative steps in that direction. In October, 1940, Lord Reith was appointed Minister of Works and Buildings so that he might make plans for the physical reconstruction of England after the war. On January 6, 1941, Mr. Arthur Greenwood (who had served on the staff of Mr. Lloyd George's Ministry of Reconstruction) was designated to supervise plans for reconstruction in political and social fields.

Meantime private or semi-official efforts have essayed to indicate lines along which reconstruction may come. Three conferences were held in January, 1941, by groups of people trying to guarantee the future. The least important was a conference of the National Peace Council held at St. Hilda's College, Oxford, to discuss peace aims, and attended by a varied group of middle-class professional people. The second was the People's Convention held in London where a program supported by many younger trades-unionists and some middle-class radicals was set forth. Their program included amongst other items friendship with the Soviet Union, a "people's government," and a "people's peace." The group was widely opposed as an organization attempting to take the leadership of the worker away from the Labor party and give it to the Communists.[51] The third and most important meeting was held at Malvern at the call of the Archbishop of York to discuss Christianity and the New Order of Society. Among the lay speakers were T. S. Eliot, J. Middleton Murry, Dorothy Sayers, and Sir Richard Acland, M. P. Many clergy attended, including twenty-three bishops. It was called "to consider from the Anglican point of view what are the fundamental facts which are directly relevant to the ordering of the new society that is quite evidently emerging and how Christian thought can be shaped to play a leading part in the reconstruction when the war is over." Necessarily vague as to expedients, its resolutions were definite as to principles. The Archbishop's resolution, agreed to by all, included the statements that "Christian doctrine must insist that wealth exists for consumption," and that "after the war our aim must be the unification of Europe as a cooperative commonwealth." Not all members of the Church of England would agree with these principles today, but a surprising number of its leaders do.[52]

The greatest achievement of the English government in wartime is that the constructive forces of society have not been quieted by the destruction that surrounds them, or by the organization of the country for military effort. In trying to preserve a free and popular government while engaged in war, England has set herself a standard no other belligerent country has tried to attain. Her success, in the first twenty months of the war, is evidence that a free popular government can be second to none in efficiency.

CHAPTER II

Policy and Administration in Wartime England

BY W. HARDY WICKWAR
Rockford College

POLICY WITHOUT PLAN

BRITISH political institutions have seldom displayed their many-sidedness both to such advantage and to such disadvantage as during the first year of the present war. They have shown a resilience and an adaptability that have already carried them far towards compensating for some of the shortcomings and ineptitudes of the recent past. Their strength is to be measured by their success in overcoming the very great weaknesses which had been allowed to creep into the British position.

The greatest weakness revealed by Britain during 1939-40, as also by the French and American democracies, was the failure to think of policy in anything like such broad terms as its totalitarian antagonist. Throughout Neville Chamberlain's premiership, the British government continued to envisage national policy in the traditional way as armed diplomacy engaged in the rectification of alleged injustices and the modification of the balance of power. Its failure to understand the expansionist nature of Nazism was accompanied by a complete inability to understand the implications of *Wehrwirtschaft*, the "economics of force." The very terms "total

43

defense" and "preparedness economy" would seem to have originated in the United States and not in the United Kingdom. And although Mr. Churchill saw some of the military and diplomatic perils clearly, and expressed the people's sense of them with great eloquence and firmness, there has been little evidence that he has envisaged economic mobilization in anything more than a commissariat sense.

In February, 1940, Sir William Beveridge could write:

The separate Government Departments are full of able and devoted administrators—civil servants and business men and others; departmentally the war had been planned, and is probably being conducted, with high efficiency. But whenever we meet an economic problem that spreads across several departments, whether it be price policy or exports, or full use of man-power, or relations of food control and agriculture, we find confusion and weakness.[1]

And in September, 1940, after Mr. Churchill became prime minister and after the absorption of Sir William Beveridge, Sir Walter Layton, Sir Arthur Salter, and Mr. J. M. Keynes into government departments, Professor F. A. Hayek could still write: "The trouble is that in the economic sphere—at least so far as the concerns of the people as a whole are affected—we still lack the intelligent and inspiring leadership which we now have in the political sphere." [2]

During the earlier phases of the war, the systematic thinking that should have been done years before in a government department was being begun in such pamphlets as Mr. Keynes' "How to Pay for the War," Sir John Orr's and Mr. David Lubbock's "Feeding the People in War-time," and the anonymous Penguin Special on "Science in War." Only one bit of credit can be given to the government for this belated activity; it was at least liberal enough to allow private citizens to do some of the thinking of which public authorities proved incapable, even though this freedom of thought and this liberty of press contributed eventually to a change of government.

With proper planning, it should have been possible to set a "siege economy" against an "economics of force." In the beleaguered Britain of 1940 it should have been possible, with adequate foresight, to guarantee to every man, woman, and child an iron ration of food, a roof over their head, and a bed to sleep in at night, in return for the government's claim to move them about and conscript their labor, their earnings, their savings, and their wealth. Instead of calling on the farmer to grow more, and on the consumer to spend less, it might have thought out exactly what it ought to have induced the farmer to grow, and which consumers it ought to have obliged to spend less on what. Instead of ordering the farmer to plow more acres, and enticing his labor away to work at the airfields, it might have stationed every man where he could do his duty most effectively. Instead of letting wages and prices chase one another upwards, it could have held both prices and wages steady, or at least coordinated their movement on some sort of plan. Instead of maintaining the traditional distinction between civilian and soldier, it might have understood earlier that in total war the whole nation is under arms and the whole island one armed camp.

Basic problems have been handled only with velvet gloves. For too many months, excessive reliance was placed upon price movements as the time-honored mechanism for diverting production from one channel into another. Indirect controls such as taxation, bulk purchasing, subsidies, and the pillorying of profiteers were relied upon to keep the inevitable instability and dislocation within bounds. Clumsily applied, these old-fashioned indirect controls sometimes actually accentuated the instability, as when taxes on consumption resulted in wage increases and therefore in further price rises, owing to the automatic operation of sliding-scale wage-contracts previously signed between employers and labor unions. Only in the early part of 1940 were more direct controls introduced, such as Germany had developed between 1936 and 1939, so as to canalize the actual movement of commodities by rationing and priorities. Not until the middle of 1940 was a serious beginning made in the application of direct controls to the canalizing of labor. Only then did it become possible to think seriously of the planned coordination of the whole national economy for the political object of winning the war.[3]

For this lack of overall planning, two reasons may be adduced. The one lies in the all-pervading moral atmosphere, the other in institutional shortcomings.

An atmosphere conducive to rational planning for so irrational a purpose as war is not easily created. Neville Chamberlain aroused enthusiasm neither for racial aggrandisement nor for international solidarity. Without the preparations over which he presided, Britain would have been even less prepared for war than she was. Yet he failed to awaken his people to a conviction that he was himself aware of the gravity of the situation. No people could seriously be expected to step straight from "peace in our time" into a totally-planned war economy. An atmosphere of peace and appeasement is ill suited to war planning.

Institutional shortcomings were no less important. One is struck not only by the absence of plan but also by the absence of any body of men whose function was to study war economics in all its many possibilities and ramifications, and prepare an intelligent plan for meeting the inevitable. Had a different course been pursued, the government might not have been driven from pillar to post by emergency after emergency and pressure after pressure, but might have kept the initiative and been to a greater extent the master of its fate.

The failure of the Treasury to perform this function has been one of the major tragedies of British government in the twentieth century. The expert leadership which a liberal Treasury was able to give to the whole economic life of the nation in the age of *laissez-faire,* a conservative Treasury has failed to give in this age, when economics and politics have again become so inextricably interwoven that a merely fiscal thread is no longer enough to bind together these aspects of the nation's life. Yet the general control which the Treasury exercises over all other departments should have enabled it not only to plan for them all but also to enforce the plans that it made. In the light of this year's shortcomings, new point has been given to the time-honored suggestion of an Economic General Staff.

With this failure of the Treasury to provide constructive and imaginative leadership has been associated a certain inadequacy in the personnel of the Civil Service. Any one who has worked much with candidates for the Administrative grade of the British Civil Service must be as much impressed by the charming mediocrity of the many as by the brilliance of the few. The competitive examination for recent graduates had at least the merit of an attempt at impartial assessment of candidates according to an intellectual standard; the method of recruitment by influence, resorted to in staffing some of the newer ministries in Chamberlain's day, regardless of the compilation of a National Register by the Ministry of Labor, had not even that modest merit; it had not then been discovered that this war might have to be won by brains and not by social graces. A better case than ever has now been made out for recruitment also at a later age of men of sufficient breadth of vision to engage in staff work of the planning type. The

inadequacies of the unreformed Civil Service were shown up
by the Crimean War; and it may be that the present war is
showing up some no less dangerous defects.

Most noticeable of all defects, the War Cabinet has proved
to be less well adapted to its job of overall coordination
than might have been an Inner Cabinet rationally composed
of Chief Ministers, each of whom could in his turn have coordinated a group of closely allied ministries. Only by means
such as these could responsibility have been clearly located
and a fair chance created that a more-than-departmental approach to current problems might have been worked out.

To these defects and deficiencies might also perhaps be
added a more positive obstacle to overall planning. This is
the tendency under a democratic government and a welfare
economy to equate the general interest with the sum of such
particular interests as are articulate and influential. In present-
day Britain, such organized interests tend not to be left in
the lobby, but to be integrated into the framework of government itself. The good organizer, whether of a department
store like Lord Woolton, or of the iron and steel industry
like Sir Andrew Duncan, whether of a political party like
Mr. Herbert Morrison, or of a trade union like Mr. Ernest
Bevin, whether of a popular newspaper like Lord Beaverbrook or of a cooperative like Mr. A. V. Alexander, proves
himself a born ruler of men and becomes in England *ipso
facto* a member of a new aristocracy of organizing ability.
The history of England throughout these last six hundred
years has seen the rise of one "new nobility" after another.
Each different age has produced its own particular brand of
"new nobility." The "governing class" of England has never
been a closed and hereditary caste, but has retained its power
in proportion to its willingness to recruit new blood and new
ability and imbue the newcomers with its own tradition of

practical responsibility, social solidarity, and liberal conservatism. Its aristocracy is democratic, its democracy aristocratic. This broadening-out process answers well enough to Tocqueville's description of the march of democracy: looked at from one angle, it is part of that "tendency towards equality" which, through the centuries, has enabled people from a continually widening range of social groups to take part in the processes of government. In the form however which it takes in this present age, this tendency does have and has had the defect of filling the seats of authority with men whose training and outlook tend to be sectional and who, at any rate when first assuming office, are not all particularly well qualified to view the national life as a whole. One is reminded of the antinomy of the "corporative" and the "totalitarian" that has long been latent in Italian fascism. Such "corporative" tendencies, as Mussolini discovered in the Ethiopian war, may be ill-suited to an epoch of war economy when national survival looms larger than the welfare of particular interests.

What planning there has been, has been a vague sort of idea at the back of a man's mind. What preparation there has been, has been by particular departments. What economic control there has been, has been by the economic interests to be controlled. And now that broad-visioned men have been brought into the government's service, it is into individual departments that they have been drafted. Where overall planning was possible, departmental efficiency has been chosen; and departmentalism costs happiness, costs lives, and may cost victory.

Public Finance

For the fiscal year April 1, 1939, to March 31, 1940, the British Parliament appropriated nearly £2 billion. One third of this sum was voted in supplementary estimates. In that one year, two budgets were presented to Parliament, a peace budget in April and a war budget in September. Yet it was characteristic of that phase of Britain's war effort that the fiscal year ended with more than £100 million still in hand.

During the following fiscal year, 1940-41, appropriations rose steadily until they have approximated £4 billion. And for a second consecutive time it was necessary to present two budgets, the one by Sir John Simon in April and the other by Sir Kingsley Wood in July, 1940.

Tax revenue during the year 1939-40 passed the one-billion mark, and it promised to be somewhat higher in 1940-41. This tax revenue was increased in four principal ways.

The first was an extension of the historic British policy of taxing "conventional necessities." Increased taxes were levied not only on drinking and smoking, but also on railway, postal, and telephone services.

What was more novel was that in 1940 for the first time the United Kingdom joined the ranks of the countries with sales taxes. After considerable floundering in Parliament, this "purchase tax" eventually took the form of a 33⅓% tax on the wholesale price of luxuries, and 16⅔% on that of necessities other than food.

The war budget of 1939 also imposed an "excess profits duty" on all profits above those attained during a base period. In fixing the base period, a considerable choice was allowed to the taxpayer; but this had to be made from the years 1935 and 1936, or an average for either 1935-36 or 1936-37. That is to say, it had to be calculated from a period well ahead of the armaments boom. The excess profits duty rate, fixed at 60% on the outbreak of war in September, 1939, was raised to 100% after the German occupation of the Channel ports in May, 1940.

The income tax proved as flexible as usual. The standard

rate rose from 22½% before April, 1939, to 42½% in July, 1940, and finally to 50% in April, 1941. Exemptions were lowered, and for high incomes the graduation was made so steep that the tax rate reached 90% above the £20,000 level.

Beyond these tax sources, the government had to augment its revenue by borrowing. To make this easier, the Treasury closed the money market to municipalities and took powers to prohibit new capital issues by business corporations except for defense purposes. In enjoyment of what amounted to a virtual monopoly, it was able to borrow at unprecedentedly low wartime interest rates varying between 2% and 3% for medium and long-term issues. By issuing treasury bills, it was able to borrow large sums for short terms at still lower rates. No forced loans were made, as in New Zealand; no compulsory saving of wartime wages was attempted, along such lines as Mr. Keynes advocated, until April, 1941. Nevertheless, by the end of 1940, about £1 billion was attracted into baby bonds of low denominations.

The war has obliged the British government to spend money abroad as well as at home. During 1940, for instance, nearly one tenth of British governmental expenditure occurred in the United States alone. Before the war began, the Treasury imposed restrictions on the sale or transfer of securities which might prove marketable abroad; and on February 18, 1940, it began the process of compelling British holders of American securities to sell them, at the New York market price, to the Exchange Equalization Fund, which raised the necessary money by the issue of bills.[4] All told, however, British-held American securities were not worth more than one billion dollars and not all of them were readily marketable.[5] In the long run therefore other means were needed to enable the British Treasury to continue to place orders and finance plant construction abroad. One such means was exchange control. Between March and June, 1940, this method took the form of insisting that an increasingly extensive list of exports from the sterling area should be paid for at the official exchange rate, which at that time was some fifty cents higher than the free market rate. More important were a whole series of commercial controls which had to be manipulated by the Board of Trade and other government departments. These were aimed partly at diminishing British internal consumption while maintaining British exports; for only so could foreign exchange be made available for war purchases. They aimed also at the importation of indispensable raw materials and foodstuffs by means of special purchase contracts negotiated with countries in a weaker bargaining position than the United States, and the signing with these countries of bilateral clearance and payment agreements that enabled Britain to conserve her dollars by crediting them with sterling. The fiscal necessities of modern war thus led to the establishment of a whole series of British governmental controls over international commercial transactions.[6]

British fiscal policy has thus had many and far-reaching social and economic implications. It has tended to discourage private consumption, diminish the private demand on shipping facilities and dollar exchange, attract investment and small savings into the service of the government, put obstacles in the way of the making of wartime fortunes, and enable the government to purchase war materials overseas. The chief criticism to which this policy has been exposed, is that it pursued these ends with inadequate speed, vigor, system, and imagination. A sensational confession of these defects was the presentation of three budgets within the first twelve months of war. For this hesitancy, the moral unpreparedness of the government, the business world, and the people generally must be held responsible. For this moral unpreparedness however the blame rests equally on the blind and vacillating leadership of all British administrations throughout the decade before the outbreak of hostilities.

SOCIAL SERVICES

During the 1930's it became axiomatic in Britain that Britain was becoming to some extent a "social-service state." That is to say, both the leading political parties took it for granted that the worst forms of insecurity and the most glaring extremes of inequality inherent in the economic and social system ought to be mitigated by governmental action.

These governmental social services have moved in three particularly important directions: (1) social insurance; (2) special provision for children; and (3) below-cost housing. In the first at least of these well-worn paths, some advance has been made during the war.

In the field of social insurance, the age at which women may qualify for a contributory old-age pension has been lowered from 65 to 60. It thus provides for the woman wage earner who finds it difficult to hold her job after she is 60, as well as for the younger wife of the 65-year-old male pensioner. This extension of coverage owed practically nothing to the war. It was the outcome of several years' agitation for "spinsters' pensions." It relieved the health-insurance system of some of the burden of "sickness benefit"—the weekly sum paid to the sick in lieu of wages—which is specially heavy in the older age-groups. Above all, it promised to be self-financing: every insured woman wage earner would have to contribute another 2d a week and her employer another 1d, and every insured man wage earner and his employer 1d each.

The coverage for unemployment has also been broadened, by raising from £250 to £400 a year the income level beneath which it is obligatory on employers, employees, and the State to contribute to the unemployment insurance fund. This extension had been widely desired for many years. It took the war and the shock of wartime unemployment among non-manual workers to bring about this much-needed reform. Even now, one unjustifiable anomaly persists: the manual worker is insured, however high his income; the non-manual worker only if his income is below £400. In the absence of universal compulsory unemployment insurance, it is impossible to state definitely whether or not the non-manual worker's risk of unemployment is less than that run by his manual colleague. The depression and the early months of this war throw some doubt on this assumption. An additional anomaly has also been created, in that compulsory health and old-age insurance still stop at £250 a year.

The inadequacy of all social insurance systems is well known. They may offer the most practicable means of helping the majority of people to help themselves in the majority of circumstances. Even with the best-devised social insurance systems in the world, there must always be a minority of people and a minority of circumstances that no compulsory insurance can provide for adequately. For these cases Great Britain seems to be on its way towards making nation-wide provision.

The first step in the establishment of this new national assistance system for plugging the holes left by social insurance was taken in 1934. At that time a national Unemployment Assistance Board was set up to render assistance to unemployed insured persons whose unemployment benefit rights were exhausted or inadequate. The first step in the extension of the UAB's activities came in September, 1939, when something had to be done for those persons who lost their livelihoods because of the war, and who had never been insured, either because their salaries were above the income limit, or because they had been their own employers. An Unemployment Assistance (Emergency Powers) Act met their problem by empowering the Minister of Labor to extend the act of 1934 to assist additional classes of persons "in distress as the result of circumstances caused by the war." A second step in the same direction was taken under the Old Age and Widows Pensions Act of 1940, whose insurance provisions we have already considered. This act allowed the Assistance Board to pay "supplementary pensions," through the Post Office, to widows and aged persons whose insurance benefits were inadequate to sustain them. It only remains now to extend the scope of the Assistance Board a little further, so as to supplement contributory blind pensions, disability pensions, and sickness benefit in this same manner; and it will then be possible to say that effective national machinery has been set up to prevent all insured persons from having to have recourse to local poor relief.

In the field of special assistance for children, the war-time advance has been less great, but it is nevertheless noteworthy. Great Britain has thus far been a country in which family allowances, as practiced in Australia and France, have found but little favor with wage earners as a means of supplementing the wages of labor; but they have found increasing favor as a means of supporting families whose heads are not regularly employed. For the recipients of unemployment insurance benefit, allowances for dependents are almost as old as unemployment insurance itself; and these allowances were slightly increased in 1940; allowances for soldiers' dependents have also been made a little more ample. The big advance has been in extending this principle to workmen's compensation. By an act of Parliament passed in the face of strong trade-union criticism shortly before Neville Chamberlain's fall, supplementary allowances were made available for wives and children, with the proviso that the total compensation should not exceed seven-eighths of the wage that had been paid before the accident. The nearest approach that has been made towards family allowances for the family whose head is a wage earner in regular work, has been the shouldering by the government of responsibility for contributing at a flat rate towards the living costs of evacuees whom it has itself billeted. In some other respects there may even have been some setback to the various tendencies at work for supplementing family incomes out of sources other than earnings. An extension of the free milk scheme for some may have been offset by the rise in the price of milk for many. And less medical and dental care has probably been available free or below cost at school clinics as the result of the widespread dislocation of the educational system.

A setback to housing was inevitable. Local authorities had to call a stop to their slum-clearance and "de-overcrowding" projects, partly because the national government wished to have a monopoly on the money market and partly because of the rising cost of materials. Municipal housing projects were continued only in such places as the ill-fated city of Coventry, where the rapid expansion of defense industries made additional housing indispensable.

Of this piecemeal extension of the social services in wartime, several criticisms could be made.

The first arises from the difficulty of adapting social insurance systems to an epoch of sharply changing living costs. The difficulty is even more noticeable in the British system of social insurance than it would be in the United States, because British social insurance aims at flat-rate benefits adequate for the bare necessities of life, whereas American social insurance aims at benefits proportionate to previous wage earnings. Any

rise in living costs is therefore apt to make British social insurance benefits inadequate to provide the bare necessities of
life for which they are designed. No attempt has been made
to institute a sliding scale of benefits, rising or falling according to variations in the cost-of-living index. Apart from a few
changes in benefit rate, all that has been done to meet this need
is to extend the scope of the national Assistance Board. This
however does not meet the problem; because "assistance" is at
the discretion of the Board, whereas "insurance benefits" are
a matter of covenanted legal right.

A second criticism, allied to the first, arises from the failure
to cope adequately with the need for supplementing wages
in order that families might meet increasing living costs. It
seems highly probable that a straightforward family-allowance
system, whether paid for by the State as in Australia or insured for by the employer as in France, would have brought
the additional income to the families where it was most
needed, without precipitating the "vicious spiral" of rising
wages and rising prices. It might also have been a measure of
justice in that it would have tended to flatten out some of the
gross inequalities of income that arise from the accidents of
war, when one man gets the fattest pay envelope of his life in
an aircraft factory while another gets only tobacco money in
the army.

A third criticism, and perhaps the most serious, comes from
the failure of those who are in authority to think of urban
wartime problems in terms of the family. The sin of social
atomism and social abstraction has seldom or never been committed on such a grand scale. Officials seem to have thought
that they could just evacuate women and children from urban
areas, and all would be well. They seem completely to have
forgotten the human aspect of the problem at both ends.
They thought in terms of providing a roof over the heads of

the evacuees, and bandages and incinerators for those who stayed behind and were wounded or killed. They forgot the need for carefully adjusting evacuee to host in the reception areas, in spite of Britain's long experience in the boarding out of children. They likewise forgot that the father and elder brothers who stayed near their work would need feeding, and that this social function is still normally performed on a family basis, unless the community provides an acceptable substitute. History's judgment on the evacuation fiasco was written twelve months later in letters of blood when the "Blitz" broke over London's dockland.[7]

This brings us to the cardinal weakness of British social service administration. This is its piecemeal growth, its compartmental organization, its lack of coordination, and its lack of sound working principle. Neither locally nor centrally is there any authority whose duty is to survey and know and organize the whole field of public welfare activities. Authority is dissipated and responsibility is spread in the worst possible manner. The first year of war showed where the administrative house cleaning needs doing. It did not get it done.

PUBLIC SERVICES

Modern Britain has steadily lengthened its list of "public services," that is to say, of the undertakings that are widely recognized as being "affected with a public interest" and therefore in need of some form of public control. In wartime it is natural that this already long list should have been considerably lengthened.

The all-important consideration has been how best to maintain a service. Before this consideration all else has had to give way.

As in all countries, competition was ceasing to be a fetish

in prewar years in Great Britain; and in an increasing number of fields it has now become taboo. The motorist can no longer choose between "Shell" and "Standard," but must buy his motor fuel ration and oil from a government-organized "pool." The tendency towards monopoly that is inherent in this phase of our economic development has in Britain, as everywhere, received tremendous impetus from the war.

The divorce between ownership and control, that is equally characteristic of contemporary economic development, has here also come into play on a gigantic scale. For a generation or more, businessmen have become so accustomed to this divorce that without much interference with private ownership it has been the easiest thing in the world for the controls to be centralized and for them then to be exercised in the name of the government. Moreover the development of this governmental control at the nodal points of the economic system has left a wide field for private ownership, in the lower reaches of the economic system.

This tendency, to which the exigencies of war economy have driven the nations at breakneck speed, has shown itself clearly in the development of the two Ministries of Food and of Supply.

To ensure the regular flow of foodstuffs from producer to consumer, a Ministry of Food was set up. At one end of this process, the ministry became the monopolistic wholesale purchaser of many imported foods and of British-raised meat. At the other end it had to see to it that every consumer became registered with a particular retail store, and that the store was supplied with an adequate quantity or a fair proportion of rationed foods. For rationed commodities, the freedom of the market thus virtually disappeared. Nor did the Ministry of Food pay its way. On the contrary, it deliberately ran at a loss; for from December, 1939, it poured out a subsidy of

£1,000,000 a week in order to keep down the retail price of bread and meat.[8]

While the Ministry of Food was making food available, the Ministry of Agriculture was paying farmers £2 an acre to increase the number of arable acres from 9,000,000 to 11,-000,000; but it offered no guarantee that seed would be available. It was nobody's business to store fodder for cattle and poultry, or seed for sowing, before the war began; and the first winter of war therefore saw a reduction of these sources of food supply.

To ensure the flow of raw materials to industry at a reasonable price, a Ministry of Supply was set up, with control over the strategic reserves accumulated since 1938, the power to buy and sell within the limit of its available funds, and the power to fix prices, allocate supplies, and establish priorities. For most commodities, the controllers were drawn from the industry most vitally concerned. The process of "cartelization" or "industrial self-government," which had received considerable recognition from parliament throughout the 1930's, thus took a new form. Industrialists could be sure that their needs were being looked after by a man who in nearly every case was one of themselves. For the smooth working of a system of governmental control, this was a considerable advantage. Yet it had the counterbalancing disadvantage that in many cases the controller was likely to give too much attention to the economic survival of the industry and too little to the prior needs of the government and of export. The war was more than seven months old before the "priorities" system became a reality. Not until April, 1940, was domestic sale of textiles slashed by one-third in order to provide a surplus for export. The control failed moreover to prevent a rise in wholesale commodity prices (1930 base) from 98 in August, 1939, to 128 in December, 1939, and on to 148 in December,

1940.[9] For this development, however, it would be unfair to hold the British government altogether responsible: the controllers and other importers were buying in a world market, with rising prices, rising freight charges, rising insurance rates, and above all a depreciated exchange that made the pound sterling worth only $4 instead of $5.

Immediately after the outbreak of war the Ministry of Transport took over control of all important British railway undertakings. As in the previous war, the Ministry turned over their actual operation to an Executive Committee composed of representatives of the principal systems to be controlled. This policy differed from that pursued in 1914 in only two particulars. The one was that in the previous war it had been necessary to pick and choose among the heads of the fifty different railway companies, whereas in this war, owing to the consolidation that had meanwhile been forced upon the railways, there were only four railway systems left, and their heads were almost automatically appointed to the new committee. The railways that they had previously managed separately as individuals, they now managed conjointly as a committee. The other difference was that the London Passenger Transport Board now took the fifth seat, along with the four great railway companies.

When the financial agreement between the Treasury and these five transportation systems was announced more than six months later, it too followed the 1914 pattern. In other words, it guaranteed to the stockholders the highest net revenue earned during recent years. In 1914, this was the single year 1913, when net revenue reached the all-time high of £51 million. In 1939, this was the average of the years 1935-36-37, when business was brisker than in the single prewar year 1938, and net revenue reached £40 million, the highest it had touched between 1921 and 1939. Over and above this guarantee, the railway pool is to be free to keep all profits up to £43.5 million; beyond that point it is to keep half its profits until it reaches the "standard net revenue" of £51 million. In order to reach these figures, the railways have been allowed to raise their rates. Thus, at the very same time as the Ministry of Food was pouring out a weekly subsidy so as to keep prices down in order to prevent a rise in wages, the Ministry of Transport was sending prices up in order to effect a rise in dividends.[10]

The Ministry of Shipping, set up in October, 1939, was manned mostly by shipping men and partly by survivors from its first World War namesake. At the beginning it exercised control by forbidding British ships to clear from any port without its license; but by the end of the year it was actually requisitioning both tramp and liner shipping.

In an important respect one prewar trend was reversed. Responsibility for control was exercised by a ministry whose political head shared in the collective responsibility of the cabinet to parliament. Responsibility was not, as was often true previously, delegated to an autonomous government-owned corporation. This reversal was perhaps a natural one; for the work done by the ministries was essentially political, not economic, and its continued performance could not be contingent on financial return. As a rule the work did not and could not pay its way. The only noteworthy exception to this rule was the English Commercial Corporation, Ltd., set up with government capital in April, 1940; but this corporation was actually established to buy and sell in the Balkans and other countries as a commercial concern, in an effort to offset the German economic penetration of Southeastern Europe.

GOVERNMENT AND LABOR

Before the war began, the German government took the power to conscript men and women for industrial labor and to determine for what employer they should work; and on the outbreak of the war, France set many of her conscripts to work in industry. Britain took no such step in 1939. On the contrary, the first Emergency Powers Act expressly forbade the government to use its otherwise almost unlimited powers for the purpose of introducing "industrial conscription."

Quite apart from a free people's traditional dislike of compulsory labor for the profit of a private employer, this omission from the Emergency Powers Act could be partly justified also by the survival at that date of a labor reserve of more than a million unemployed. Many future defense plants were still months from completion, owing to the government's tardiness and lack of foresight. And the army's demand for manpower was so limited that the Ministry of Labor and National Service was able to schedule a long list of occupations, which demanded skill or experience, of sufficient national importance, to justify exemption from military service.[11]

This maintenance of a free market for labor had certain serious consequences.

One was that competition in the more restricted segments of the labor market tended to stimulate a rise in wages. This in its turn was bound to raise prices to the government and to the consumer. The benefit to the worker was bound in many cases to be illusory, as a general price rise would offset the rise in his money wages and make his real wages no more than before. If he belonged to the fortunate minority whose money wages rose sufficiently to raise his real wages despite the upswing in prices, he tended to increase consumption, importation, and the demand on shipping tonnage, at a time when reduction was desirable. Meanwhile the vast majority, who were not in strategic positions for improving their earnings, were bound to find their purchasing power and real income consequently diminished.[12]

A no less serious result was that labor was attracted away from such ill-paid work as agriculture and mining, at the very moment when the demand for foodcrops and coal was increasing. The government lacked adequate power to cope with the problem.

The Emergency Powers Act of May 22, 1940, removed this limitation on the government's powers. By an "anti-poaching" order, Mr. Ernest Bevin, the new Minister of Labor, thereupon forbade employers to entice machine-tool and construction workers, coal miners and farm laborers, into other industries. These employees became tied to their trade, though not to any particular employer. At the same time employers in these industries were forbidden to hire labor except through employment offices run by the state or by trade unions. And national and local Labor Supply Boards, representing the government, the unions, and the employers, were established in order to make sure that skilled labor was being used and supplemented in the most effective way. The first steps were thus taken towards eventual universal industrial conscription, if this should prove to be necessary at some later stage of the war.[13]

Restrictions could not be applied to the liberty of labor without management and ownership being subjected to equal restraints. Not only was the excess profits tax raised to 100%, but the government reserved to itself the right to take over property as well as persons.

When workers were deprived of the opportunity to better their conditions by moving from worse-paid to better-paid work, the government had to assume an increased measure of responsibility for their working conditions. In particular, it had to make the farm laborer's lot more palatable by securing him a nation-wide raise in wages. The national Agricultural Wages Board of 1917-21 was revived; it brought a national weekly minimum of 48s. into effect on July 1, 1940; and several county boards fixed somewhat higher minima.

Trade Board procedure was also speeded up in the spring of 1940 in order to facilitate wage rate increases in the comparatively ill-organized industries covered by these government-appointed boards. Prewar governmental machinery was similarly used for raising the wage rates of coal miners, railwaymen, and road-transport workers. All this was in addition to the raises obtained by the ordinary process of collective bargaining, with or without the help of official conciliators or arbitrators. On the whole, however, the government can take little pride in the £2,000,000 increase in weekly wage rates granted during the first ten months of the war. It was necessitated by a rise in the cost of living, and was a measure of the government's failure to stabilize prices and mobilize labor at the commencement of the war.

As the Ministry became more and more responsible for labor conditions, it inevitably went beyond the fixing of wages and the matching of men and jobs. It began for almost the first time to consider the general welfare of workers in industry. By an order in council of June 7, 1940, the administration of the Factory Acts was transferred from the Home Office to the Ministry of Labor. Thus here, as in many other fields, a long-needed reform was accomplished under the stress of temporary emergency, and a channel opened to the more effective future collaboration of Great Britain in the work of international labor legislation.

The relations between the government and the organized labor movement passed through two distinct phases, which might be called "outside" and "inside" collaboration.

The first eight months saw a considerable measure of outside collaboration. The trade unions had no official responsibility for the formation or administration of policy; yet they
participated energetically in this process. This they did, not
as mere pressure groups, but through a regularly constituted
Consultative Committee, on which an equal number of representatives of the General Council of the Trades Union Congress and of the British Employers' Confederation might
confer together on matters of common interest. This body
discussed freely with the government all matters of current
labor legislation and administration. It played a part, for instance, in working out means by which Factory Acts might
be modified in wartime with the agreement of all parties concerned. Some Area Advisory Committees, composed likewise
of equal numbers of trade-union and employer representatives, were also set up early in 1940 to help thresh out some
of the problems of expanding output.

After the fall of Neville Chamberlain on May 10, 1940,
the active participation of organized labor in the inner councils of the government became possible. With Mr. Ernest
Bevin at the Ministry of Labor, the trade unions had nothing
to fear in agreeing to a temporary increase in governmental
authority. When the Consultative Committee was consulted
by the new minister on the best means of avoiding the inter-
ruption of war production by strikes or lockouts, it recommended a National Arbitration Tribunal to settle disputes
that had not been settled by the usual procedure of negotia-
tion. This recommendation the Minister accepted. In actual
practice this tribunal has not prevented small stoppages; it
has served to represent a moral principle rather than the enforcement of penal law.

Throughout the war, the attitude of organized labor whether
in the hold or at the helm, has been constant and unchanged.[14]

"If we fail at this critical moment to gain the victory over the dark forces which assail us, all hope of freedom and progress have gone (*sic*) for generations to come," the secretary of the movement has written. "The Trade Unions as we know them will vanish. We shall be completely unable to protect the interests of the workers, and to vindicate those principles on which the movement is based." [15]

GOVERNMENT AND EDUCATION

England continues to have its two systems of education, the one privately paid for by those who can afford it, and the other publicly tax-supported.

With the private system we are not directly concerned; for, in spite of more taxes and less births, this private system of "preparatory" and "public" schools has not yet had to accept government aid or make concessions to democratic principles in order to earn such aid.

It is the tax-supported system alone that is to be discussed here. The present war has not yet produced any educational revolution comparable to that effected by the late H. A. L. Fisher toward the end of the first World War, when the government offered state aid to endowed "grammar schools" in return for the granting of free places, gave special grants for the building up of "sixth forms" in municipal secondary schools, provided several hundred "state scholarships" [16] for school-leavers going to universities, and established nation-wide minimum scales for the payment of elementary and secondary school teachers. No similar experiment in educational democratization has yet been attempted.

Instead, some retrogression has occurred. This has arisen partly from the process of evacuation without due consideration being given to reception. Rural reception areas have seldom had as good educational facilities to offer as urban evacuation areas. Romantics who believe that country life is inherently more educative than city life see advantages in the shift. Romantics who believe that country air is more health-giving than adequate clinical following-up of periodic school medical examinations also see physical advantages in this change of environment. During the first year of war, however, the number of school children evacuees seems never to have amounted to more than 750,000 out of a tax-supported school population of over 5,000,000; and only a limited number of these settled down for any considerable length of time in the reception areas. Before the war began the government invested £1,000,000 in a non-profit Camps Corporation which was to meet a large part of its expenses in peacetime by renting cabins to holiday-makers. In wartime these fifty camps were to become schools for 350 evacuees each; yet six months after the outbreak of the war, and twelve months after the conquest of Czechoslovakia, only twenty of these much-publicized camps were ready. The chief merit of this first great evacuation in the autumn of 1939 was that its unlimited failure made possible the comparative success of the second evacuation at the end of 1940.

Worse than the evacuation has been the commandeering of school buildings for other governmental purposes. In some areas this meant that when the first evacuation failed in the winter of 1939-40, the children found on their return that they had no school to which they could go. Several months would elapse before buildings could once more be made available for teaching. Even then, school had to be taught in two shifts a day in many buildings. By April, 1940, only 20% of the children in evacuation areas were in full-time attendance.

Under the circumstances, compulsory school attendance

broke down. Evacuees who returned could not be compelled to attend schools that did not exist. Local education authorities in evacuation areas were unwilling to assume responsibility for herding hundreds of children together in buildings devoid of bombproof shelters. Only when a second chance of voluntary evacuation had been offered and neglected in the spring of 1940 did the Board of Education feel justified in urging local authorities to restore half-time compulsory attendance. Even in "neutral" areas—that is, areas that were designated neither for "evacuation" nor for "reception"— the local education authorities often refrained from enforcing compulsory attendance, especially in infants' schools. A demoralizing break has thus occurred in what seemed to be the well-established social habit of regular school attendance.

Special setbacks were received by the powerful movement making for increased provision of educational opportunities for adolescents. The law raising the national minimum school-leaving age to 15 was due to come into operation in September, 1939; it was postponed. The new workmen's compensation law of 1940 provides no allowances for children after the age of 15. Vocational training by employers, in agreement with trade unions, and under government supervision, has been greatly stressed; but it has inevitably been to a great extent in jobs that will prove to be blind alleys if Britain ever again has peace.

Compulsory military training has begun at 20; deferment has been wisely granted to students; and education in the army has not been neglected.

Between leaving school at 14 or 15—the age varies from one locality to another—and induction into the army at 20, a considerable gap has thus remained. Attempts to bridge this gap by government grants-in-aid to voluntary agencies for physical education have not yet resulted in the emergence of any well-established patterns of governmental action.

LOCAL ADMINISTRATION

Next to the burning problem of how to raise policy-determining to a level more worthy of man as a rational being, the striking lesson of the first year and a half of war has probably been a series of changes in relations between the national government and the local authorities.

For many years past, British local government authorities have been developing into local administrators of national policies. Hitherto, this has been mainly in such fields of social policy as health, infant welfare, education, and poor relief. Now, however, the exigencies of total war have thrust upon these civilian bodies the responsibility for recruiting and training over one million Air Raid Precautions volunteers, besides quadrupling their fire brigades, enlarging their police forces, controlling the retail trade in rationed foods, arranging to repair damaged houses, establishing rest-centers and feeding-centers for those who have lost their homes, sending 1,500,000 persons from evacuation areas (which was easy) to reception areas—where it was hard to know what to do with them, or to ascertain which authority exactly was responsible for what—and coping with them when they streamed back home unbidden to find their schools commandeered for other purposes. No equitable formula could possibly have been devised for sharing the cost of such civil defense services between the central and the local authorities. This financial problem was particularly troublesome, as the Home Office, which was initially responsible for civil defense, was addicted to the outworn practice of making percentage grants. Such a system led to endless haggling and

wasted efforts. Yet in the emergency we have seen a few instances where the national government trusted the discretion
of elective local authorities so absolutely as to break all precedent and make 100% grants for some purposes. This confidence, it might be added, was foreshadowed ten years earlier
by the Ministry of Health's famous experiment in block
grants.[17]

Such mutual trust as this is so intimately bound up with
the present partnership of danger, that it may well not survive the emergency to its present extent. But other more
complicated changes have taken place in the patterns of
central-local relationships, changes which meet long felt needs
and may be expected to stand a good chance of survival. For
the first time, to illustrate, the state has coordinated such
local services as fire fighting and hospitalization on a regional
scale, making the services of the city available in the coun-
tryside, and overriding many vested antipathies. Moreover,
these overdue reforms have been effected by emergency regulations issued under the first Emergency Powers Act.

More and more the old lines of demarcation between local
and national functions are being blurred; but new lines of
demarcation are becoming slowly clearer. Little by little, for
a whole generation now, the national government has been
taking over responsibility for the payment of monetary assistance to the needy. In this process 1940's great step, mentioned earlier in this chapter, was the transformation of the
national Unemployment Assistance Board into an Assistance
Board *tout court*, with the duty of relieving unemployed
persons who had never been insured, and old-age pensioners
and widows whose pensions were inadequate. By this transfer, local Public Assistance Committees were relieved of
some £5,000,000 of liabilities, although their block grant
was at the same time reduced by £1,000,000. Thus even

wartime distress has helped in the breakup of local poor relief, the concentration in the hands of the national government of this as of so much other economic power, and the reintegration in the hands of a single authority of more and more aspects of home assistance.

Thus far, the local authorities have survived; but for how long? When in 1939 one hundred local War Agricultural Executive Committees were set up to force farmers to plow up 2,000,000 acres of grassland, they were nominated by the Minister of Agriculture, instead of being chosen by the county councils as in the previous war. This example, however, has not been generally followed. Above all, the central government has made but little use of its power to supersede previously-existing local authorities in the way that the Ministry of Health formerly superseded recalcitrant Boards of Guardians; that is, by substituting commissioners for mayor and council. No ministry seems even to have had much recourse to the default powers vested in it by the Civil Defense Act. Elective councils have been made co-optative so long as the emergency may last; some queer and muddled experiments have been made in places where local councils have delegated considerable powers to Emergency Committees; and their clerks have shown some sign of developing into central agents by being named Air Raid Precautions Controllers, National Registration Officers, and Food Executive Officers. Yet even at the height of the aerial attack on London, when cabinet ministers had to tour the worst-bombed boroughs nightly, the central government did not yield to the widespread demand that it appoint a "dictator" for Greater London. Certainly, if the metropolitan police can be under the direct control of the Home Office in time of peace, there seems no good reason why civil defense services and public utility undertakings, at the very least, should not pass under

similar control in time of war. At present the twelve Regional
Commissioners are slowly finding their feet and even Washington, D. C.—or would it be better to say the T. V. A.?—
may yet become a model for Greater London.

The continued existence of local self-government, shorn
of some social service functions, but burdened with new
national defense responsibilities, leads us straight back however to the problem with which we started. The local authority is not only a maid of all work: it is everybody's maid
of all work. How can it, for example, pay the many bills
that all central departments insist on charging to its account? [18]
The city chamberlain of Edinburgh struck at the core of the
problem when he wrote:

Local authorities are attacked, as they say, by a multitude of
enemies. There is no department of State solely concerned with
the impact of the war on local authority finances, and consequently each department makes its own attack. If it is the Ministry of Home Security on Civil Defense at one moment, it is the
Ministry of Health on First Aid Posts at another. The Ministry
of Agriculture hammers away at allotments, while the Education Department and the Health Ministry deal with evacuation.
The Home Office deals with Watching, and the Ministry of
Transport with Roads. One is tempted to ask how much coordination there is at the center. Has the Treasury no obligation to the localities as well as to the central departments?

When there is no over-all plan and no unity in national
policy making, it is not easy for the local administrator to
serve his many masters intelligently.

CHAPTER III

The Effects of the War on the
Government of Germany

BY FRITZ MORSTEIN MARX
Queens College

"**G**ERMANY today resembles a besieged fortress."
These words were addressed to a mass meeting of
German workers. The speaker: Dr. Robert Ley, Chief of
Staff of the Political Organization of the National Socialist
Party. Time: 1935.[1] The simile was both strained and persuasive. It was strained because "peace in our time" was still
in the offing, and all avenues of international intercourse,
political and economic, were wide open. It was persuasive
because it drove home the speaker's keynote—Hitler's Mil-
lennium would have to rest on superior force, and the policy
of total preparedness would require the systematic organization of a closed war economy as peacetime "normalcy."

We know now that Dr. Ley outlined not only the intentions of his master but also the practical realities of subsequent years. When the invasion of Poland got under way,
the Third Reich stood poised for the kill. Each cog in the
vast war machinery worked with almost automatic precision.
Clausewitz could not have dreamed of a smoother shift from
diplomatic to military means in the pursuit of national self-
interest. The people sensed that the fateful hour had struck.
But the transition from peace to war involved no noticeable
change in the community processes, political, economic or

74

social. What happened was merely a tightening of controls, a bracing for the crucial test.

THE MINISTER COUNCIL FOR NATIONAL DEFENSE

Political systems centered on the symbolism of personal leadership are likely to die with the death of the recognized Leader unless the line of succession is made clear in advance. For years it remained a moot question who would follow Hitler. The moody mystic who personifies the Third Reich, fond of alluding with choked voice to his inevitable departure, preferred to leave it to rumor on whom the toga of authority would fall. Meanwhile the achievements and the prestige of his lieutenants could be trusted to facilitate his eventual choice. When on the eve of war he was finally ready to commit himself, disclosure of the secret that he had guarded so long did not cause surprise. In the emergency session of the Reichstag, he marked Hermann Göring as the Leader to come; after him, Rudolf Hess,* Hitler's Substitute in Party Affairs; "should anything happen" to Hess, a special Senate would have to "select from among its members the next worthiest, that is, the bravest." No reference was made to acid-tongued Dr. Joseph Goebbels, manipulator of bold words, now eclipsed by men of action.

This order of succession had been foreshadowed by the creation of a new Minister Council for National Defense, established while Germany was still technically at peace. One of the most bothersome problems of modern warfare, on which Lloyd George has supplied us with a classic commentary in his memoirs, arises from the contest between civil and military authorities for supremacy of decision. The Minister

---

* Hess, in a fantastic flight from Germany, crashed and was captured in Scotland, May 10, 1941.

Council represents an ingenious solution by interlocking the respective control mechanisms in a body that does not require the constant attention of the Leader in person.[2] Hitler has kept himself outside and thus above the Council. When assuming the title of "First Soldier" he merely underscored the implications of the "leadership principle"—that all ultimate authority is merged in him, military as well as civil.[3] Political primacy embraces both aspects, and in the National Socialist scheme political primacy rests with the Leader alone.

However, in order to be workable such an arrangement presupposes essential homogeneity on the immediately subordinate level at which the Minister Council is lodged. To make sure of this homogeneity Hitler lifted into the Council exclusively men of proven capacity for anticipating his mind and of fundamental agreement in inclination and outlook among themselves. There was not one single new face; no one "borrowed" from outside the "inner ring" around the Führer; no captain of industry; and, needless to say, no labor leader since only organization functionaries are left. What is perhaps more important: each one of those drafted for the Minister Council belongs to the group known as "sound and sane," in contrast with the radical wing of the Party eager to push social experimentation or to chart the New World. As an invitation addressed to the whole people to forget the extravagant partisanship of National Socialism and to put its mind on national unity, the Council could hardly have looked more attractive.

The Minister Council's chairman is mountain-moving and widely popular Marshal Göring, who simultaneously remains in charge of the Four-Year Plan. The other members are stalwart Hess, businesslike and wakeful, second in succession; efficiency-minded Dr. Wilhelm Frick, Reich Minister of the Interior, as coordinator of the national administration; Dr.

Walther Funk, Reich Minister of Commerce, who prefers results to political orthodoxy, as coordinator of the national economy; Reich Minister Dr. Lammers, a career civil servant, head of the Chancellor's Bureau; and strategist Wilhelm Keitel, chief of the High Command of the Armed Forces. This six-man body has the task of "unified direction of the administration and the economy." It is authorized to issue ordinances "having statutory effect," limited only by the power of the Leader to assign the adoption of individual laws either to the Reich cabinet or the national parliament. The Council is hence not only a consultative organ available to the Leader but also a full-fledged agency of legislation, quite apart from its executive function. While it is not to absorb the broad ordinance-making powers conferred upon Göring as the coordinator for the Four-Year Plan, the Council has virtually superseded the cabinet as a legislative body, just as the cabinet, under the Enabling Act of 1933, had relieved the national parliament of practically all of its lawmaking business.

Thus a narrowly limited group of key people, each with the resources of his own vast organization behind him, has been set up in order to secure the highest degree of elasticity, dispatch, and unity in reaching and enforcing policy decisions. The Leader has freed his mind, save for exceptional circumstances, from the burden of insuring technical direction and synthesis of expert judgments. He can confine himself to the determination of the general line of policy without being drawn into the cumbersome planning of ways and means, for which he never had much taste. He can sit in at Council meetings and get the advice of those he trusts most, but he need not bother with the intricacies of coordination and execution that confront the chairman, and Göring has native talent in these matters. Moreover, there is no likelihood of serious friction in the Council and between it and the *Führer*. Each member has worked in increasingly close contact with Hitler for quite some time, most of them in fact since 1933. And their team spirit is as highly developed as is their deference to Göring's leadership. No better working nucleus could have been brought together from among all those who at one juncture or another occupied prominent positions in the New Germany.

REGIONAL ORGANIZATION

One of the first measures taken by the Minister Council for National Defense was to provide itself with its own regional machinery for the effective correlation of all activities bearing upon warfare. For each army area a regional commissioner has been appointed to serve as the Council's agent. He is responsible for all of the non-military aspects of defense. His chief duty is to secure unity of planning and operations within his district and to effect harmonious cooperation with the army area command. Though not as such at the helm of the existing regional administration, the commissioners have tended to become the pivots of control in all matters of major importance, for in times of war defense needs claim priority over anything else. This priority found early recognition in the Leader's Decree on Administrative Simplification, promulgated half a week before the first German soldier crossed the Polish frontier.

The Simplification Decree also concerned itself with other equally significant questions. It called for full departmental self-exertion, for quick unbureaucratic and independent decision, and for joint administrative effort without jurisdictional squabbles and delay. It further authorized the delegation to subordinate agencies of powers reserved by law for the central departments, thus giving the field services greater leeway, and wider opportunities for immediate determination in their respective districts. At the same time, those agencies charged with the supervision of local authorities and other public corporations were empowered to issue binding directions beyond the scope of their supervisory prerogatives.[4] Finally, as coordinators of the national administration and the national economy, Dr. Frick and Dr. Funk received a special mandate to design and carry out additional simplifications of the administrative process. With so much stress on vigorous action, it is not startling that the decree virtually abolished litigation before administrative courts, substituting simple complaint procedure for judicial review. Acting on this broad authorization, Dr. Funk immediately entrusted the responsible integration of all economic measures within each army area to the regional level of the administrative hierarchy, primarily the national governors and in Prussia the provincial prefects. The Food Estate, proud of the specious autonomy that it had maintained thus far, was abruptly placed at the direct command of the Reich Minister of Agriculture, and drawn into the governmental structure through the establishment of regional and local food offices.

The demand for flexibility and speed, expressed in the Simplification Decree, initiated a distinct trend toward deconcentration of operative responsibility throughout the executive branch. However, the trend did not carry over into the local sphere. Anticipating difficulties in the coordination of municipal authorities, the decree on the contrary strengthened the supervisory agencies by giving them the power to bring local government in line by fiat. In practice, the exercise of this power proved to be a complicating factor, resulting as it did in conflict and duplication. In February, 1940, Dr. Frick deemed it imperative to reaffirm the initiative of municipal authorities. He instructed the supervisory agencies to rely on their extraordinary power only in very exceptional cases. Since local government, in his words, had "carried out the manifold war tasks left to it with a sense of responsibility and in commendable orientation toward the aims of the Reich," he saw no need for extraordinary powers beyond those means of central supervision provided in such laws as the Municipal Act of 1935. Press comment rejoiced at the explicit recognition of the accomplishments of "German self-government." It is more to the point to say that the "running" of local administration from the supervisory level produced too much waste motion without appreciable gains. One must bear in mind that on the whole the standards of German municipal management are not inferior to those prevailing in the national and state services.

With local government largely restored to its former functions, the innovations of wartime organization may be summed up as a resolute effort to re-enforce administrative responsibility at the appropriate levels of action. The tendency itself suggests sound counsel; the man primarily identified with it is that embodiment of permanency, Dr. Lammers, whose government career spans across the entire sequence of régimes that twentieth century Germany has witnessed. And he is merely the most conspicuous exponent of an inconspicuous force whose influence is often inadequately assessed—the merit bureaucracy, permeated by a service tradition that in strength and continuity dwarfs that of National Socialism. The career element has also contributed of its experience in the experimental approach to fuller regional integration. Conquest has opened new outlets for laboratory tests in search of *Reichsreform*.[5]

The territorial changes that took place after the Polish campaign included the incorporation into the Third Reich of those areas of Poland which before Versailles had been the Prussian provinces of West Prussia and Posen. Like Austria and the Sudeten districts, the "liberated regions," as they are being called, entered Germany in a novel status, that of Reich *Gaue*. As such they were placed under the immediate jurisdiction of the central authorities. In structure, the two new Reich *Gaue* were modeled on the Sudeten *Gau* Act, the most advanced pattern of integration. This law made the national governor, who at the same time was to serve as the *Gau* leader of the National Socialist Party, a real center of political and administrative control. In him all branches of the national administration were for the first time combined on the regional level, save for revenue collection, railroads, communications, and the courts. Like other national governors, he was empowered to demand information from every administrative agency located in his area. But beyond that, he was enabled to issue binding directions "within the framework of the laws and the instructions of the central departments" independent of exceptional urgency. This was a new page in the evolution of regional organization.

For the Reich *Gaue* Danzig and Posen, however, still another page was added.[6] The national governors were put also at the helm of those regional establishments left technically independent under the Sudeten *Gau* Act. While the regional head of the revenue administration, for instance, would continue to receive most of his orders from the Reich Ministry of Finance, such orders were to clear through the governor's office, thereby giving the governor an opportunity of securing complete coordination of action in harmony with the needs of the area and his general administrative program. On the subordinate level, the same concentration has been insured by grouping the local offices of the different branches of national administration under the county prefect. The experimental character of these arrangements is indicated by

the fact that the Minister of the Interior can subsequently
separate individual field services from the governor's and
the county prefect's offices. But the line of regional consolidation marked by the Sudeten *Gau* Act and its elaboration in
the Reich *Gaue* Danzig and Posen may well be intended to
furnish the general formula for central-regional relationships
in the definitive administrative subdivision of National Socialist Germany.

In Austria *Reichsreform* apparently proceeded on the principle of political caution. While Austrian army units reaped
glory on Poland's plains and in Norway's mountains, administrative reorganization swept the last testimonials of the
Hapsburg Empire into the gutter. The biggest sweep occurred in January, 1940, through two executive orders passed
under the *Ostmark* Act.[7] As if to counteract autonomist tendencies, the functions of the former central government in
Vienna were distributed among the Berlin Ministries and the
seven Austrian Reich *Gaue*. The entire field of school policy
and supervision, including the universities, was taken over
by the Reich Ministry of Education. All matters of regional
concern were assigned to the *Gau* governors. The former
Austrian Supreme Court was allowed to live on as its own
shadow; its jurisdiction is now confined to administrative
litigation (of which little is left under the Leader's Simplification Decree), and it was expressly prohibited from review-
ing measures passed by the central departments. In March,
1938, Austria had been welcomed into Hitler's realm as a
"*Land* of the German Reich." The *Land* was no longer; all
that was left was seven regions. Dr. Seyss-Inquart, the special governor for the central administration of the former
Austrian government, closed his offices for good.

ECONOMIC MANAGEMENT

The self-imposed restrictions of occupational and consumer freedom to which Dr. Ley alluded in his phrase of the "besieged fortress" have long been a typical feature of the National Socialist economy.[8] Step by step a highly complex looking but essentially simple system of regulation was evolved, slowly perfected into a "black art," particularly in its fiscal features. In its initial phase, the Hitler cabinet, duly adorned by Dr. Schacht's presence, gratefully acknowledged the encouraging nod of the German capitalist. Once entrenched it could afford to turn the tables. What followed was the equivalent of an embargo on ownership and investment. Title remained in private hands, but its holder found himself placed on political probation.[9] As for the worker, free labor was transformed into a governmentally controlled service function.[10] Ideological ministrations meanwhile kept alive the thought of things to come—a Greater Reich, a richer life, fat years after lean ones. And there was work for all, even though guns had precedence over butter.

Rationing both as a principle of distribution and commodity planning had stealthily crept into the Third Reich as early as 1935. Being a necessity, it was soon glorified as a Spartan test. It was also inconspicuously developed into a smoothly running administrative technique. Most Germans, however, rubbed their eyes when they saw the batch of ordinances, all dated alike, that elevated rationing to a comprehensive system several days before the first shot was fired. Every detail of these measures had been worked out before the event, and all that was required at the critical moment was the ministerial signature. Literally overnight the personal purchase certificate had made its appearance, covering important foodstuffs, nearly all textiles and shoeware, coal, motor fuel, and soap. With the same dispatch a nation-wide allocation service was set up, divided into local and regional offices. In the preceding years the emphasis had been upon "steering" the consumer away from supplies that were running short, such as butter, meat, and coffee. Now it was a demand of prudence, in official language, to safeguard "justice and equality" among all classes by commandeering the supply of nearly all vital goods. As during the first World War, workers engaged in physically exacting labor were promoted into a privileged category as recipients of additional food rations.

While taking credit for such providence, the authorities let it be understood that for some time they had been building up considerable inventories of crucial raw materials. They also cited facts and figures to show that livestock was way up, owing to the earlier restrictions of meat consumption, and that grain storage was exceptionally plentiful. With memories of the first World War still widespread, Germans needed no reminder that it was better to economize right at the beginning than to be careless at first and reduced to starvation in the end.[11] They knew purchase certificates to be a nuisance, but certainly only a minor nuisance as long as their essential purpose could be achieved: to preserve the home front. Moreover, one consolation remained; bread, flour, potatoes, and vegetables had been left unrationed—for the time being. It could have been worse, and the demonstration of government foresight made the striking step on second thought a perfectly normal thing. There was no opportunity for a run on the stores. In a few weeks the ensuing inconveniences had become routine transactions, for officials and citizens alike.

Within little more than a week universal rationing was followed by a War Economy Ordinance passed by the Min-

ister Council for National Defense.[12] It combined an appeal
for equality of sacrifices with pragmatic considerations of
war finance.[13] The wage earner had to take a downward revision of the industrial wage scales. All other incomes were
burdened with substantial surtaxes, especially through imple-
mentation of the graduated income tax. In addition, entre-
preneurs were directed to translate any gains derived from
the war conditions solely into lower prices. There was to
be no profiteering. These measures were expected to do two
things: to bolster morale and to ease the pressure on the Reich
Treasury through both additional revenue and price reductions on the vast bulk of government orders, thus minimizing
the need for borrowing. If we may trust official statistics,
the result seems to have proved satisfactory. In spite of the
loss of overseas trade connections, the national tax revenue
for fiscal 1939-1940 reached a new high, with almost 24 billion *Reichsmark*, and fiscal 1940-1941 gives some promise of
passing this mark. Nevertheless, the Reich's funded debt had
risen to nearly 30 billions at the end of the first quarter of
1940, representing an increase of about 3 billions within the
preceding three months alone. Whether the undisclosed in-
debtedness has also gone up is anybody's guess, but wage and
price control buttressed by rationing have enabled the government to check the normal signs and disruptions of inflation. It is probable, however, that in the War Economy Ordinance the Minister Council discovered that it had reached
the ceiling. For after twelve months overtime compensation
was restored,[14] and the income surtax was limited to one tax
year.[15] Were the vanquished nations west of the Rhine expected to chip in?

As to the entrepreneur's duties under the War Economy
Ordinance, it was soon made plain that his fulfillment of the
obligation to reduce prices would be looked upon as a sign

of patriotism—and woe to those who failed to be patriots! General price limits decreed heretofore were no legal excuse for sitting tight. Only the actual cost situation could serve as a standard. And the cost calculation was not permitted to include factors such as general war risks or losses through war damages; nor special social services maintained by the plant for the workers beyond the new wage level; nor ill-considered and hence expensive rush purchases of raw materials. On the other hand, all savings caused by lower wages and market prices would have to go to the public in terms of price reductions. This had to apply also to the area of imperfect competition governed by cartels and monopolistic formations.

The British blockade and the spectre of a war of attrition were bound to produce mounting pressure in the direction of utmost precision of economic regulation. By January, 1940, Marshal Göring had added another ring to his sprawling circus by quietly relieving Dr. Funk of much of his assignment as coordinator of the national economy. Direction of the entire war economy fell to the man who today unquestionably ranks as the organizational star of the régime. Apart from his chairmanship in the Minister Council for National Defense, Göring undertook to boss a new General Economic Council that meets once or twice a week, bringing together an array of administrative officers responsible for the actual operations of a variety of central agencies. Its members are the permanent undersecretaries of the Ministries of Commerce, Agriculture, Labor, Transportation, and the Interior, the National Forest Office and the Four-Year Plan Administration, besides the High Command's chief of ordnance, the Reich Price Commissioner and a representative of Rudolf Hess, for the National Socialist Party.

Depending on the nature of its deliberations, the council

calls for the presence of spokesmen for the Ministry of Finance, the Reich Bank, or the bureaus of the national coordinators. Its deputy chairman is Undersecretary Körner of the Göring entourage; he is the central cog of the organization. With a face-saving gesture, Göring has designated Dr. Funk as his substitute in case he is afield for longer periods, but only for major decisions of economic policy, in which Funk is hardly expected to improvise. Thus the strongest of Hitler's associates has been forced to assume the functions of a dynamo working on two different levels: policy-making, as the dominant figure in the Minister Council for National Defense; and policy-executing, as the hard-driving go-getter of the General Economic Council.

In the control of industry, particularly the allocation of raw materials, the Reich Ministries can confine themselves to general direction. The spade work is done by special agencies installed for each major branch of production. Most are staffed in about equal proportion with civil servants and with experts who have practical familiarity with the specific sector. These government agencies have come to exercise stewardship over all so-called "economic self-government," such as the Estates and similar corporative hierarchies.[16] The latter are utilized as regional distribution machinery. The basic relationship between government and business is well epitomized in that ominous passage that has made the rounds in Germany in innumerable variations: "It is left to the initiative of business so to organize that the government need not step in." Under the late Karl Bosch, Nobel Prize winner, board chairman of the German Dye Trust and Hitler's *Wehrwirtschaftsführer*, the theme acquired an undertone of dignified inevitability.

No less inevitable was the gradual submission of the small entrepreneur and craftsman to the pressure for broader com-

binations at the price of independence. As cartels and syn-
dicates bloomed forth throughout the economy, it could be
only a question of time until small-scale enterprise would
have to join hands the same way.[17] Under an ordinance issued
early in September, 1939, such concentrations of minor plants
and workshops may be achieved by decree. In the bland
language of an editorial, "Now the public interest has become
exclusively decisive; it will be realized by ministerial decision,
a decision that weighs all factors, as can not be doubted, with
a just hand." [18] The new old-age insurance for craftsmen will
probably somewhat cushion the blow, while the resulting
amalgamations have a chance of benefiting from the present
policy of "strewing" government contracts widely enough
to reach all middle-sized business units.

The Quest of National Solidarity

From the very beginning, the régime has been profoundly
mindful of one paramount premise: that the war will be won
or lost at the home front rather than on the battlefields.
The lesson of 1918 stands out too clearly in Hitler's mind to
let him simply trust his stars. To generate and re-enforce
popular support is a government task that ranks first.[19] It is
inseparably related to sacrifice, food and victories, but it
overshadows everything else. The quest of national solidarity
has taken many forms, but it is instructive to focus on some
of the *Leitmotive* in the symphony of government propaganda. One of them is that the exigencies of war involve no
basic departure from what was commonplace in peace. Editorial comment before the event put it as follows:[20]

Every worker, employee and entrepreneur has been trained
for years to orient himself toward the public interest as a whole
and to follow governmental direction, quite apart from the fact

that owing to the progressive development of market organization and control, small leeway is left for unsound individual deviations. In addition, national discipline has been practiced long enough, and no alarm call need go out should further steps become necessary to transform the governmentally directed peace economy into a war economy.

How to manage in case of war is a question that has found attention for considerable time, as Undersecretary Dr. Landfried pointed out the other day at the opening of the German East Fair in Königsberg. An economic general staff under the Reich Minister of Commerce has the task of satisfying, on the basis of uniform standards, those needs which war creates in every walk of life. It is clear that all war economy measures must be taken with due regard for the close relationship between the commodity and the money supply. . . . In the first place, the scarcities of labor, raw materials, and machines must be overcome or minimized. That is different only in degree and means, but not in principle, from the governmentally directed peace economy. What is required is a rank order of war needs and their adequate satisfaction both singly and in their entirety. . . . Since there is no problem of government revenues, the only question is to secure, by taxation and the utilization of savings, a constant back flow of the money and bills of credit which the government channelizes into industry, so that the ill effects of surplus purchasing power will be avoided. For this too the necessary devices are already present in the governmentally directed peace economy. Price stop and wage stop, old and conceivably also new taxes must be relied upon under such conditions for arresting undesirable consumption and for placing at the disposal of warfare all available goods and services. Unquestionably, unfamiliar demands would nevertheless have to be made on the government and the citizen. War experience, above anything else, is apt to show that *greatest determination* of governmental direction in the commodity as well as the monetary fields is indispensable.

Another leading tune is a favorite of Hitler's—"They Wanted War," that is, Chamberlain, Daladier, and the rest "wanted war." Dr. Rudolf Kircher, once an Anglophile and still the editor-in-chief of the *Frankfurter Zeitung*, presented his readers, at the threshold of war, with this persuasive elucidation:[21]

The German people stands united behind its Leader, wishing nothing more anxiously than that his great statesmanship and diplomacy may again enable him to reach his goal without war. The certainty, however, that the struggle does not only involve Danzig, which is bound to fall into our lap like a ripe fruit, but that England and France have arbitrarily singled out the Polish question for a showdown with the National Socialist Reich, so that Germany's future itself is at stake, has made the German people ready for every sacrifice. . . . Unwilling and unable to establish a new order because that would necessarily be to Germany's advantage, they (England and France) knew no other course than to abuse the East European states for one system of alliance after another. That must end. And it will end. . . . We want neither England and France nor Poland for eternal foes. But the hour has come in which the Polish question must be solved.

When Hitler after the Polish campaign met again with the Reichstag early in October, 1939, he gave his plea for a German Peace a fine turn by intoning:

Has Germany presented England with any demand that would threaten the British Empire or put its existence in question? No, on the contrary, Germany has made such a demand neither of France nor of England. . . . If (the problems of the European Continent) have to be met anyway sooner or later, it would be more reasonable to tackle the solution before millions of men have spilled their blood and billions of values have been destroyed without purpose.

Now, however, that the incredible has become a *fait accompli*, that France is prostrate, even the mute skeptic under the swastika is compelled to concede the Hitler Utopia a distinct winning chance. Continental hegemony, after all, is so much closer that it appears worth while in a new sense to "stick it out." The Leader showed himself again an astute slogan-maker when he said of the Great Western Offensive: "The fight beginning today determines the fate of the German nation for the next thousand years." And as the fury of the Battle of Britain increased, few Germans, National Socialist or not, could be expected to ignore the fundamental implications. These summed up to a plain alternative—"either we or they." Propaganda was able to embellish the formula,[22] but it was not in need of embellishment. There was no other way of getting out of the war. To plot for the downfall of the régime and hope for the victor's consideration? That had failed to work once, and the aftermath of 1918 had lived on as a poignant lesson.[23]

This was certainly not a war of enthusiasm, as even the German press frankly stated.[24] The man in the street had not wanted anything of the sort, even if he thought the liquidation of Poland entirely in order. Needless to say, he has not come to like the war now, though matters look better than at the start. However, he cannot well close his eyes to the conclusion that peace will be achieved only through victory or defeat, and there is nothing on the horizon that would induce him to prefer defeat. Hence the strange paradox that the Third Reich at war, at least at the present juncture, is a more truly united and more solidified Germany than she was a few years ago.[25] This explains why the boisterous shouts of "popular enlightenment" that Dr. Goebbels used to set off serially have largely died away. Aside from the skillful exploitation of the "we or they" alternative, the home front, by comparison with bygone days, is grimly quiet. The drums of propaganda are muffled, for the obvious is explicit. Extraordinary as it may seem, that is a source of strength which no one should underestimate. It would be bold to assume that even the politically controlling group anticipated this development.

Air raids do not distinguish between men and women, old and young, but quite aside from that, totalitarian war is everybody's business. Hundreds of thousands of pensioners have come back to pinch-hit on chores that called for additional man power. Youth has filled other gaps. The Labor Service took up front duties.[26] Nearly 600 detachments followed the troops into Poland, while others worked in the advanced positions of the West Wall. The Woman's Labor Service was rapidly expanded. There are now more than 2,000 training camps for girls who prepare for farm responsibilities; enlistment is by draft. The same principle was applied to recruitment for the Hitler Youth. Until then membership had remained voluntary in law,[27] although in the past years fewer and fewer parents had resisted official pressure for inclusion of all eligible youngsters. Those who are now entering in compliance with legal obligation must undergo a period of political probation. The rules, however, stress that "only attainment and sense of duty are decisive." During the first month of war, more than 1,000,000 boys and girls of the Hitler Youth served as volunteers for urgent tasks, especially agricultural work.[28]

While most Germans have not yet undergone the ordeal to which England's population is exposed with harrowing frequency, the stress and strain of war conditions cannot escape notice. With so many demands that tax the individual's nervous balance, there is widest opportunity for misgivings, suspicions and exasperations. As early as December, 1939, Göring saw good reasons for providing a safety valve by opening a new channel for public grievances, in addition to the regular complaint procedure before the administrative authorities. He called on studious Philip Bouhler, head of the Leader's Bureau of the National Socialist Party, to take charge of all such troublesome matters that did not find attention elsewhere, and to hold culprits fully accountable. It seems that the announcement itself had a wholesome effect. That many turned to another pacifier may be inferred from the fact that beer consumption has reached an unprecedented high.

THE NEW ORDER OF HIERARCHIES

Among the Third Reich's hierarchies, the National Socialist Party had always claimed first rank. Its competitors were the bureaucracy and the army. War proved no blessing to the Party.

Mobilization orders meant the same for the citizen and for the rank and file of the National Socialist organizations, but the apparatus of functionaries was largely retained in order to "strengthen the inner front of the German people," in Dr. Ley's words. In the execution of its tasks, the Party tightened the screws by demanding "military precision" of its officialdom.[29] Regulations were issued to secure increased control of the *Gau* and district leaders over the political activities within their areas. Noncompliance with their orders would bring upon the responsible functionary punishment according to military law. Only those projects sponsored by the Party were to be continued that related clearly to war necessities.

Party personnel would concern itself primarily with assistance to the victims of air raids and refugees, and with consultation of these and other groups. The various special formations of the Party were instructed to devote their time to their individual aims and to combine with them supplementary services. Thus the Labor Front, while concentrating on its program for social peace in plant and shop, was to extend its recreational and entertainment facilities to the soldiers in the war zone. The National Socialist Welfare

Organization would have to branch out in order to take care of those made temporarily homeless. The Storm Troop detachments, the National Socialist Motor Corps, and the Hitler Youth were directed to place themselves at the disposal of the authorities and help out wherever needs might arise.

Much of the old glory is gone, however. With so large a number of men under the colors, it is a dubious distinction to walk about in the uniform of the Party. Whatever the attainments of the Brownshirts in "strengthening the inner front of the German people," [30] more real was the triumph of the soldier. Torn out of their civilian routines and the habits of deference to high-booted functionaries, the men in field-gray are less impressed by political ritual and those who administered it. Many a "small Hitler," until then something of a local demigod, stumbled from his pedestal. His patronizing gestures had become pointless, and the magic of terror worked no longer. The political control group had to adjust itself to the new situation. Significantly, the government canceled the usual general display of flags in commemoration of the day of the National Revolution (January 30). Party celebrations are being reduced to a minimum.

"Military precision" indeed was a descriptive password. As the command centers of the Party gained in power, the responsibilities of the corps of functionaries increased. In his Reichstag address at the outbreak of war, Hitler had defined the Party's new mandate by roaring at his assembled chieftains: "Let no one ever report to me that spirits are low in his region, his district, his local group or his cell! You are the ones accountable for sustaining public morale!" That was a large order; moreover, it called for a vast modification of established techniques.

Heretofore the persuasion of propaganda had operated hand in hand with intimidation. But morale cannot be built up by fear, and mere passive acceptance of political decisions does not suffice. War morale, in fact, requires not only a reasonable prospect of victory but also the assurance that the government does its utmost to ease the burden on the people. It is clear that such assurance must find expression in more than words, particularly in National Socialist Germany, where oratory, owing to oversupply, has a pretty low rating. Keeping the people's spirits up is therefore an assignment that of necessity compels the *Gau* and district leaders of the Party to demonstrate a deeper concern for the feelings of the ordinary citizen. Only time can tell how well they will succeed. But the forced reorientation of the Party's domestic strategy itself is a cardinal factor in wartime Germany.

While the Party lost ground, the corporative formations which it had done so much to shape were taken in tow by the central departments. The maneuver signified the growing strength of the bureaucracy.[31] With organizational and administrative skill at a premium, it is but natural that the civil service has continued to rise in the esteem of the political control group. Once the target of bitter attacks for its indifference toward National Socialism, the bureaucracy in recent years has earned the praise of the new régime. Said Frick in February, 1940, before a mass meeting of public personnel in Munich:

There is no period of German history in which such gigantic tasks have been accomplished in so little time as in the past seven years. The German civil servant may take pride in having assumed a prominent place in achieving this work of construction as one of the supporting pillars of the State.

The very composition of the Minister Council for National Defense shows the marked preponderance of men who mean business over ideologues and politicos. In no comparable body that ever graced the Third Reich has the career element been so widely represented, directly and indirectly. Since the establishment of the Council, recognition of the Party has remained confined to the enlistment of its outstanding technical talent. An example is the appointment of Dr. Todt, creator of the new national highway system, to the post of Reich Minister for Armament and Munitions.[32]

In general, the dominant tendency toward highest efficiency has caused the public administrator to outshine the political functionary. As if to demonstrate that this is not just an accident, Hitler lately promoted Civil Servant Lammers *honoris causa* to one of the top ranks of his Special Guard *(Schutzstaffel)*. Half a year earlier, he had attempted to clarify the relationships between county prefects, agents of the central government, and their counterparts in the organization of the Party, the district leaders. The decree made it the exclusive duty of each district leader to promote a positive attitude among the population of his area.[33] All governmental and administrative responsibility, however, would have to stay where it belonged: with the county prefect. District leaders were sharply warned never to interfere with the decisions of the county prefects.

Civil service personnel has also been relied upon for the administration of the occupied territories. Thus the National Socialist Governor General in what is left of Poland has some 3,000 German civil servants under him. These occupy all the important posts; their subordinates are largely Poles. The present eastern boundary of Germany is pushed beyond the frontier of 1918, but between it and the Soviet border remains a territory holding about 14 million people. The regions now included in the Third Reich proper are designated for settlement by German farmers repatriated from the Baltic countries and East Poland, although large-scale execution of this project is to wait until the end of the war. As to the atmosphere in the Governor General's domain, little is said in the German press. Some six months after the collapse of Polish resistance, a German reporter ventured east to cover the ground for his paper. Tucked away in one of his installments was this graphic item:[34]

A district administrator told us that he considered it safe to drive about in the country, accompanied solely by his assistant. "Recently we had a little trouble on the road. Our car got stuck in the snow. But the Polish peasants helped us get out of the drift. You know, we didn't even have a pistol with us."

Although the Party has not been slighted in the distribution of political posts throughout the occupied territories, the executive type was favored quite consistently over the agitator and the rabble-rouser.[35] Between the former and the civil servant, there is naturally a better understanding than characterizes the relationships between the Party personnel and the bureaucracy in general. Thus the changing order of rank of the hierarchies has even led to a certain rearrangement of the prestige scale within the Party. And the gains of the bureaucracy are duplicated by the army.[36] The military hierarchy, identified with the fabulous successes of *Blitzkrieg*, has all but cornered the market of honors. Worse still for the National Socialist functionary, in contrast with the former barrage of political verbiage, the High Command's terse bulletins have made the taciturn army figures peculiarly awe-inspiring. The distinction between words and deeds, so long ignored by the Party, was put in focus by mere implication.

But it is not only this distinction that has given the army higher standing. The very nature of its business, under a conscription system, brings the military hierarchy face to face with the large body of citizens. Moreover, technological warfare has added emphasis to Clausewitz's observation: "The war instrument resembles a machine working with tremen-

dous friction, and it is everywhere in contact with a host of
unpredictable events." The self-exertion of the common soldier, more than ever before, is basic to the effective execution
of strategic plans and tactical coordination. Awareness of this
fact on Hitler's part probably accounts for the statutory
prohibition of politics within the armed forces. While in army
uniform, National Socialists must refrain from all political
activities. There is to be no dual standard, and each man is
considered as good a National Socialist as any one else. Under
the colors, Germans achieve real political equality.

Hence the military hierarchy rests on a more genuine
popular basis than the Party, with its representative preten-
sions. The officer corps, far less homogeneous in social background than a generation ago, has viewed it as something of
a professional necessity to keep the rank and file preoccupied
with straight soldiering. That means today not only intensive
training, with a great variety of technical equipment, but also
the cultivation of individual initiative and group leadership.
Widest devolution of line responsibility is imperative for
offensive movements involving great masses of men. Preparation for independent judgment and decision could not stop
with the officer; it had to reach further.[37] The diffusion of
formerly compact units into innumerable small teams such as
the tank, the plane, and the infantry squad calls for an unusual degree of resourceful cooperation by every team member. Such cooperation cannot be coerced; it must emanate
from the spirit that permeates the soldier. And the soldier is
the ordinary German. Battle experience has furnished proof
that army morale is superior to general political morale. The
lesson must be unmistakable to both High Command and
Party—the aggressive partisanship through which National
Socialism has divided the people is no asset in totalitarian war.

Outlook

It is hardly too bold an assumption that none of the political systems drawn into the second World War will emerge from it unscathed. It is eminently clear, however, that for the Third Reich defeat will mean the end of the Hitler régime. Whether or not such an outcome would merely set off another cycle of humiliation, frustration, and eventual dictatorial resurgence would seem to depend primarily on the character of the peace to follow.[38] There is no certainty that it will differ from the Versailles precedent.

The position which Germany has won thus far is such as to make it impossible for England to acquiesce in it. Peace on the basis of the present situation would spell Britain's surrender. For the British Empire could not live except in amity with the controlling power on the Continent. It therefore looks like the initial phase in an exchange of ever harder blows. No doubt that will tax the Third Reich to the utmost. But one should not underestimate Germany's strength. The inexorable logic of the "we or they" alternative tacitly pleads for perseverance. It effectively substitutes for a positively stated common cause. It does not arise from mere speculation, nor is it confined to the anxieties of a few. What happened in 1918 and thereafter is engraved in the minds of the entire people.[39]

Moreover, in organization, technical facilities, and resources National Socialist Germany represents a more formidable opponent than the *Kaiserreich*. Management of supplies is on a respectable plane of efficiency, rations on the whole have not been cut down, and loss of lives in action was far below reasonable expectations. Decisive campaigns were won in a few weeks of concentrated effort. Time and again the nation held its breath, conscious of the unpredictable risks that it

was forced to face. In each case, it was in the end over-
whelmed by the conclusion that there was merit in taking
chances. The border line between possibility and impossibility
had ceased to be a valid conception. Things could be done
that but yesterday were laughable boasts.

In spite of the widespread desire for peace among the population, psychological factors such as these may well offset the
physical impact of warfare on the German masses for time to
come. There is ground to expect the régime to slow down
further on its domestic mission of National Socialist indoctrin-
ation,[40] to foster those tendencies that are apt to give it the
appearance of a truly national institution, and to infuse into
its higher councils as much competence and *expertise* as is
available. The relative decline of the political functionary is
a feature that may have lasting consequences—should there be
a *Pax Germanica*. And the relegation of the Party hierarchy
to inferior rank would carry with it a modification of the
totalitarian formula of far-reaching import. For it is clear that
the weakening of the Party must bring forth a more direct
relationship between the political control group and the
people itself. Such a relationship is not conceivable without
a considerable degree of formalization. Is it possible that
totalitarianism will produce one day its own brand of constitutionalism?

CHAPTER IV

Wartime Theories and Policies of the Third Reich

BY TAYLOR COLE

Duke University

THERE has been no dearth of explanations for the German expansionist policies which led, step by step, to the outbreak of the war in September, 1939. Among those mentioned have been the growing difficulties within the Third Reich and the necessity of finding some external solution for the internal problems created by Germany's military economy; the related Marxist contention that contradictions in Germany's capitalistic system determined the course of Nazi foreign policy; the ever recurrent necessity of finding a psychological shock to justify an internal *status quo*; the expansion of a missionary political religion; the Nazi equivalent of manifest destiny rendered vague but more impelling by direction from Teutonic gods; the fulfillment of the pan-German dream of a de Lagarde, a Schönerer, and a Naumann, or the realization of the more ambitious program of a Karl Haushofer; the natural sequel to the end of economic man; contradictions between economic and geographic factors; and the personal ambitions of a revolutionist coupled with the irresistible drives of a psychopath, seeking world domination. All of these and others are offered as the *real* causes which explain Germany's militant foreign policy. Some of the explanations have merit and some have not; some are complementary and some inconsistent. By way of evaluation it is sufficient to say that the leaders of Germany planned, expected, and wanted the present war; that Germany was prepared for the present conflict and struck at the peak of her economic and military strength; and that this struggle has evolved into a true "war against the West."

TRENDS IN NAZI THEORY

In the light of these explanations, some attention may be directed to the Nazi theories regarding the war. These theories are not offered as furnishing any serious clues to the expansionist policy followed by the National Socialist régime.

To Adolf Hitler, beginning with the boundaries of Germany in 1933, territorial readjustments which would violate the provisions of the "iniquitous" Treaty of Versailles were justified on two major counts. The first was the right of "self-determination of peoples," which had been flagrantly violated to Germany's detriment, and the second was the right to secure sustenance for an already over-crowded Germany with a growing population. Necessity for self-defense, in the light of previous "aggressions" and anticipated dangers, was joined with the above-mentioned considerations in the discussions leading up to the Munich Conference in 1938 and the subsequent dismemberment of Czechoslovakia. With this stage the cry for the "union of all Germans in one Great Germany by the right of self-determination of peoples" could no longer serve a purpose even for internal propagandistic purposes. The stress was now placed upon the right to *Lebensraum* and upon the necessity of defense against "encirclement." Protest against encirclement was the heart of the Goebbels' campaign against Poland. Despite the hatred of Poland in Germany and some belief in an encirclement plot, this campaign struck deaf German ears which were accustomed to the usual build-up and the inevitable crescendo.

After war had been declared on Germany by the "warmongers" in the "encircling" states, Hitler fell back upon his old arguments to justify his many actions. But mindful of the Russian commercial treaty and non-aggression pact signed in August, 1939, and keenly appreciative of the usefulness of revolutionary slogans, he began placing more and more emphasis upon the capitalistic lechery of Germany's enemies. The fullest expression of Hitler's latest interpretation of the present conflict was presented in his speech of December 10, 1940, before the arms workers in Berlin.[1] He contended that the present conflict involves more than the victory of one combatant over another; it is essentially the struggle of two worlds and two philosophies of life. On the one hand, there are the "so-called democracies" in which capitalism rules supreme, domination is exercised by a privileged few hundred, gold is an instrument for subjugating peoples, and liberty means essentially a "freedom of economy," with its consequent poverty and unemployment. On the other hand, there is National Socialist Germany with an economic system built on the "conception of work" and in which gold is no factor of importance. A state in which "birth matters nothing, achievement means everything" was depicted; a new epoch of "cooperative labor" and "cooperative duties" was envisaged. In the words of one commentator, "England is the representative fighter of the old world struggling not only against *national* Germany, in order to prevent it from securing equal rights, but above all against *social* Germany which has through its emphasis on 'labor and performance' reduced privileges based on riches and birth, and which has a vision of a new and more righteous order for the future." [2]

National sovereignty, self-determination of peoples, *Lebens-*

raum, defense against encirclement, and the missionary goal
of the Leader in a conflict between "two worlds" are all steps
in an unfolding pattern of justification. From Germany of
1933, to Greater Germany with Austria, to European regionalism, to two worlds, has been the sequence. "One of these
two worlds must crack up," Hitler has warned, and the next
step in *der Führer's* moves must await a decision as to which
one it will be. Some solace has been offered the inhabitants of
the "plutocracies" in advance, for only when the "other world
cracks will it be free."

The writings of Nazi legal theorists have followed closely
both the utterances of Hitler and the movement of the German armies. During the early days after 1933, they were
stressing the iniquities of a system which denied Germany
"justice" and "equality." The racial basis of law and international law could be appealed to when German minorities,
or territories containing German minorities, were still sepa-
rated from the homeland. Hardly had Hitler entered Hrad-
schin in 1939 before adaptable Carl Schmitt had presented his
legal foundations for the division of the earth's surface among
a few large powers.[3] Precedent is furnished by the Monroe
Doctrine, in its original and unperverted form, for the "enlarged living spaces" composed of a central Reich as the
"leading and directing power," and of various territories that
reflect the rays of the central sun. Only when there has been
a recognition in international law of these enlarged living
spaces and a denial of the right of spatially foreign powers
to intervene in these areas, will there be any legal basis for a
truly meaningful division of the earth's surface.[4] In any case,
the old concept of state as the central concept in international
law corresponds to neither "truth nor reality." [5]

The essential thesis of Schmitt is imbedded in the recent
remarks of E. R. Huber before the Academy of German

Law.[6] A distinction, he maintains, must be drawn between the national territory in a narrower sense and the "greater space" (*Grossraum*) of the Reich. The old territory embodies the areas incorporated in the former German states, the new national districts (*Gaue*) and the new national territories, such as the Government-General of Poland. The *Grossraum* extends beyond these areas to those territories which retain their "independence" but which also fall under the "guidance" of the Reich. This guidance, we are assured, is quite different from the old imperialistic domination, for it involves a responsibility to the inhabitants of these areas. There is, in short, a "European responsibility in the constitution of the Reich." [7]

Thus Hitler now finds the mission of Germany is to realize an international "socialistic" and planned totalitarian order which will come when the opposing "world" has been de-troyed.[8] The lawyers are still providing legal justification for the *Grossraum* stage of German expansion. They remain one full step behind their leader, but there are always possibilities for juristic progress in those hidden springs from which Nazi law flows.

Prior to the outbreak of hostilities, the self-styled international lawyers in Germany had followed the political charts with facile pens.[9] There was a tendency on their part to minimize but not to exclude entirely the binding effects of international law. Insofar as the laws of war were concerned, this minimization took the form of objections to attempts to distinguish between "just" and "unjust" wars,[10] and between wars of defense and wars of aggression, where defined as "just" and "unjust" wars. The widening of the scope of the international law of war—its "inflation" in the words of G. A. Walz [11]—was condemned, especially insofar as this inflation represented the embodiment of rules based on the "British conception of sea warfare" as distinguished from the "Continental conception of land warfare." The Continental conception, it was maintained, limited the effects of war to the actual military participants. The British conception, on the other hand, involved the enemy citizen and his property as well as neutral ships and property. The Continental conception was more "limited" and hence more humane; the British conception led to the barbarities of total war.

Despite this tendency to minimize international law, in September, 1939, the Nazi press suddenly became solicitous of the enforcement of all accepted principles of the laws of war—at least, if we are to judge by the attacks upon enemy violators or alleged violators. In the early months of the war, to take only a few illustrations, there appeared various accounts of British violations in the Mediterranean,[12] of British delivery of poison gas for use in Poland,[13] and of British "robbery" of neutral goods.[14] Even the late Neville Chamberlain was pictured as an "international legal attorney" who had a passion for violating international law.[15] The organ of the Elite Guards, *Das schwarze Korps*, carried a cartoon on May 7, 1940, picturing Chamberlain holding a holy book and dipping his pen in the blood of a fallen neutral. The same paper depicted Churchill with a vicious grip (called *ein Doppel-Nelson*) on a desperate and scantily clad maiden who represented neutrality. The maiden, in turn, stood on a torn and trampled document entitled "international law." [16] German occupation of such countries as Norway and Holland was preceded in each case by "irrefutable information" that Britain was planning to violate the territorial integrity of these states. These attacks on Britain have gradually declined with repeated German military aggression leading to the occupation of several of the former neutral states. Nevertheless, occasional accounts of British "piratical" acts still appear.[17] The decision in August, 1940, to create out of the two New

Guinea territories a new military district which would be part of the Australian northern command was denounced by the Nazi press as "a gross breach of international law."[18] And at the annual meeting of the Academy of German Law, Reichsminister Frank, after charging foreign states with "countless violations" of the rights of German soldiers and citizens, urged his hearers to cooperate with the official offices in their search for breaches of international law.[19] It would, of course, be absurd to take seriously most of the German charges. But it is certainly not farfetched to recognize in this new respect for international legal rights another example of the Nazi screen technique used to conceal true aims and anticipated acts.[20]

In the present conflict, total war has come to mean more than the use of military power alone, for it includes psychological and economic warfare as well. Far in advance of any outbreak of hostilities, Germany was refining the economic techniques of total war.[21] Reference may be made to only one of the developments in the writings of the military economists. Where German writers during the earlier years of National Socialist control had placed heavy emphasis upon agriculture and agricultural production, they have more recently stressed industry and industrial production.[22] According to Nazi claims, countries with highly developed industries are in a better position than "agricultural countries" to secure from both foreign and domestic sources needed war materials. The necessary dependence of a modern army upon the industrial development has thus been reflected in these writings of students of military economy. This emphasis will explain the current tendency to concentrate heavy industry in Germany and to make of the conquered areas satellite agricultural regions. Such concentration, in turn, will furnish the means for

German domination, of at least Europe, when victory has been won.

In sum, the true motives of Hitler and the logical end of those forces which are driving him on are being made clearer even in the *Führer's* own speeches. His policies have been rationalized by Nazi jurists before and after the outbreak of the war. The moral conscience of Dr. Goebbels has been deeply disturbed by western violations of international law, which Nazi lawyers had so greatly minimized before the outbreak of hostilities and which Nazi leaders have done so much afterward to destroy. A part of the German success may be attributed to the new science of *Wehrwirtschaft* which finds application in various of the wartime policies of the Nazi régime.

GERMAN LABOR AND THE WAR

The general position of labor in the German political and economic system up to 1939 is well known. Membership in the German Labor Front was virtually compulsory; wages and conditions of work were determined by agencies over which the worker had no direct control. Almost the last vestiges of a free labor market had been removed, at first by measures to care for the unemployment situation, then by steps to deal with the labor shortage under the Four-Year Plan of 1936,[23] and finally by the restrictive measures in the years immediately preceding the war. The war economy of prewar days had largely accomplished the task of freezing wages and of allocating and confining the laborer to those employments which state officials designated.[24] The general task of allocating, training and supervising labor, as well as determining its material and non-material return, involved directly such agencies as the Ministry of Labor and the labor trustees, the German Labor Front, the social honor courts, the criminal and labor courts, the school officials, the National Institution for Employment Exchanges and Unemployment Insurance, and a host of other agencies more indirectly involved.

The actual outbreak of hostilities furnished the authorities with no new tasks and with few new problems. The essential object was to secure the maximum degree of productivity for war purposes which was commensurate with the most effective type of control and the minimum of return allowable for non-military purposes. In the light of this primary purpose, some attention may be directed to the wartime control of labor and to wartime labor legislation and policies.[25]

The Control of Labor.—

The regimentation of labor has gone on apace during the war period. The controls by the state have been sharpened and refined. Among other developments, the powers of the labor trustees have been gradually increased. Early in September, 1939, these officials were authorized to issue individual rules for separate establishments and were no longer bound to issue them solely for groups of establishments or common employments in different establishments. They were also freed from the rather meaningless requirement, provided in the National Labor Law of 1934, that they secure the advice of the Statutory Committee of Experts before formulating their rules. In December, 1939, they received a further increment to their wide powers, when they were given authority to punish summarily with fines all persons violating their regulations in individual enterprises and branches of industry.[26]

Additions were made to the broad jurisdiction of the State Employment Exchanges over the labor market. The authorization of these offices was necessary, in accordance with an order of September 1, 1939, before one could enter any employment except agriculture, mining, or certain domestic employments. The consent of these offices usually was required before employment could be terminated, and even where this consent was not necessary, the offices had to be notified. "Bound to duty" contracts were by no means new or seldom used. However, the tenor of the wartime regulations extending the scope of jurisdiction of the Labor Exchange Offices in this respect and the changes necessary in order to replace soldiers called to the colors, indicate a rapidly growing use of this device which had come into such prominence in connection with the building of the West Wall.[27] In short, the process of centralizing control over the hiring, dismissal and transfer of laborers was greatly accelerated.

There have been some changes in the organization and the procedure of the labor courts which eliminate completely such "due process of law" in procedural matters as may have been retained by the labor courts. The local labor courts which formerly consisted of a regular judge and two assessors saw the elimination on September 1, 1939, of the assessors and an almost unlimited discretion placed in the hands of the local labor court judges in the application of procedural rules.[28] Each labor judge may make such adaptations to individual cases as "special circumstances" may dictate. Furthermore, the proposals of the Criminal Law Commission to increase the criminal penalties in labor legislation had borne fruit in a number of respects prior to the war, and under wartime conditions the criminal and non-criminal penalties have been increased.[29] For example, regulations of January 30, 1940, provided for imprisonment up to 90 days for women who opposed or refused to perform the required labor service.[30] The elimination of these procedural guarantees, coupled with the penal provisions in labor legislation, furnishes a good example of the extent to which the emphasis has been placed upon the *control*, in contrast to the *rights* of labor.

In 1938, Dr. Ley, who had undertaken various experiments in the "communal" organization of the factories and work-shops, spoke of a new organizational unit known as the "shop troops." "Should Germany once more have to undergo a severe trial of strength and should this process lead to serious disturbances in the factories as it did during the last war," he said, "every factory must be organized so that it will itself be able to take the measures necessary for the creation of order." [31] Actually these shop troops consist of small groups recruited from the entire force of the plant, who serve to prevent disturbances in the organization. Anticipating future internal troubles, they act as a "factory police agency appropriating certain fraternal characteristics and veiled by the community ideology." [32] Their organization has kept in step with the din of the battle, and their activities have become more evident to foreign observers. Stress is being laid upon the assurance of safety and efficiency in the work of the factories, the setting of proper examples to "comrades," and the furnishing of instruction and education in the true fundaments of the *Weltanschauung*.[33] Coupled with an increase in membership of the Elite Guards and their reported circulation in the plants of Germany, the activities of the shop troops may not suggest serious unrest, but they do indicate that there is unending work to be done, even in the days of victory.

Labor Legislation and Policies.—

If the system of control has not been fundamentally changed, there has been a rather sharp shift during the war period in the legislative policies. Apparently well prepared for the eventuality and with evident determination, the Minister Council for National Defense and the Minister of Labor issued a number of orders and regulations in September, 1939, extending the hours of labor, making allowance for child labor, altering somewhat the system of paying unemployment benefits, and making available new sources of labor supply.

Allowance was made for extending the hours of work. In the case of male workers over 18 years of age, the previous limitations on maximum hours were effectively removed. Special arrangements were made for other classes of workers. On September 11, for example, the Minister of Labor permitted boys between 16 and 18 years of age and women, in "cases of emergency," to work up to 10 hours a day and 56 hours a week, inclusive of the time spent in attending technical training courses. For children under 16 years of age, a maximum of 48 hours was permitted. Women between the ages of 17 and 25 were subject to call to the labor service unless they were fully employed, or were receiving instruction, or were needed for specific kinds of work. Students above the age of 17 were to be available for work during vacations and those between the ages of 10 and 16 were subject to light duties outside of school hours.

Other regulations were also issued. With the purpose of simplifying the system of administration and of extending the benefits, some changes were made in the system of paying unemployment benefits. For example, workers capable of employment, who were unemployed against their wishes, were to receive benefits regardless of their lack of insurance or lack of insurability. In view of the almost complete absence of present or anticipated unemployment, these changes were obviously in the nature of a gesture. The positions of workers called to the colors were guaranteed upon their return from service in the army, except at the request of the individual worker or at the request of the employer with the consent of the labor trustee.

The most significant developments were reflected in the various orders and regulations issued in September and October, 1939, designed primarily to increase state revenues and to prevent a rise in consumer demand. They provided that supplementary wages for overtime, night and holiday work should be paid to the state, together with any savings which were occasioned by the regulation of wages.[34] However, the Price Fixing Commissioner could exempt an employer from making the payment in case it would result in increased prices or in case the employer reduced his prices to an extent that was commensurate with his savings. Restrictions were placed upon increases or decreases in wages, with exceptions allowable in some cases by a Minister and in others by the labor trustees. The German authorities have been optimistic in terming this policy a "wartime policy"; they were certainly correct in characterizing it as a "general wage-stop." [35] In short, the old wage schedules were to be kept, despite increased hours of work, and the state was to receive the increment that even under previous Nazi laws would have gone to the laborer. These regulations represented a natural culmination of an essential part of the program so effectively used by Germany to finance her rearmament.[36]

The severity of these new regulations led to unexpected and undesired results. Reported increases in sickness, absences from work, and declining efficiency due to fatigue led quickly to an appraisal of the results and to considerable changes. The increased consumption of beer had perhaps given a fleeting but inadequate escape for the workers. After the middle of November, 1939, the wage supplements for night, holiday, and Sunday work were restored in part, with overtime pay for work up to 10 hours to revert to the state as previously. Finally, on September 6, 1940,[37] the Minister of Labor, "in view of the demands on labor during the previous months and to simplify the administration," decreed that the prewar provisions governing payment for overtime would apply in the future. Hours of labor were restricted somewhat by the provision that after January 1, 1940, the "normal" eight hour day was not to be extended to more than 10 hours except under prescribed circumstances. The employment of women and children on night shifts was, with exceptions, prohibited. The ban on paid vacations was likewise relaxed.

In view of the wide discretion which still remained in the hands of various officials, it is impossible to say just what the net effects of these changes were. The mere fact that they came at all, however, might well indicate that the goal of maximum productivity had been adversely affected by the severity of the earlier regulations. And even the labor short-age, indicated by the 1,500,000 places reported open in No-vember, 1940, despite the extensive use of foreign labor and prisoners of war, has not led to an attempt to return to the earlier hours of labor policy.[38] Furthermore, the reduction during 1940 of 200,000 in the number of women employed, along with a reported failure to put into effect the measures prepared for calling employable women between the ages of 16 and 40 (who were not "bound to the home"), would sug-gest that there has been no increased pressure on women laborers.[39] There would thus appear to have been no funda-mental change in labor policy since the beginning of 1940.

Since concessions can be made only up to a certain point at present, the German laborer recently has been showered with promises which will be fulfilled "after the war." In Septem-ber, 1940, Dr. Ley, the head of the German Labor Front, an-nounced that Hitler intends to reduce drastically hours of labor, to insure annual ten-day vacations, and to guarantee a free weekend from Saturday noon until Monday morning. Compulsory labor and military service will also be discontinued.[40] Somewhat later the housing problem was solved. "After the war" between 500,000 and 600,000 homes are to be constructed annually, and they are to rent for fantastically low prices. In ten years the housing problem will no longer exist. The details of construction were discussed; the details of financing were omitted.[41] Old-age pensions were next added to the list. There is to be a general insurance plan which will make old-age insurance a matter of "legal right" and which will allow for payments adequate to maintain a standard of physical and cultural life "that is natural to the German." [42] Visions of the world-to-be do not indicate any break in the home front in the labor ranks. However, this picture of a laborer's Utopia suggests a new solicitude for *rewards* and *rights*, in contrast to the *duties* of labor in a postwar reconstruction.

CHURCH AND STATE RELATIONS

The conflict of religions, political and non-political, which marked the period from 1933-1939, has not been particularly in evidence since the outbreak of the war. To date the several parties involved in the religious conflict have taken no positive or uncompromising positions that would be considered as "disruptive of the national community." [43] The relative quiescence may be attributed in part to the fact that grievances cannot be too openly discussed and that, if discussed, they cannot be reported in full. Be that as it may, such fundamental questions as those involved in the trial and imprisonment of Pastor Niemöller, those raised in the earlier sermons of Cardinal Faulhaber, and those involving the future of church property or centering around the financial support of the churches have not been frequently raised.[44]

The Nazi press has made brief mention of claims that Catholic contributions to soldiers at Christmas time have been heavy and that the relief rôle of priests and pastors for the dependents of those fallen at the front has been great. A large number of chaplains who have received various decorations for bravery at the front have been commended. Exhortations to soldiers to fight bravely and to be loyal, reputed to have been made in many Catholic and Protestant churches at the beginning of the war, were reported. In other words, to the limited extent that the churches have received attention in the Nazi press, their spirit and acts of cooperation have normally been stressed. Even *Das schwarze Korps,* which was in the vanguard of the anti-Catholic Movement, has been significantly silent on church and religious questions.

Nevertheless, all has by no means been peace, unity and quiescence. Evidence of opposition in Protestant ranks is not lacking. For example, large percentages of Protestant seminarians were not certified as having passed the state examinations in 1940. But, since the Catholic church has a more unified organization than the Protestant, and since the papal newspaper and radio allow for greater publicity to protests coming from Catholic quarters, it is to be expected that more evidences of conflict would appear in Nazi-Catholic relations than in the Nazi-Protestant relations. In any event, the degree of positive enthusiasm for the war, not marked in any part of Germany except among the youth and the fanatical fringe of the Party, has reached its lowest ebb in some of the predominantly Catholic areas.

Among the reported instances of rifts between the Catholic and Nazi hierarchies, the following might be mentioned. The First Encyclical of Pope Pius XII, containing some sharp strictures on totalitarian governments, could not be read in Germany in October, 1939. The Pope protested this suppression.[45] Rome reports of the closing of large numbers of convents and monasteries and bans on the collection of alms were based on evidence submitted by the Papal Nuncio in Berlin [46] —reports made, it might be added, shortly before the Pope congratulated Hitler on escaping the bombing attempt made on his life in November, 1939. The exhortation of Heinrich Himmler in December, 1939 to the Elite Guards to beget children during the war, in or out of wedlock, and the subsequent promise of Rudolph Hess that the Party would stand sponsor for illegitimate children could not fall on deaf Catholic ears.[47] One instance of charges that church taxes were being used by the Reich was reported. Especially sharp attacks were made by the Vatican on the persecution of Catholics in Poland by a movement that was tending toward "National Bolshevism." [48] Pope Pius is reputed to have told a group of pilgrims on May 15, 1940, that "neo-pagans" were responsible for the "newest extension" of the war in Belgium and Holland.[49] On November 20, 1940, a Spanish newspaper was rebuked for writing that Christian ideals were reconcilable with National Socialism.[50] In addition, many other reports based upon supposition and rumor have been made. Wartime reporting can at best give only a vague picture.

While foreign enemies are to be met, the leaders of the Nazi state may well afford to temper their ultimate aims. By and large, the Protestant churches, except for minor sects which were bitterly persecuted even before the war began, have fallen in line.[51] The Pope has avoided any open break with Hitler, although protesting with varying degrees of vehemence many actions of the present regime. The Catholics still refer to the Concordat of 1933, which realistic observers considered to have been buried in its violations; and there is room for the suspicion that the Nazis today owe an unpaid debt to Martin Luther, who is remembered in some respects and forgotten in all others. Since one cannot speak of a lasting truce between competing philosophies of life, the church-state relationships might have been characterized by a former President of the United States as being in a state of "animated suspension."

THE WAR AND THE NAZI REVOLUTION

There were at one time many serious misunderstandings of the true nature of National Socialism. There are still some divergencies in the interpretations that are being offered. On one point, however, there seems to be a growing agreement—namely, that National Socialism represents a fundamental revolution in a social and civilizational sense. It involves a complete reordering of the lives of the individuals in Germany and the imposition of a new set of values. A final query might consequently be directed at the effects of the war on the revolution in progress.

Some arguments are being presented to the effect that the Nazi revolution *is* beginning or *may begin* soon or *probably will begin* soon to show signs of leveling off and of reaching a Thermidor stage. Various facts and opinions are presented to support this point of view. The precedent of past revolutions which have a "natural history" or which follow a certain "pattern" or "process," the growing age of the Nazi leaders with a possible decline in the technique of violence which appeals to youth and perhaps to "youthful movements,"[52] the suggestion that there may be a saturation point in conquest itself which in turn will act as an internal "stabilizer," and the declining influence during the war of the Party which has been considered the dynamic factor—the pathfinder for the *Bewegung*—are all matters that are pointed to in support of one or the other of the above-mentioned points of view.

Up to the present time in the conflict, however, there appears to be no serious evidence of a tapering off in the revolution. While the life of the average non-military citizen has not been greatly changed since the outbreak of hostilities, there has been in some respects a continued trend toward greater coordination in the cultural sphere. The existing family ties have not been strengthened through the discussion of illegitimacy by the head of the *Gestapo* or by the patronage distributor of the Party. As yet there appears no evidence of a developing constitutionalism, if one implies by this term certain formal and effective limitations on the exercise of arbitrary power. The elimination of the meager safeguards furnished by the administrative courts [53] and the almost unlimited discretion placed in the hands of the local labor court judges to adopt their own rules of procedure are merely examples of the extension of the "prerogative state." [54] Further deviations from the limited residue of a capitalistic system, the consequence in part of the war developments, have been evident. Hitler's speeches and those of his designated and self-appointed spokesmen show no indications to observers of a dimming of revolutionary ardor.

And if one may conjecture, it is difficult to see how the present conflict with its psychological, social, political and economic aftermath, can lead to a return of any kind of "post revolutionary normalcy" in Germany. The late Emil Lederer, albeit writing in a new vein, has pointed in the right direction in his *State of the Masses*.[55] Group life has not been *completely* destroyed in Germany, as Lederer would suggest, but the trend is in that direction. The war has increased rather than lessened this tendency to eliminate the little remaining "society and privacy" and to stress the institutionalized masses in the emotional unity of which the dictatorship has its basis. It is in this sense that the revolution has continued and to date shows signs of further continuation, for this trend is the revolution. And since this type of mass state in its entirety is a new phenomenon in history, its course cannot be predicted in the light of past experience.

CHAPTER V

The Impact of the War on Soviet Political and Economic Institutions

BY JOHN N. HAZARD

Institute of Current World Affairs and Columbia University

MAJOR military engagements of the present European war have not yet embroiled the Soviet Union, but the conflict is leaving its mark. Considerable territory has been acquired since September, 1939, and an additional twenty-three million people have been brought under Soviet jurisdiction.[1] Five new constituent republics have been admitted to the Union,[2] and large sections of former Poland, as well as Northern Bukovina and parts of Bessarabia, have been added to the already existing Republics of the Ukraine and White Russia. A relatively short war has been fought with Finland,[3] and border clashes have occasionally been reported with the troops of Japan and Manchukuo. A new political and economic international orientation has evolved, with consequences which cannot yet be fully determined.

These developments are important to any broad study of the effect of the war upon the Soviet Union and its political institutions, but they must be placed aside in this discussion to permit a fuller consideration than would otherwise be possible of the effect of the general war situation upon the relationship between the Soviet state and its citizens.

An analysis of Soviet affairs should probably be prefaced with the warning that cause and effect are often even more

difficult to discern in studying the Soviet Union than in studying some other states. To find evidence of this fact one need
only review the differing interpretations placed upon Soviet
events by responsible students. There are those who deny that
the war has had any direct measurable effect upon Soviet political institutions. They lay all change on the Soviet scene to
the thirst for power and to the desire for self-preservation
which they find in a small ruling group, if not in a single man.
There is a second group which takes the position that change
in Soviet political institutions is due primarily to a pressing
need for increased production, a need which it believes accentuated by, but not created by, the war. A third group
explains every event in terms of the war alone, and Soviet
history is cited to prove that since the inception of the Soviet
state, there has been the almost perpetual peril of war.

It is deemed impossible at this time to do more than chroni-
cle major events and policies of the "war period." It is still too
early to draw a final conclusion as to whether the war is alone
responsible. There will be found herein, however, the underlying thesis that the influence of the war can be traced in
varying but important degrees throughout most of the events
of the recent past. There will also be found the underlying
assumption that the reader is familiar with Soviet political
theory and institutions, as they had developed before the war.

Some of the events selected for consideration occurred prior
to the outbreak of hostilities in Poland. Reasonable support
for tracing the events of the "war period" from a date prior
to the outbreak of military activity may be found in the fact
that Soviet statesmen, in explaining their activity for a lengthy
period before the first battles of the war occurred, enunciated
the theory that the second great war had commenced even
though battles had not yet been fought.

POLITICAL THEORY

Few students of Soviet affairs begin their analysis of daily
events until they have examined current Soviet political theory. On the eve of the present war there appeared a novel
interpretation of Marxian theory which was to set the stage
for much of what has happened. To understand the importance of this interpretation and the manner in which it has
been developed one must turn back to the XVI Communist
Party Congress, held in 1930. Stalin told the Party members
that the state, as an apparatus of compulsion, would not
"wither away" by degrees.[4] His declaration caused excitement
because many authoritative Soviet theorists of that period
were on record as understanding Marx, Engels and Lenin to
have meant in their writings that the gradual approach toward
a socialist economy would be accomplished by the gradual
disappearance of the repressive powers of the state. Stalin's
statement was in such sharp contrast to the beliefs of many
of these theorists that they consciously or unconsciously
thrust it aside and continued to preach and practice their beliefs, sometimes from the tribunes of important state positions.

On December 1, 1934, an assassin's bullet was directed at
the Leningrad Party Secretary, Sergei Kirov. This bullet may
be said to have brought an end to the dreams of those who
preached the early withering away of the state. They were
slowly eliminated and finally silenced completely in the great
housecleaning which swept through the ranks of Soviet political theorists in the early spring of 1937. The principle of the
survival of the state, as an instrument of compulsion and re-
pression, became thoroughly established, and every one was
warned that the approach to a socialist economy would not
be accompanied by lessening in the number or power of political instrumentalities.

There are many who say that the assassination of Kirov was the opening gun in the international intrigue preparing for the war, and that the influence of the war upon Soviet political theory and institutions may be traced from this event. Certainly the record is replete with material indicating a change of policy after December, 1934, from one evidencing relaxation of enforced discipline to one based upon the iron discipline of the present day.

Although Soviet theorists after 1930 came to accept the principle of a *socialist* economy thriving in company with a state apparatus which retained its compulsory function, they never uttered a belief that a *communist* economy, symbolized by the slogan, "From each according to his ability, to each according to his needs," could be achieved while the state continued to function as an apparatus of compulsion. There were still those who looked for an eventual relaxation of laws based upon a rule of iron discipline. At this point the present European war, which had not yet taken military form but which the Soviet leaders had long anticipated, became a factor and took its toll of basic Soviet political theory.

At the XVIII Communist Party Congress, held in March, 1939, Stalin set forth what he called a development of Marxian theory to fit a new situation.[5] He reviewed the peril of what he termed a "new imperialist war," and he declared that in the face of such a peril, the Soviet Union could not relax in vigilance. He found that the times required the preservation of the state apparatus for external protection, even though a *communist* economy were in the offing and might be achieved within the Soviet Union.

The significance of the new interpretation of Marxian political theory appears to lie in this: The economic development of the Soviet Union has become completely dissociated from its political development in Soviet policy-making circles, at least for the time being. The citizens who look for the day to come when bread and other staples are distributed to each individual in accordance with his needs have been advised that they may still look forward to such an eventuality, even though the international situation does not permit relaxation of vigilance and elimination of the state. Those who expected the withering away of the state, at least under communism, have been told to wait for a world in which there is no peril of war.

The Franchise

Evidence of the effect of war upon the political institutions of a nation is often looked for first in the electoral law. Less than three years before the beginning of hostilities in Poland, the Soviet citizen had become the beneficiary of a considerable liberalization of the election procedure, with the introduction of direct, secret elections, open to all citizens, regardless of their economic status before the revolution or since the introduction of the Soviet form of government.[6] No one in the Soviet Union expected that this liberalization of the election procedure envisaged the appearance of a set of candidates who would stand upon a platform calling for a return to pre-revolutionary economic and political forms. On the other hand, the citizens anticipated that they would be able to choose between various candidates standing upon their political records of efficiency, if not upon varying political beliefs. Stalin had indicated as much in an interview given to the American editor, Roy Howard, on March 1, 1936, when he said, "You think there will be no election contests. But there will be, and I foresee very lively election campaigns." [7]

As the time for the first elections held under the new Constitution approached, however, the international picture became increasingly ominous. The Anti-Comintern Pact had been anticipated and even exposed on November 28, 1936, from the tribune of the Congress of Soviets considering the new Constitution.[8] It subsequently became a reality, and Germany and Japan became increasingly hostile to the Soviet Union. Defense of the fatherland became the theme of countless Soviet lectures and speeches. Without explanation the number of candidates in the first elections was reduced to one in each electoral district. The first elections held on December 12, 1937, could hardly have been called contests, as Stalin had declared they would be, for the voter was given a blank with a single name, which he could scratch but not replace with another name.[9] Some voters asserted their privilege to dissent, for in the elections of 1937 for the Soviet of the Union names were scratched by 632,074 persons or .69 per centum of the persons casting ballots. A smaller number scratched the names of candidates for election to the Soviet of Nationalities, for in this instance 562,402 persons dissented, or .61 per centum of the persons casting ballots. The Soviet of the Union and the Soviet of Nationalities comprise the two chambers of the Supreme Soviet of the U.S.S.R.

Since the first elections under the new Constitution, there have been numerous elections for local and regional Soviets in all parts of the Union and in the newly acquired territories, several of these elections having taken place after the opening of European hostilities. In each election the procedure has been the same. Candidates have been proposed by meetings in collective farms, factories, schools and other institutions. The names have been forwarded to the specially constituted electoral commission in each electoral district. If several candidates have been proposed, all but one withdraws his name. This withdrawal is dictated by the Communist Party for Party members, in accordance with the usual discipline of the Party. If the person withdrawing his name is not

a Party member, he is presumably informed of the unde-
sirability of his candidacy by the Party or some allied agency.
The candidate chosen to run in the election conducts a vigorous speaking tour in which he assumes the rôle of chief "go-
between," complaint bureau, and government spokesman for
the district, and on election day a printed ballot with his name
upon it is presented to the electorate for approval. After
his election he continues to interpret government policies to
his constituency, and he opens an office to which constituents
can and do write or recount orally their complaints about
bureaucratic abuses of local officials, or inadequate housing or
school facilities, or other such subjects.

It cannot be said that the outbreak of military hostilities in
Europe has had any direct effect upon the citizen's choice of
his representative in the government, for the procedure has
been the same for all elections held under the new Constitution of 1936, whether these elections were held before or after
the outbreak of hostilities in Poland. On the other hand, it
would be hard to prove, until more evidence is available, that
the restrictions upon the selection of representatives which
appeared prior to the first battles in Poland were not introduced because of the anticipation of war and the need for
a thoroughly controlled state apparatus whose members could
be trusted to remain loyal to the central authorities.

THE COMMUNIST PARTY

The one-party system has long been in force in the Soviet
Union, although there was no provision to this effect in early
Constitutions. The sole constitutional basis for the institution
in the early days of Soviet political life has been said to lie
in Article 23 of the first Constitution of 1918, in which the
republic was permitted to deprive individual persons or

groups of their rights if used to the detriment of the socialist revolution. The Constitution of 1936 departed from this indirect language and provided in Article 126 for a single Party, by stating: "The most active and politically conscious citizens in the ranks of the working class and other strata of the toilers unite in the Communist Party of the U.S.S.R., which is the vanguard of the toilers in their struggle to strengthen the socialist system and which represents the leading core of all organizations both public and state."

Membership in Party ranks has always been extremely limited. Lenin early advocated a small disciplined Party, from which mere sympathizers were to be excluded from membership.[10] He was outvoted in the 1903 session of the Party, but won his point in the vote of 1905, and the principle he introduced has remained the major principle of the Party's organization to the present day. Membership has grown immensely, however, as the Party has passed from the minority party fighting for revolution to the Party of today. From some 200,000 members at the time of the 1917 revolution, the Party has grown to approximately ten times its pre-revolutionary size. Membership has varied from year to year, as indicated by the following statistics on membership:[11]

1927	721,486
1930	1,169,689
1933	1,895,411
1939	1,588,852
1941	2,515,481

To discover possible effects of the war situation upon the Party, one must look to the purges as well as to statements of what the Party was expected to become after the introduction of the Constitution of 1936. Some of these expectations were being discussed in Party circles in Moscow in 1936. At that time some responsibly placed Party members were heard to

foretell extensive expansion of the Party to include all workers and collective farmers who became prominent because
of their qualities of leadership, initiative and productive capacity. It was said that the time had come when it was
no longer necessary to retain the Party as a militant unit,
providing the key personnel for a vigorous struggle against
the forces of opposition, since those forces had been reduced
to a minimum, and the vast majority of the population had
become imbued with the ideals of the Party.

The war situation developed fast after 1936, and no expansion in Party membership occurred. On the contrary,
members were expelled as the need for a small selective leadership became apparent, and opposition within the Party
became intolerable. Treason trials were held of world-famous
Party members,[12] and lesser persons were quietly removed.
In these housecleanings, many have seen the urge for expansion of personal power on the part of Stalin himself. While
such an allegation has been made by too many persons to
be overlooked, it is believed that it should be evaluated in
the light of other possible reasons for the purges. These other
possible explanations come to mind when one considers the
general trend of Soviet policy during the years when the
international situation was deteriorating. It may be that the international situation will be found, when all evidence is
made available, to have been a more plausible explanation
of the leadership's fear for its continued existence in the face
of a war situation than the difficulties on the home front,
or any desire for increased personal power.

For whatever reason it may eventually turn out to be,
Party ranks were decreased rather than increased until
recent years, and this small Party has found it desirable to
unite with sympathizers of tested loyalty to present candidates in the elections. This unified slate of candidates has

become known as the union of party and non-party Bolsheviks, and has been in evidence everywhere during elections, even when these elections have been held in territories acquired after the outbreak of the war in Poland. The results of the elections indicate the extent to which Party members hold office. 76.2 per centum of the delegates in the Supreme Soviet of the U.S.S.R. belong to the Party.[13] In local elections the non-party adherents have played a more important part, for only 42 per centum of the delegates to local urban soviets are Party members, and no more than 18.9 per centum of the delegates to local village soviets are Party members.

While Party members have retained their status as the leaders in each community, they have lost some of the peculiar rights they were formerly granted by decree. In the Army during the trying days of the civil war following the last World War, the system of political commissars was created to provide a check on the possible treason of officers trained under the Tsars. The system of political commissars rose and fell in importance during the years following upon the civil war, and was reintroduced in all its vigor by decree of May 10, 1937, at the time of the announced disaffection among officers in the Red Army.[14] The political commissar in each military unit was given equal authority with its military commander, and the Red Army man took his oath to obey the political commissar as well as the military commander. One of the outstanding changes in Soviet political institutions brought by the war has been the reversal of this policy, for a decree has been issued restoring the military commander to full control and responsibility,[15] while the military oath has been revised to eliminate the oath to obey the political commissar.[16] Soviet commentators explain that political commissars, while remaining for various purposes, including that of a complaint bureau for the men and for education in Party matters, are no longer necessary as policemen watching over the possible disaffections of officers, since these officers are largely Party members who combine in their single persons the attributes of a military expert and a politically educated citizen. While there is certainly much of importance in this explanation, there is probably a further explanation. This is the fact that it is to the advantage of the officer of a modern army to be in a position where he can act quickly and without the necessity for justifying each move as it is made to a man who is not primarily a military man, and who, therefore, requires extensive time-consuming explanations before he is willing to accept the joint responsibility which was his under the law.[17]

In the Red Army it appears that the political commissar has become the chief morale officer for the men, and encourages them to deeds of heroism by recommending them for Party membership when they prove their worth upon the battlefield. Such was apparently the practice during the war between the Soviet Union and Finland. Whether this policy caused the recent augmentation of Party membership has yet to be discovered.

Party Secretaries have also found their position altered in industry, for they no longer have the right to share with the factory director the decision on questions of administration. In 1937, Stalin denounced the former "triangle" system as an outmoded form. This form had combined the local Party Secretary and the local Trade Union Secretary with the director of the factory as a board of three to make all important decisions. Today the Party Secretary of the factory can advise, and his advice may carry great weight, due often to the fact that the director is a Party member, but his advice can be disregarded and the director's decision stands until the appeal of the Party Secretary results in an adverse decision by the higher authorities.

It would probably be a mistake to draw the conclusion that the Party is losing its power as the war proceeds, for it is still the key force in each local community. Young members have been admitted in increasingly greater numbers under the revisions of the Party Rules in March, 1939,[18] but these men appear to be receiving Party membership as a reward for merit in fulfilling the program of the day rather than as a means of creating a nucleus for a militant revolutionary effort, as was the case in earlier years. These men are no longer required to master the Party program before being admitted, but they may be admitted if they "accept" this program, which amounts to little more than an affirmation of faith, based, of course, upon compulsory general instruction in Party principles. The Party member continues to be the chief molder of opinion and builder of morale in the unit in which he operates, and, as such, he is extremely important in a state in which no other political party is at work. He provides the backbone of the political system and gives it the strength with which it may withstand the shocks of war and difficult times.

THE DRIVE FOR PRODUCTION

"Discipline" and "production" are not new watchwords of Soviet policy, but their use has been multiplied since fighting in the west began. On some occasions the drive for production has been linked directly to the exigencies of war, as when the Soviet press stated that the national productivity had been adversely affected by the reduction in the number of workers due to the Finnish war. Workers were urged to do their best to compensate for the undermanning of factories.[19]

Some of the efforts to increase production have had little
direct effect on the individual, as when commissariats were
increased in number to provide less centralization of administration. This policy has been in the process of realization
since 1936, but it has been accelerated since the outbreak
of hostilities. In the face of decentralization of administration,
the Commission of Soviet Control has been raised from its
informal status to the position of a full-fledged commissariat,
to provide what has been announced to be a system of vigi-
lant supervision of plan fulfillment.[20]

The Commission was formerly a body which heard complaints and sent its inspectors throughout Soviet organizations
to gather facts independently of any formal organ. It was
the eyes and ears of the highest Party and government officials to provide information independently of any of the
other fact-finding organs. The new commissariat is given a
similar function, defined by *Pravda* as follows:[21] "To check
upon the fulfillment of government decrees so that there will
not be a single administrative department, not a single economic or social organization in the country which does not
feel focused upon it the all-seeing eye of state control." The
new commissariat, by virtue of its formal position, is now
more than a listening post. It is empowered by law to give
orders to any organization it examines and to fine or cause
the dismissal of any person who misuses state property. It
may instigate criminal prosecution, if violation of the criminal laws is believed to have occurred.

Another organizational change has been the expansion of
the Economic Council under the Council of People's Commissars, with the avowed purpose of improving the work of
coordination between industries.[22]

The drive for production vitally affected the average citizen after the outbreak of hostilities, when, on June 26, 1940,

the eight-hour day and seven-day week were restored in all except dangerous or unhealthy occupations.[23] Soviet workers were called upon to accept an increase in working hours without a compensating increase in wages.[24] The reason given was that the worker must make a sacrifice in the face of the peril of war, and the Chairman of the Central Council of Trade Unions reviewed the sacrifices forced upon workers in the countries at war as sufficient reason to ask the Soviet workers to throw their full weight into production as an essential weapon of the Soviet Union in its preparation for defense.[25] Perhaps only those who have followed Soviet writing during the past ten years can appreciate the momentous nature of the change in the workday and work week. It involved the partial abandonment of principles on which the government had relied heavily as justification for the sacrifice of much political liberty. It meant losing some of the benefit of the oft-heard argument that there is no objection to vigorous discipline when it results in lessening of hours of work and improvement of economic position.

Labor discipline had received considerable attention before the government went to the extreme of lengthening the workday. Efforts had been made to assure full use of the seven-hour workday as early as December 28, 1938, when a law was enacted providing for the dismissal of workers who were tardy three times during a month or four times during two consecutive months.[26] Subsequently, any single tardiness in excess of twenty minutes was considered as absence for one day and sufficient reason to cause dismissal. Since the outbreak of war, these disciplinary measures have been stiffened, for an Order of the People's Commissariat of Justice of the U.S.S.R. has provided that a worker shall be dismissed who goes to lunch more than twenty minutes early or returns more than twenty minutes late.[27] Other decrees have changed court procedure in actions concerning labor discipline. One of these decrees provides that a single judge shall hear the case, instead of the regular three-judge court, comprising two lay judges with the professional judge.[28] An Order of the Supreme Court of the U.S.S.R. eliminates the usual preliminary hearing before the case is heard formally.[29] Courts have apparently been reluctant to enforce the strict penalties of the law for infractions of labor discipline, and reports have been published of the sentencing of judges themselves for failing to enforce the law.[30]

The law lengthening the workday and work week also denied to workers in factories and offices the right to leave their jobs without permission from the administration.[31] Permission could be withheld except in cases involving ill-health or withdrawal to enter a technical training school. This latter reason for permitting departure from a job provides a convenient method of avoiding the severity of the rule—at least for younger workers. The same principle of enforced continuation at a job was extended by a law, dated July 17, 1940, to tractor drivers employed by Machine Tractor Stations, which are the units serving the collective farms.[32] The Supreme Court of the U.S.S.R. has issued an order to all lower courts to the effect that the law shall be vigorously enforced and the full penalties exacted.[33] The new laws put teeth into a policy which had long been developing, and which had previously taken the visible form of labor passports, in which a state enterprise, which had been the employer, listed the reasons for severing the worker's connection with his job. These passports were carried by each worker and presented for examination by a prospective employer. They were intended to bring social pressure to bear upon the worker who moved from job to job.

Efforts to prevent labor turnover with consequent reduction in production have now passed beyond the period in which public censure was the primary source of restriction, and the worker is now restricted in freedom of movement. Perhaps no other method of control was possible in view of the fact that the war increased the labor shortage, thus upsetting the social controls which might otherwise have proved adequate to induce an employer not to employ a man who had a bad record for moving from job to job.

A law complementary to the laws requiring workers to remain at their jobs was issued on October 19, 1940.[34] It granted to the People's Commissars of the U.S.S.R. the right of obligatory transfer of special categories of professional people and skilled workmen from one enterprise or institution to another, regardless of the territorial location of the institutions or enterprises. Special arrangements were made for the payment of bonuses in salaries and the expenses involved in moving a family to the locality designated. Persons refusing to carry out the instructions of the People's Commissars fall within the classification of workers who have left their jobs arbitrarily. They are to be tried pursuant to the provisions of the law of June 26, 1940, already discussed.

Penalties have long existed for those who produce goods below fixed standards of quality.[35] The present crisis has brought forth a law which lays the responsibility for producing underquality products squarely at the door of the director of the factory and his staff with stiff penalties for failure of the factory to turn out goods of the required standard.[36]

Production has been further encouraged by the introduction of a system of conscription of labor from urban and collective farm centers. Each center has been required by the law of October 2, 1940,[37] to send forward for training in technical schools a fixed number of boys and young men between the ages of 14 and 17. Each graduate of the training school must serve for a five-year period in a post assigned by the government officials. This principle of limited compulsory labor service after the completion of state-financed education has long been applied to students of the state-operated schools of medicine, law, education and engineering,[38] but recruiting for these schools has always been, and apparently will remain, upon a voluntary basis. The new law makes possible the drafting of man power for the technical aspects of the productive process, and introduces an important innovation into the relationship between the state and the citizen. It so happens that to date the compulsory aspects of the law have not been enforced, as sufficient youths have come forward voluntarily to fill the quotas.

The drive for production has reached beyond industry to agriculture. Various important decrees have appeared changing the system of computation of deliveries to the state by the collective farms,[39] but the one concerning directly the individual and his relationship to the state will alone be considered at this point. To understand the effect of this decree, one must bear in mind that one of the concessions to the peasant who entered the collective farm system was the privilege of tilling a small plot of ground, covering an area from one-fourth to one-half hectare,[40] as he and the members of his family wished. There was no control from the authorities of the collective farm or the government. Those who have studied Soviet agriculture are aware of the part these family plots have played in the life of the collective farm household. Much time was spent by the members of the household in tilling the land during the long summer evenings, and the products were not only consumed by the family but cash income was derived from a sale of the products on the open markets. Restriction upon the use of the plot first appeared in the law of May 27, 1939,[41] which urged the limitation of the amount of time to be spent on the plot, and required the collective farmer to spend at least from sixty to one hundred "workdays" on the collective farm land. Only the balance of his time was free for work on the family plot.

Unlimited control of the family plot was reduced by the law dated February 21, 1940,[42] requiring collective farm households to plant fruit trees in the plots so as to increase the amount of fruit available for local consumption. The decree also made available state supplies of fruit trees for planting in these plots.

On April 11, 1940,[43] the unbridled use of the family plot was further limited by a decree providing that collective farmers who raise grain of their own on the family plot must sell a portion of the grain to the state at the fixed price, which is less than the open market price for the same product. Part of the product of the family plot thus comes under state control, although the nature of the control is nothing more radical than a form of taxation.

SOVIET INSTITUTIONS IN THE NEW TERRITORIES

Acquisition of large sections of Poland, of Bessarabia and Northern Bukovina, and of the Baltic States has resulted in the expansion of Soviet political institutions in varying forms in these territories. It is still too early to tell with accuracy precisely what has happened, but published accounts indicate that the Soviet government has proceeded in accordance with Communist Party teachings to introduce the Soviet form of government slowly, making certain, however, at the very start that the means of production, i.e., the land, banks, large industries and trading enterprises, would not remain privately owned. A student of Soviet political theory will quickly recognize that such essential means of production have long been considered the residuum of political power for the forces opposed to the Soviet system of socialism, and it can afford no surprise that property of this nature was quickly removed from the ownership of private individuals and placed in the hands of the State to be administered by committees of local citizens.

The form of the transitional period has differed in the territories accepted for membership in the Union. In some instances, the citizens of the territory, led by Communist Party members of the local Communist Party, and supported by Communist Party members and state officials from the Soviet Union, organized local Soviet governments which proceeded to enact decrees providing for the elimination of private ownership of essential means of production and banks before the territory became a part of the Soviet Union. This was the procedure in the territories acquired from Poland.[44] In the Baltic States the entire state apparatus was held intact, while the Parliaments under the supervision of communist elements, which had remained quiescent until granted their opportunity to work openly with the advent of Soviet military forces under the treaties signed with these states after the outbreak of the war in Poland, voted the familiar Soviet measures prior to applying for admission to the Soviet Union as constituent Republics.[45]

In carrying out the program, the *Seims* of Latvia and Lithuania and the *Duma* of Esthonia declared land the property of the state on July 22 and 23, 1940. The land was then distributed to peasants on the basis of not more than thirty hectares per peasant. If a peasant held less than this amount of land, it was left in his control. If he held more, he was deprived of the use of his excess land, and it was placed in a state land fund, from which it was withdrawn and given to the landless or small-landed peasantry. The declaration making land the property of the state contained in each of the three Baltic states a guaranty against collectivization and declared that any attempts to force collective farming would be punished as being harmful to the interests of the state and the people. Peasants who were still paying the debts contracted when they purchased their land under the land reforms introduced before sovietization were given the benefit of cancellation of these debts.

Another important decree provided for the nationalization of banks and large industry, which occurred in Latvia on July 22, and in Lithuania and Esthonia on July 23, 1940.

Not until the end of August, 1940, did the parliaments of the three Baltic states declare themselves Temporary Supreme Soviets, while the decrees issued during July became the bases for their constitutions, which were formally adopted on August 25, 1940, by extraordinary parliamentary sessions in the three states which had become by that time Republics of the Soviet Union. The first decrees issued after the states became constituent Republics related to the nationalization of the banks, railroad and water transport, and communications. Industry was not entirely nationalized. In Lithuania, for example, only some 600 industrial enterprises were nationalized.

The constitutions of the new Baltic Soviet Republics list the types of permissible property and indicate that only large factories and large apartment houses are state-owned property. By thus failing to include all factories and all large houses as state-owned property, these constitutions reflect the difference in the economy of the Baltic Republics and of the older parts of the Soviet Union.

The principle of nationalization of large property holdings

which provide income in excess of that earned by a single man, or a few men toiling for themselves, is carried into shipping, so that in the decree of October 8, 1940, the Lithuanian Supreme Soviet declared that all ships, not mechanically propelled, were nationalized if they exceeded fifty tons capacity and were seagoing vessels, or five tons capacity and were river vessels. All mechanically propelled seagoing vessels of more than fifteen horsepower and all mechanically propelled river vessels of more than ten horsepower were also nationalized. Compensation of 25 per centum of value was provided for owners of nationalized vessels. Small vessels used for fishing or hunting and providing their owners with a living wage were specifically excluded from such regulations.

Similar limitations appeared in the decree of October 28, 1940, of the Latvian Supreme Soviet in which buildings were nationalized only if the living space in the house exceeded 220 square meters in area in the large cities, and 170 square meters in the smaller places. Both of these decrees bring to mind the decrees of the early years in Russia where socialization was undertaken slowly and with an effort to avoid antagonizing the small property owner. The decrees on nationalization were identical in Lithuania and Esthonia. The steps toward socialization have been small, for it is estimated, for example, that in Esthonia the socialized economy accounts for only ten per centum of the total economy of the villages.

An unusual concession, for Soviet legislators, has been made to the Church in the Baltic States, in that priests have been permitted to retain a small parcel of land for their use, and the clergy using the land are classed as peasants. It is explained that this concession has been made because of the highly religious character of some communities.

Citizens of the former Baltic States have become citizens of the U.S.S.R., and all have the right to use their native language in schools and courts. Laws in each Baltic Republic are published in the language of the Republic, as well as in Russian. On November 6, 1940, the Presidium of the Supreme Soviet of the U.S.S.R. acceded to the demand of the governments of the Latvian, Lithuanian and Esthonian Republics for the application of the existing codes of the R.S.F.S.R.[46] to the three territories; these codes being the civil, criminal, labor and family codes, and the codes of civil and criminal procedure. These codes form part of a legal system which has been extensively developed of recent years in the U.S.S.R. so that personal property rights, of a nature not affecting political power, as well as family relations and other branches of law, have been subjected to strict control and protection.

In the former provinces of Poland which have become parts of the Soviet Union, a similar hesitancy to move immediately towards Soviet socialism, is to be found. Thus, all of industry and trade has not been nationalized, although banks, land and large industry, as well as the insurance business, have become the property of the nation. This action was taken by the National Assemblies of Western Ukraine and Western White Russia before the areas were admitted to the Soviet Union and made parts of the Ukrainian and White Russian Republics, respectively.

Elections in the new areas were open to all persons, regardless of whether they had been formerly members of the working class, of the peasantry, or of the bourgeoisie. This step represents a departure from the rule extant in Russia in the early years after the revolution, when former members of the bourgeoisie and priests were automatically disenfranchised, and may have been responsible for the appearance of 99.3 per centum of the population at the polls in Western Ukraine for the first elections and 99.21 per centum of the population in Western White Russia.

Collective farming has been pushed more extensively in Western Ukraine and Western White Russia than has been the case in the former Baltic States. Machine Tractor Stations and State Farms have been set up. In considering the difference in the approach to the peasantry of the former sections of Poland on the one hand, and to the peasantry of the Baltic States on the other, one must recall that the level of the peasantry in the Polish area was probably lower than that of the Baltic area, and fewer of the peasants owned their own land. Another factor which may have accounted for the different approach is the inclusion of the former Polish provinces as integral parts of Soviet Republics which have long developed collective farming as the major form of agricultural production, while the Baltic States have been incorporated as Soviet Republics without being united with parts of the Soviet Union already collectivized. To this statement there is one exception, for parts of the long-existing Soviet Republic of White Russia were added to the Lithuanian Soviet Republic on its entrance into the Soviet Union since residents of these areas were largely Lithuanian in racial characteristics and language.

CONCLUSION

A survey of the events which have occurred in the Soviet Union since the outbreak of war in Poland in 1939 indicates in most instances the same tension and restriction upon freedom of movement which is to be found in the warring countries of Western Europe. If one pushes back the point at which the survey commences to late in the year 1936 when the Soviet leaders began to talk openly of the peril of attack, one finds that institutions which have remained unchanged during the period of actual hostilities in Europe have been altered from what they were, or from what they were expected to be, prior to 1936.

While the record of decrees restricting the citizen has been laid upon the books, the precise cause of the increasing restriction is still a matter of conjecture. Students of geography point to the position of the Soviet Union and its openness to attack, as reason for the Soviet leaders to expect extreme danger and therefore to take measures which will assure mobilization of all resources—human as well as material. Students of production needs of a country upon a wartime footing point to the fact that the Soviet Union has taken many of the same steps which are to be found in other areas of Europe to insure the increased production which is so persistent a need for countries at war or about to go to war.

On the other hand, no one who has lived in the Soviet Union prior to the war would take the position that production was a new problem brought by the war. The government and people have clamored for more goods ever since the end of the last World War. Some observers lay the shortage to the social and economic system and see no hope of improvement. Others lay the shortage to the backwardness of a nation only recently emerged from feudalism and trying desperately to keep up with its needs while laboring under the constant fear that expert assistance from abroad is only a ruse to obtain positions from which espionage and sabotage may be carried on.

In the face of these varying interpretations, each of which has been well documented by its proponents, it would be foolhardy to draw a general conclusion at this time that one or the other is correct, and, by like token, one cannot say that the war situation has been solely responsible for recent trends in the development of Soviet political institutions. Yet the pattern has changed and the change has coincided with the war, and the months preceding the war. It would seem that all would agree that the war has had a marked effect upon life in the Soviet Union, and such disagreement as would arise would center about the question of whether the war and its anticipation gave rise to the trend or merely accentuated a trend which had already developed because of previously existing circumstances.

CHAPTER VI

The Impact of the Second World War on Italian Fascism

BY WILLIAM EBENSTEIN
University of Wisconsin

ANY understanding of the influence of the present war upon the position, and perhaps the fate, of the Fascist régime in Italy must take particular account of Italian developments since 1922. There is no need, however, to recount again the political and economic history of this period.[1] It must suffice to say that during these years Fascist politics and politicians failed to give Italy economic prosperity and social security and that there was a progressive degeneration of Fascism into a kind of totalitarian socialism, which substantially amounted to the sacrifice of good macaroni for poor guns. At a price of increased taxation and lowered living standards between 1935 and 1939, Mussolini successively engineered the conquest of Ethiopia, helped plunge Spain into a civil war and finally completed the seizure of Albania. Ignoring the cultural and historical factors which would have suggested other courses of action, and conveniently forgetting that he had ordered troops to the Brenner Pass in 1934, he allowed Italy to be drawn more and more into the German orbit after 1935. Too late did it dawn upon many Italians that the fate of Fascism had become intertwined with that of Nazism and that the hold of Nazism upon Italy would increase,

rather than diminish, with the growing divergence between
the interests of Italy and of Italian Fascism.

THE EFFECT OF NON-BELLIGERENCY ON FASCISM AT HOME

Only a full appreciation of the psychological evolution of
the Italian people in the years prior to the outbreak of the
present war will make comprehensible the significant and
dramatic changes which have subsequently occurred. These
changes have fundamentally affected the régime both inter-
nally and externally and have also vitally altered the attitude
of the Italian people toward Fascism.

The effects of the shot in the arm which Italy's successful
"defiance of 52 nations" provided during the conquest of
Ethiopia had worn away by 1939. At this time the low morale
of the people evidenced a growing realization that Mussolini's
imperialistic ventures could offer few tangible results outside
of confiscations of capital at home and the sacrifice of Italian
youths abroad. With the outbreak of the present war in 1939,
however, Fascism had again a golden opportunity to awaken
the Italian people from the apathy and despondency with
which they regarded the Fascist régime. After seventeen years
of progressive pauperization, and continuous warfare since
1935, the people were tired and psychologically exhausted.
Especially after the long and unprofitable wars in Ethiopia
and Spain the desire for peace in Italy was profound, and
the satisfaction of this longing would have persuaded many
former opponents of Fascism to forget its earlier misdeeds.
It is a matter of record that Fascism failed to take advantage
of the opportunity, and the analysis of that failure throws as
much light upon the transformation of the Fascist régime
during the war as does any of its positive actions.

In the first world war Italy sprang a surprise when she

abandoned her Teutonic allies and joined the enemy camp. In the second world war she again surprised many people all over the world who had confidently expected the Fascist government to betray its ally, this time Nazi Germany. Instead, the Fascist government, after a period of over nine months of hesitation and preparation, tied itself to the Nazi war machine and thus disappointed the expectations of those who were confident that the Italian dictator would never live up to the pledges given to his German colleague.

The military alliance of May 22, 1939, between Germany and Italy stated in Article 3 that if one of the contracting parties should be involved in an armed conflict, "the other contracting party will immediately come to its aid with all its armed forces on land, in the air, and on sea." When Germany invaded Poland on September 1, 1939, Great Britain and France went to war with Germany in pursuance of their obligations to the Polish Republic; Mussolini announced that Italy would not engage in any military operations. Herr Hitler not only accepted this decision of Signor Mussolini, but even thanked him for political and diplomatic support, adding that Germany would be well capable of bringing the military conflict to a successful end by herself.

To the Italian people this declaration was received with deep satisfaction, and many even admired the régime for out-smarting the Teutons by not going to their aid, as Article 3 of the German-Italian military alliance of May, 1939, un-equivocally stipulated. The rank and file of the nation, not too interested in diplomatic issues as such, felt gratitude to the régime not only for sparing Italy the horrors of war in terms of human sacrifices and physical destruction, but especially for putting, as it seemed, the interests of Italy, which sorely needed peace and tranquillity, above the interests of Fascism that had always preached and lately practiced war.

To many Italians, even to anti-Fascists, it seemed in the fall
of 1939 that Nazism had staked the future of Germany on the
necessity of its own survival, whereas Fascism had shown
itself more patriotic by serving first the main interest of
Italy: peace and recovery from the Ethiopian and Spanish
wars. Naturally, the Italian people would have looked up to
Fascism with even greater admiration and gratitude had the
government come forth with the assurance that Italy would
not join the war at all. Although such a declaration was never
made, and although the Italian people were kept in subservience by the Fascist propaganda that *il Duce* must be blindly
followed in the critical days ahead as "one must not disturb
the pilot, especially during stormy navigation," [2] the failure
of the government to enter the war at once came as such an
unexpected relief and blessing that most people were too busy
enjoying the sweet moments of peace to gaze with much
apprehension into the future.

This period of genuine popular sympathy for the régime
was to last only very briefly. The Italians were soon taught
that Fascist non-intervention was not motivated by considerations of a higher patriotism, and that they had been the victims
of ignorance deliberately fostered by the responsible heads of
the régime. Foreign Minister Count Ciano reported to the
Italian Chamber, on December 16, 1939, his contention, made
at the meeting with Hitler in Salzburg in the middle of
August of the same year, that "as a consequence of the ex-
haustion of Italian resources caused by two wars a minimum
period of three years would be necessary for Italy to bring
her military preparation to the desired level of efficiency.
The outbreak of the military conflict could not change the
facts of the situation." Similarly, Signor Farinacci, an old
Fascist extremist and one of the outstanding Italian-speaking
Nazi leaders in Italy, wrote, in April, 1940, that Italy could

not join Germany in September, 1939, because the war "had just broken out after four years of Italian war," [3] meaning the wars of Ethiopia, Spain, and Albania. These three wars had drained the economic, financial, and military resources of Italy. Another high Fascist official stated on January 17, 1940, in an address before the Fascist district leaders of Italy, that "we must not remain in the illusion that the present position of Italy with regard to the war can last. Fascist Italy must get ready to step into the war at any moment." [4]

Official statements of this sort quickly dispelled any illusions held by Italians with regard to Fascist patriotism, and rapidly widened the gap between the régime and the people. First, the people were shocked to learn that, if Count Ciano was to be believed, the military alliance between Nazism and Fascism contained a secret clause that would exempt Italy from fulfilling her part for three years; this made the "unbreakable union of our wills and our forces" [5] appear in an entirely new light. However, what was distressing in the eyes of many Italians was the official admission that Fascism did not enter the war at once, solely for reasons of economic and military weakness. This admission came after Fascism had preached for seventeen years that a new world conflagration was coming, and that the preparation and complete militarization of Italy demanded sacrifices in political liberties and economic welfare, "even if it should mean the wiping out of all that is called civil life." [6] This official acknowledgement of weakness made many wonder on what grounds their privations over almost two decades could be justified if, at the very moment of the new "collision of rivalling imperialisms," Fascism admitted that it was incapable of participating in the struggle, the supreme form of existence according to Fascist philosophy. Not a sudden awakening of Italian patriotism, many Italians woefully realized, was responsible for the failure of Fascism to enter the struggle at once, but its bank-ruptcy with regard to the very aspect of national life which it had always extolled and prepared for: war.

Wishful thinking abroad was convinced that the real rea-sons for Italy's status of non-belligerency from September to June were to be found in the attitude of the Italian king, a gentleman of western upbringing and tradition and anti-Prussian at heart, in the intercession of the Pope on behalf of peace, and in the desire of the Italian nation to avoid a war in which it would have to fight its Latin sister, France, and the old friend of Italy, Great Britain. All these reasons were continually advanced in the western nations on the assump-tion that if Italy, from a historical, sane and liberal point of view, knew her own enlightened self-interest, she could not possibly act in any other manner.

However, the mechanics of totalitarianism work differ-ently; the most important reason for Italy's non-belligerency from September to June was the belief of Mussolini and the Fascist hierarchs, shared with many military experts and ordinary people in democracies as well as dictatorships, that the Maginot line was virtually impregnable and that the French army could not be beaten in open combat. This belief, we may note, was widespread not only in the demo-cratic nations; even men less well disposed toward the French republic, including Herr Hitler and the German military staff, seemed to share this view until Herr Hitler took his gigantic gamble in May, 1940, with the invasion of Holland and Bel-gium.

In the period from the outbreak of war up to the invasion of Norway and Denmark, Mussolini and even his pro-Nazi aides were obviously uncertain who was going to win. Fas-cism therefore shrewdly retained the Axis alliance, putting it for the time being, however, if not into cold storage, at least into a cool safe, while exploiting simultaneously the illusions of the western nations concerning Fascist ambitions and policies. The British and French governments actually permitted British and French factories to accept Italian orders amounting to $240,000,000. These orders covered such vital war material as ships, machines, cars, motors, coal, and minerals which Italy sorely needed. In return, Italy continually postponed payment, slowed up deliveries, and tried to flood Britain and France with bumper crops of lemons and dried fruits that she could not get rid of elsewhere.

MILITARY AND POLITICAL CHANGES IN THE REGIME

The turning point in the attitude of Fascism was the Russian-Finnish war and the German campaign in Norway. In both cases, Mussolini was impressed by the fact that Franco-British military power was actually much inferior to what he had been led to believe. He therefore ordered the Italian press to follow the German propaganda leads in handling both of these wars. Then, on May 10, 1940, Herr Hitler issued his command to the German army to invade the Lowlands and France in order to settle the fate of the world once and for all, or at least for a few thousand years. This was the moment, if there ever was one for the Fascist government, to join the war because the conflict had now entered the phase in which men and machines and not spirited discourses by Signor Gayda or Signor Ansaldo were needed.

However, Mussolini continued to believe firmly in the strength of the Maginot line and in the military genius of the French army. Only after France was already beaten did the Fascist government declare war on France and Britain on June 10, 1940, confident of dealing with Herr Hitler in the same way as it had dealt with the British and French appeasers before; that is, on the principle of getting something for nothing. In his speech of June 10, 1940, announcing the declaration of war to the massed Blackshirts in Rome, Mussolini stated that although Italy had solved the problem of her continental frontiers in the first world war, she was now intent on solving the problem of her maritime frontiers because "a country of 45,000,000 is not truly free if it has not free access to the ocean." Mussolini also attacked in this speech the "plutocratic and reactionary democracies who always have blocked the march and frequently have plotted against the existence of the Italian people," and predicted victory for "proletarian, Fascist Italy." In the first three-quarters of his speech, Mussolini himself did not even mention that Italy had gone to war on the side of Germany because she was bound to do so by virtue of the German-Italian military pact of May 22, 1940. Only in the last part of his address did he say that "according to the rules of Fascist morals when one has a friend, one marches with him to the end. This we have done and will continue to do with Germany, her people, and her victorious armed forces."

Seven days after Italy entered the war (despite her entry, one might almost say) France sued for an armistice, and *il Duce* now received the first real defeat in his career. As a result of the German-French armistice, Germany occupied two-thirds of France, the cost of occupation being borne by France. Included in this occupied area was the whole Atlantic coast of France and territory giving her a direct contact with the Spanish frontier. Germany, that is, took everything from France that in her opinion was necessary for the prosecution of the war against Britain. In addition, the direct territorial aspirations concerning Alsace-Lorraine were realized immediately, and Alsace-Lorraine is already being administered as an integral part of the German Reich, although no peace between France and Germany has been concluded as yet.

Italy, on the other hand, received none of the territorial prizes she had been demanding for many years: neither Corsica nor Tunisia; neither Nice nor Savoy; even under conditions of temporary occupation. Nor did Herr Hitler allow any of the Mediterranean bases of France to fall into the hands of Italy, although Italy too was at war with England. The only rather meager results of the French-Italian armistice were the demilitarization of the Franco-Italian frontier and of the French colonies bordering Italian possessions in Africa. Italy also obtained full rights in Jibuti and on the railway line from Jibuti to Addis Ababa.

Subsequent to the defeat of France, Germany tried to make good her failure to conquer Britain by subjugating the remaining neutral countries in the southeast of Europe. In Roumania she fully succeeded, and the new government following the abdication of King Carol was a puppet in the hands of the Nazi masters. In October, 1940, Germany even occupied the vital industrial and commercial centers of Roumania. To this date about all Mussolini and his so-called belligerent régime have done in the war is to talk a good deal, give "moral" support to the Axis partner, keep the Italian navy in poorly protected hideouts, and otherwise rely on the German army, in short—give to Germany all war short of aid.

The unprovoked aggression against Greece at the end of October, 1940, is to be understood not only as a part of the Fascist campaign to get to the Suez Canal and smash the British Empire, but also as a protest of *il Duce* Mussolini against being relegated to the status of *Gauleiter* Mussolini in a Slovakia in which the official language is Italian. The Italian fiasco in Greece and Albania proved that Fascism was safe as long as it was not too optimistic about the quality and equipment of the Italian armed forces.

On October 28 at 3 o'clock in the morning the Fascist government confronted Greece with an ultimatum in which it demanded the right to occupy various Greek ports and naval and air bases for the prosecution of the war against Britain. Copying the lightning diplomacy of Germany, Italy gave Greece only three hours in which she might accept the ultimatum. This action was taken in spite of Mussolini's solemn assurance on June 10, 1940, that "Italy does not intend to drag other peoples bordering on her sea or land into the conflict," and the specific mention, in this connection, of Greece. Again copying Germany, Italian troops invaded Greece even before the three hours had expired. Up to that point Italy had imitated all the new techniques of totalitarian diplomacy and lightning warfare. Here the differences begin, for where Germany brilliantly succeeded in her campaigns in Norway and the Low Countries, Italy in contrast suffered a military débâcle in Greece and Albania. A Turkish newspaper warned early in December, 1940, against exaggerating the ultimate significance of the Greek victories in Greece and Albania as Italy might call into action a secret weapon—one German regiment. At that time Fascist spokesmen, still convinced of the singular virility of Fascist warriors, indignantly ridiculed such a suggestion as violating the honor of Fascist Italy. Since January, 1941, the secret weapon was introduced in increasing quantities into Italy, especially in southern Italy and Sicily, and has been aiding Italy in Albania and Africa.

While the war against Greece has resulted in a serious setback for the prestige of Fascism at home, the Italian forces have at least put up some fight, stiffened by German assistance in the air and by the German invasion of Yugoslavia and Greece through Bulgaria and Roumania.[7] On the other hand, the Fascist campaign in Africa, destined to hasten the collapse of the British Empire by attacks against Egypt from the west, south and east, has turned into the major military disaster of Italy in this war. In the campaign against Greece the Fascist military machine was shown to be a thing of wood painted to look like iron. Although the number of the Fascist forces was about three to one as compared with the British forces, superior British strategy, equipment, and fighting spirit transformed a small local skirmish around Sidi Barrani early in December (1940) into a major campaign in which the Italian empire in Africa, both in the north and in the east, quickly crumbled. The vision of cities in the Fascist African empire, founded by Italian soldiers, cities in which "Italian children were born with Fascist rhythm," [8] was suddenly shattered. While there is no doubt that poor fighting spirit was not the only cause of the Fascist military collapse, it is remarkable that over 125,000 Italians, almost half of the total fighting strength in northern Africa, were captured. It is significant indeed that even the young men who grew up under the Fascist régime and who never knew any other institutional pattern, quickly gave up the fight when they felt that they had been "sold" to destruction by incompetence, concealed weaknesses, and lies (e.g., that the British were people "who are in a decline," decadent, and therefore no match for virile Italians [9]). 125,000 Italians, who were sent out to northern Africa in order to conquer Egypt as the vanguard of the expanding Fascist empire, reached Egypt more quickly than they thought they would—but as prisoners of war. It is doubtful what allegiance many of them, officers or men, still harbor for the Fascist régime. At the present time their release from captivity and return to Italy would be entirely unwelcome to the Fascist hierarchs, because they have actually encountered the glories of Fascist existence, living dangerously and conquering inferior decadents.

The effects of military defeats have already imposed their imprint upon the structure and organization of the Fascist régime. The relationship between party and army under Fascism has been essentially the same as under Nazism. In both cases the upper strata of the army, or at least some of the higher officers, might have felt contempt for the plebeian and untamed elements in the Fascist or Nazi movements, but in both cases also the common hatred of free institutions and common imperialistic ambitions finally subordinated the army completely to the political movement. It may be that in this war the higher officers of the Italian army were fundamentally split as to the wisdom of entering the war on Germany's side. However, the pro-Nazi faction finally carried the day, and the faction that was less optimistic, or more pro-Italian, or more anti-Nazi, had to submit and do its duty. Where the triumphs of the German *Wehrmacht* diverted popular sympathies and enthusiasm in Germany from the party to the army so that the party became relatively less important than before the war, in Italy the trend of events has been in the other direction so far. The continued military setbacks suffered by Fascism have produced a political situation in which someone or some group must serve as the scapegoat which can be sacrificed on the altar of popular wrath and indignation.

In democracies changes in the government usually serve as safety valves, as happened after the Franco-British débâcle in Norway in April and May, 1940, when both Daladier in France and Chamberlain in England together with some of their prominent colleagues had to leave office. Under Fascism the safety valve of comprehensive cabinet changes is by definition impossible, as the fate of the One Man is tied up with that of his cabinet, the party, the régime and, in a sense, the whole country. If the guilty system, the responsible author of defeat and disillusionment, cannot be made accountable, then prominent individuals, preferably the innocent agents in that process, must be sacrificed. Early in November, 1940, General Prasca, commander of the Fascist forces in Albania, was demoted in the first army shake-up when Greece did not fold up in terror before Fascist power. At that time General Soddu, former Under-Secretary of War, took over command. However, these changes did not produce the desired effect, and early in December the Italian armed forces underwent the most thoroughgoing changes since Fascism seized power in 1922. Marshal Badoglio, chief of the general staff, resigned, as did Admiral Cavagnari, chief of the naval staff, and General De Vecchi, governor of the strategically important Dodecanese Islands close to the Turkish southwestern coastline. In none of these cases did the official announcements even pretend that ill health or age were the causes of the "resignations." It is no exaggeration to say that Marshal Badoglio has been Italy's outstanding soldier since the foundation of the kingdom seventy years ago. In the first world war he reorganized the Italian army after the crushing defeat of Caporetto, and led it to victory in the battle of Vittorio Veneto, one of the most memorable military successes of the last war. Later on he showed remarkable skill as an organizer and strategist in the Ethiopian campaign. He is an officer of the old school who never made himself conspicuous by political activities. While there is little foundation for the occasionally cited opinion that he is anti-Fascist, he no doubt has retained some elements of loyalty to Italy, as contrasted with subservience to one man or to his foreign masters. His successor in office, General Cavallero, can in no way be called Badoglio's match as a soldier, but he has always been a soldier-politician, has organized the Fascist militia, has come out enthusiastically for the régime, and is one of the most outspoken pro-Nazis in Italy. These qualifications, rather than a military record of extraordinary brilliance, secured General Cavallero his present high position. Admiral Cavagnari was the sacrifice offered to expiate the extremely poor fighting record of the Fascist navy. It steadily refused to give battle to British vessels until the British had to attack enemy vessels in the very harbors in which they had fled for refuge. Here again the "resignation" of Admiral Cavagnari has not improved Italy's fighting position at sea, as the British naval operations during the north African campaign as well as the naval raids against Taranto, Naples, Brindisi and, most sensational of all, the shelling of Genoa early in February, 1941, amply demonstrated.

The crushing defeat of the Italian navy in the battle of the Ionian Sea on March 28, 1941, further contributed to the disintegration of Fascist military strength. The "resignation" of De Vecchi has an additional note of historical interest as he was one of the four men, so-called *quadrumviri*, who staged the March on Rome in 1922. One of them, Michele Bianchi, died several years ago under somewhat mysterious circumstances. Another of the four original Fascists, Italo Balbo, was mysteriously killed in Libya shortly after Italy's entry into the war—as mysteriously, many claim, as General von Fritsch in Poland. Now De Vecchi has been dropped, alive for the time being, and Mussolini may soon find himself the only remaining one of the four original Fascist leaders. In March, 1941, Marshal Graziani, commander of the Fascist forces in north Africa, resigned. This was no real surprise. Although Graziani stated in his report to his government of December 22, 1940, that "crushing superiority of the enemy's armed units" was the essential reason for the British success, events since that time had adequately demonstrated that the highly coordinated British air, sea, and mechanized land power was relatively little resisted by the ill-equipped Fascist forces. No matter what was the actual cause of the Fascist failure, there was little doubt that some prominent military chief, such as Graziani, would have to "resign" when the master gave the signal—at the behest of the Nazi *Wehrmacht* that has taken over in Libya since March, 1941.

However, these large-scale demotions of the old and trusted military leaders have been insufficient to check the rising feeling of frustration and disillusionment following the uninterrupted military setbacks. Numbers of high Fascist political officials have resigned from their offices, at their "own request" of course, in order to serve the régime on the battle front. Pavolini, Minister of Popular Culture, Ricci, Minister of Corporations, Cianetti, Under-Secretary of Corporations, and many other hierarchs had to volunteer, mostly for the Albanian front. Early in February, 1941, it was officially announced in Rome that thirty-three high Fascist officials had resigned from their offices, and that most of them had volunteered or had been called to go to the front. Their places were taken by true and tried veterans of the Fascist movement, although it would have seemed that at no time high offices in the Fascist hierarchy would be entrusted to persons other than true and tried Fascists. These purges were carried out in accordance with the order of Mussolini given in his speech at Rome on November 18, 1940, that "the party should free itself and the nation of the petty bourgeois ballast." These internal changes in the highest of political offices of the régime reached their climax when it was announced officially in Rome, on January 27, 1941, that Count Ciano, son-in-law of Mussolini and Foreign Minister since 1936, had gone to the front for service in the air force. As long as Fascist foreign policy was unimpeded by any resistance of the western democracies, in fact actively aided by them in the era of appeasement, Mussolini unhesitatingly harvested the fruits of publicity, glorifying what was described by the Fascist press as triumphs of Fascist statesmanship and diplomacy. However, after the failure of Fascist policy to terrorize—and of Fascist arms to force—Greece into submission Ciano was sacrificed, for the time being at least, at the very time when his position seemed well-nigh impregnable. Even with Greece having to accept a settlement dictated by Germany following military penetration of Yugoslavia and Bulgaria the original failure will not be forgotten. In any case the subsequent Nazi dictate will, of course, again be glorified in Italy as a brilliant triumph of Mussolini.

SOME SOCIAL AND ECONOMIC CONSEQUENCES OF THE WAR

If it is true that ability to wage war today is conditioned more than ever before by a country's economic resources, Italy standing alone is certainly least capable among all the belligerents of resisting the pressure of a long war. In 1936 the International Labor Office published a very significant study on nutrition standards of various countries in the world. According to this study the average Italian diet has the lowest calorific content of all European countries for which statistics were available, and was considered to be substantially below what was held to be an adequate diet.[10] The people of Italy then consumed, per capita, less meat, butter, eggs, and sugar than those of any other country in Europe and of most countries overseas.

After the outbreak of the war, in September, 1939, Italy had to effect a still further serious reduction of her food consumption as a consequence of the allied blockade and general war conditions. By the time Italy entered the war in June, 1940, four out of every seven days were meatless and sugar and coffee were drastically rationed. The war added to these restrictions. The sale of coffee has been entirely prohibited, and Italy, it may be noted, is like the United States and France, a coffee-drinking country. Five days out of seven are now meatless. Fats, oils, rice, and bread have been severely rationed. Since December, 1940, even the consumption of spaghetti has been drastically curtailed to about four pounds a person per month, which is about half as much as the Italian normally consumes. Bread and flour products such as macaroni and spaghetti are the staple foods in the Italian diet, not because Italians are innately sober and hardy, as some foreigners seem to imagine, but because too many of them are too poor to eat anything more luxurious.

Food prices rose by about thirty-five per cent between 1934 and 1939 and by another forty per cent from September, 1939, to September, 1940. Signor Roberto Farinacci, secretary of the Fascist Party, wrote as follows in his paper, *La Vita Italiana*, of December 9, 1940: "The crescendo continues; with things increasing at this rate, are wages and salaries to remain unaltered?" So far no notice has come of any wage increase in Italy to offset the imposed reduction of even the barest necessities of life.

At the same time we must also remember that the British blockade hits Italy much harder than it does Germany. Whereas normally only about fifteen per cent of German trade is with overseas countries, in the case of Italy the situation is fundamentally different as eighty-six per cent of Italy's trade is sea-borne. Of Italy's total imports eighty per cent must pass through the straits of Gibraltar or through the Suez Canal and five per cent through the Dardanelles, and only ten per cent originates in ports of other Mediterranean countries. Among other items the blockade has totally stopped the imports of coffee, meats, rubber, and jute, ninety-five per cent of the imports of oils and fats, raw cotton and wool, and about seventy per cent of the normal imports of cereals.

Thanks to the Italian invasion of Greece, Britain has now occupied the island of Crete and other strategic Greek naval bases and is thus in a better position to stop Italian commerce even within the Mediterranean. The position of Italy in relation to Germany in this war is very often compared with the rôle of Austria in the last war. While there may be some resemblances insofar as both placed certain strains on Germany, we should not forget that Austria-Hungary in the last war was an empire rich in economic resources, whereas Italy is poor. Germany, for instance, now supplies Italy with 1,000,000 tons of coal a month, and these shipments are not only a drain on Germany's own coal supply but constitute also a considerable burden on the German transportation facilities. Similarly, Italy is entirely dependent on Germany for the heavy industrial equipment and machinery that Italy needs for the maintenance of her industry. The trouble from Germany's viewpoint is that Italy in turn can export nothing to her that can be called vital in any sense. Italy has none of the minerals or raw materials such as oil or foodstuffs that Germany needs and cannot obtain from overseas.

It would be a mistake to assume that the war has imposed new burdens only on the poorer sections of the people, who constitute a majority of the Italian nation. Nevertheless, the working classes and peasants have been hit hardest. Although their living standard has always been very low, it seems that the boundaries of their suffering and poverty can be stretched beyond the imagination of the satiated. Under the impact of the new sufferings of the working classes the propaganda of the régime has increasingly emphasized that this war is not fought by Fascism for the resurrection of the Roman empire, as has been proclaimed during the last eighteen years, but that it is a war "rich in revolutionary substance," [11] a war of proletarian Italy against Anglo-American plutocrats.[12] On December 1, 1940, the Charter of Labor was proclaimed a constitutional law by the Grand Council of Fascism in order to bolster the morale of the working classes.[13] However, the Charter of Labor has been in existence since 1927 as a basic declaration of the rights and duties of labor, and its elevation to the rank of a constitutional statute will not change the present trade unions from government agencies into free associations of workingmen.[14]

On December 29, 1940, Giuseppe Tassinari, Minister of Agriculture, was made virtual food dictator of Italy. He is empowered to order the declaration of foodstuffs by holders, to buy and requisition foodstuffs, to determine the amount of food to be assigned to the various sections of the country, and to organize producers, merchants, and consumers for such purposes. Heavy punishments are provided for violators, and the death penalty is foreseen for crimes concerning the hoarding of basic commodities for profiteering purposes. Similarly, mine operators and farmers are subject to penalties including loss of property and imprisonment in the case of "lack of discipline and comprehension of the superior national necessities" in the form of hoarding produce of any sort. In the business community, the war has brought the limitation of dividends for all types of business to seven per cent. In addition, the tax on interest on bonds of private companies and state agencies was raised from ten to twenty per cent. It is interesting that most of these drastic war measures in all branches of industry, agriculture, and commerce were introduced only in December, 1940; until then the Fascist conduct of the war seemed to be based on the

expectation of a short war. Only after Germany's failure to
conquer England in the fall of 1940, and after the defeats of
Italy in Greece and Africa, were measures introduced which
foresaw a protracted war. However, hard as these new economic restrictions may appear, they alone cannot seriously
undermine the functioning of the Fascist régime as a going
concern, as long as Nazism stands and can supply Italy with
the vital materials and industrial products required for the
prosecution of the war. Furthermore, while "the end of economic man" [15] may perhaps not be as complete as some
observers of the contemporary scene believe, there may be
more truth in the phrase than old-fashioned liberal or socialist
economists would be willing to admit.

The Struggle of Fascism for Survival

In addition to significant shifts in the Fascist political hierarchy as well as in the highest ranks of the military leadership,
organized threats and actual violence have been forced upon
the régime by the changed internal situation; and these have
appeared on a larger scale than ever before in the history of
Fascism. The years 1924-1927 witnessed not only the assassination of Matteotti, Amendola, and other leaders of the
opposition but also the use of violence against the rank and
file of anti-Fascist groups. These years saw more brutality in
Italy than any others in the Fascist period prior to the outbreak of this war. Now the European and not only the Italian
situation has changed insofar as the Nazis taught totalitarians
everywhere following 1933, that what they had indulged in
before was child's play compared with what could be achieved
in the way of total destruction of political opponents or
other undesirables. Italy has learned this lesson well from the
Nazis. The wave of terror in Italy since the outbreak of this

war, and especially since the setbacks in Greece and Africa, has lost those elements of humanism which dilettantism and inefficiency had to a certain extent permitted in previous episodes. All over the country concentration camps have been established in which thousands of persons have been interned; these include former leaders or members of opposition parties who had completely refrained from any political expression for the last ten or fifteen years, or who had even been converted, officially at least, to the orthodox creed. In addition, thousands of Jews (the total Jewish population of Italy is only about 50,000) have been put in these concentration camps, some of them, in fact, specifically reserved for Jewish internees. Among them are Jews of all professional and political affiliations, including ardent Fascists and former high officers, such as General Levi. In Trieste, the Capo d'Istria prison alone has over 5,000 political prisoners, most of them Slovenes and Croats, of the Slav population of Istria (over half a million) who have never willingly submitted to the Fascist procedures of forcible Italianization. Also at Trieste a huge concentration camp has been recently built to accommodate thousands of Albanian "bandits," i.e., patriots who have never given up their struggle against the Fascist conquerors. Curiously enough, in view of the Axis pact of steel, one concentration camp (in Lagonegro) has a special concentration of obstinate German Tirolese.

The appointment of Roberto Farinacci as Secretary General of the Fascist Party was another symbol of the fact that Fascism has drifted into a phase of terror and intimidation. Farinacci was Secretary General of the Party in the middle twenties, at the time when the régime established itself definitely as a dictatorship. At that time his ruthlessness against opponents was notorious, and he then had the distinction of belonging to the small but not uninfluential wing of the

Fascist party that was anti-religious, anti-Catholic, and violently anti-Jewish. Farinacci was kept out of the picture in the period when Fascism sought to build up a front of relative respectability before the respectable people at home and abroad, but since the unfolding of Fascist dynamics from the Ethiopian war onwards and the final realization of his dream of an alliance with Nazism, his influence has steadily grown. He is now probably the leading Italian-speaking Nazi in Italy, and his fortune will be determined by that of his foreign masters and protectors. He was the only man in Italy who recently dared to attack Badoglio after the latter's resignation. This he did in the following manner:

A certain person is frequenting salons, hunting preserves, and groups who received favors from him, saying that he did not favor the undertaking and that he demanded more divisions to do it. It should be known that this person undertook the task with the forces already existing in Albania and made no qualification. Everything else is contrary to the truth. It is infantile to try to put the responsibility on the political command, when it is more than clear that the military conduct of the war is solely concerned with technical organization.[16]

Mussolini's appeal of November 18, 1940, to clean out "the remaining petty bourgeois ballast" has since found repeated resonance in the Fascist press and is symptomatic of the wave of restlessness that must have affected many Italians since the ill-starred campaigns in Greece and Africa. What the Fascist officeholders and propagandists are especially afraid of is the spreading "disease" of listening in to foreign stations, including enemy broadcasts, and of reading neutral papers still accessible. The *Popolo di Roma* of December 10, 1940, vigorously attacked the scoundrels who read the French-Swiss press in order to get the British side of the news, and then continued as follows: "These are the ones who, on read-

ing the communiques of our general headquarters, always have
something to add. These are the prophets of disaster, the professional alarmists, the convinced pessimists, the empty brains,
and the sour stomachs who still exist among us here and
there. It seems to us that the time has come for some beatings."
Three days later the same paper in Rome lashed out against
the traitors who "delight to listen to the British radio night
after night, and who swear by its truth. The hour has come
to brand these traitors in a due manner. No pardon can be
given." [17] Another even more influential organ, the official
mouthpiece of Fascist labor organizations, expressed itself as
follows:

The time has come to say to our open and hidden enemies that
we have never been prouder of being Italians and Fascists. We
will take a cold, clear, pitiless vengeance, man for man, head for
head; a vengeance without forgetfulness and without mercy, an
epoch-making vengeance. That goes also for those Italians who
are falser than Greek money and doubly bastardized, who have
not the heart to hold out for victory and who are not worthy of
it. With them, fortunately, the accounting is near.[18]

This is not the language of a régime that still prides itself on
being a *blocco granitico* (granite block), but shows rather
the convulsions of collective fear and neurosis.

The persecution of the Catholic press has been resumed.
The *Osservatore Romano,* published in the Vatican City
and considered as the mouthpiece of the Vatican, has experienced various difficulties since the outbreak of the war.
Before the war, its circulation was only 20,000, but afterwards it rapidly rose to 200,000 copies daily, a very large
circulation in a country with very few papers over one
hundred thousand daily. The *Osservatore Romano* owed this
jump in circulation to the fact that it is the only paper in Italy
which is not technically subject to the orders of the Ministry

of Propaganda. As a consequence, more and more readers were anxious to get the other side of the war news, and that is the extent of anti-Fascist material that even the *Osservatore Romano* would probably desire and certainly dare to present. In the month of May, 1940, spontaneous demonstrations against news vendors selling the *Osservatore Romano* were organized in Rome and other cities, piles of papers were burned in public, and prospective buyers of the paper were intimidated. The circulation subsequently dropped very sharply due to these and other methods of "control of public opinion," although later on the editorial policies of the *Osservatore Romano* attempted to take into consideration Fascist sensitivity more carefully than before. In January, 1941, Catholic weeklies in Padua and Udine were suppressed because of "pacifist propaganda," according to the explanation of Fascist authorities.[19]

The latest symptom of a fear complex is the restriction of freedom of movement for foreigners. Even diplomats and news correspondents cannot leave Rome without special permission of the authorities, and the Fascist government requested the United States government to close its consulates in Naples and Palermo, giving as an official explanation its desire to keep foreigners out of danger. It is noteworthy that this request came in the middle of February, 1941, just after British parachutists had been dropped in southern Italy. It is also a sign of the dynamically changed internal situation that the Fascist counterpart of the Nazi *SS*, the *squadristi*, has been called to new life since the officially inaugurated campaign of terror and intimidation. In fairness to the régime it ought to be emphasized that the Fascist *squadristi*, while using threats, intimidation, and terror on a large scale, never have in any substantial degree resorted to wholesale sadism and degeneracy, as their more thorough colleagues in the north have done with deadly efficiency. It should also be emphasized that the concentration camps in Italy, while no sanitaria, have not been and are not the scenes of horror which are characteristic of Nazi concentration camps. There are differences of treatment in the Fascist concentration camps, depending on the predominant type of inmate, but so far no news of deliberate sadism and brutality has reached the outside world. All that happens is that thousands of innocent citizens or foreigners are interned because of their past or present political or religious beliefs. No trial is held in determining the fate of these innocent and mostly quite unimportant people.

It is not accurately ascertainable to what extent the introduction of these new methods of violence is due to the frequent visits of high Nazi officials of the *Gestapo* (including Heinrich Himmler, its head) and to the resulting close cooperation of Fascism and Nazism in this field. But even before the outbreak of this war the intimacy of the military staffs had been accompanied by "mutual consultation" of the secret police of both countries. Since Italy's entry into the war, and particularly since the stationing of German forces in various cities and air fields of Italy, notably in the south and in Sicily, the *Gestapo* has taken over many functions of a delicate nature deemed necessary in the interests of Nazi military efficiency.[20]

The difference between the present wave of terror and intimidation, the most intense in the record of Fascism, and that of the years 1924-1927, lies not alone in the greater volume of officially organized terror, or in the more effective application of violence; it lies primarily in the fact that the terror of the early years of Fascism was native and a symptom of Fascist consolidation of power, whereas the present large-scale wave of planned violence is, certainly to a large extent, inspired and dictated by the Nazi masters of Italy, and, furthermore, coincident with and caused by internal weakness and failure. Violence is, in a deeper sense, always the admission of weakness, but in the present situation the maintenance of Fascism on the point of the Nazi bayonet may increasingly lead more and more Italians to identify Fascism with foreign domination. Whether Italy will without resistance allow herself to be completely turned into an Italian-speaking Slovakia remains to be seen; in any event, Fascism has done its utmost, over a period of almost twenty years, to extirpate civic courage and personal dignity without which no true patriotism can flourish.

CHAPTER VII

French Government under Pétain

BY J. G. HEINBERG

University of Missouri

PREFACE FOR STUDENTS

AN ABUNDANT literature has been produced to explain the defeat of France. Much of it is obviously superficial by reason of the motives of its authors. Some authors are motivated by a desire to discredit the Third Republic, while others desire simply to discredit a handful of men. Still others are motivated by nothing more significant than a hope to publish a best seller, or to secure promotion and a higher salary from their newspaper. Nothing approaching a definitive investigation of the how and why of French defeat has yet appeared, and it seems altogether likely that a number of years must pass before our understanding of this tragedy will be clarified.

In order first to comprehend the persistent historical nature of the problem to be investigated a student of French government should be acquainted with certain passages in the works of Georges Clemenceau, the "Father of Victory" of the first World War. He should begin with the chapter entitled "The Retrograde Peace" in *Grandeur and Misery of Victory*. He should notice that the volume itself was published simultaneously in the leading countries of the world on April 12, 1930. On that date Hitler had only a small following in Germany and there were no fascist leagues in France, but Clemenceau realized the approach of the "terrible moment."

What are we doing, then, if not proceeding, article by article, to restore Germany's power, which, by a truly miraculous exercise of will, after its complete collapse during the War, is about to be built up again in the retrograde peace, which is surrendering, stage by stage, everything that human justice had gained by our victory? After the restoration of Germany's moral prestige by a lie we have the upsetting of the financial reparations by the progressive mutilations of the treaty down to the payment of the so-called debts to America! Finally, when this account is settled, or simply opened for the first cut of the final, fatal wound, it will be represented to us that the fabric of European justice according to the Treaty of Versailles has on all sides caused nothing but social disturbance and recriminations leading to outbreaks of violence. That will be the day toward which Germany has been ceaselessly striving since the Treaty of Versailles. What forces are at the disposal of the new nations of Central Europe? What help will they afford us, and what support are we in a position to offer them? All the problems raised by German aggression of 1914 will have to be dealt with at one and the same time. Germany, having regained her strength, will have inevitably bargained for arrangements from which her concern to isolate France will not be excluded.

I pause on the threshold of the terrible moment when the last great struggle will be entered upon.[1]

Chapter XVI, of the same work, "The Mutilations of the Treaty of Versailles: Mutilation by America—Separate Peace," is also assigned reading. These chapters will serve to outline the periphery of the field of investigation which must be covered if we are to explain the events of June, 1940.

Before any investigation of the French defeat is attempted, there is need for an hypothesis. For example, research into the defeat of France might conceivably proceed upon the basis of any one or a combination of hypotheses: that it was due to the incompetency of French generals, to the rottenness of the governmental system, to the conspiracies of French friends of Germany, to Fifth Columnists, to the Popular Front, to the *Croix de Feu* or to the activities of the Communists in France after the signing of the German-Soviet accord of August, 1939. Such hypotheses, based entirely upon developments *inside* France, have been advanced by the authors of the "superficial literature" mentioned above.

Clemenceau mentioned another hypothesis. On February 5, 1929, in explanation for his fear that the Germans planned "bad things" for European peace he said that:

The German conceives of war in cold-blooded fashion and consequently prepares for it; the Frenchman does not begin to think of it until the day of mobilization.[2]

We might, with better reason, adopt this hypothesis as a basis for investigation into the causes for French defeat in June of 1940. Or, in other words, we might investigate the German preparations for war as well as the slowness and inadequacy of French counter-measures. It seems altogether likely that the greater part of the responsibility for the French defeat must be accorded to the mighty yet minute German preparations for the waging of totalitarian war.

André Morize, Director of the French Ministry of Information before the military débâcle, attempts to enumerate the ten "decisive factors" that led to the French defeat.[3] If the ten are classified, with the idea of assigning responsibility, we may say that three, the force and ingenuity of German propaganda, the work of "fifth columnists," and organized German-Communist sabotage, cannot be credited to the government of the Third Republic, for they originated across the Rhine. These factors, of course, must be indefinitely increased in number to encompass the full extent of German preparations. French military men are largely responsible for three additional "decisive factors": the uncritical faithfulness of the French High Command to obsolete methods, French inferiority in air power, and inadequate information concerning German preparations. In the case of another factor practically all Frenchmen must share responsibility with the government: France, M. Morize tells us, was unprepared in that the whole nation was not organized under strict iron discipline to devote every possible bit of effort and energy to the preparation for war. What French critics or opponents of the Third Republic favored such extensive preparations? Another decisive factor, French failure to speed preparations, is one, the responsibility for which must be shared by military men, politicians, and Frenchmen generally. Two factors remain. "Democratic France was not in perfect health," Morize tells us, "to face the challenge of events." There were internal quarrels, petty party discords and a weak stand against extremist perils of Fascism or Communism. Finally, war leaders like Daladier and Reynaud were not "up to the task." These two factors may be said to be faults of the republican régime. But internal quarrels and party discords were also present during the World War from which France emerged victorious. The fact, if it can be established, that political leaders like Daladier and Reynaud were not "up to the task" affords no basis for wholesale condemnation of the republican régime, for Clemenceau was a republican who succeeded.

Morize suggests the ten factors "simply as a witness, without any specialized competence." The "responsibilities" have been assigned by the present author who was not an actual witness and who certainly claims no special competence for so wide a task. It appears, however, that fruitful inquiry into the defeat of France could be made through the employment of Morize's ten factors as leads under the hypothesis that the defeat is to be explained by the German preparations for war and the slowness and inadequacy of French counter-measures.

Having suggested this inquiry it is well to pass to a consideration of the impact of defeat upon the system of French political institutions.

The Pétain Régime

It has been said that "the collapse of France is a simple, if colossal, fact." [4] A collapse, however, may be either partial or complete. The *system* of government, known as the Third Republic, is at an end, and its political personnel is dispersed. The armed forces are completely demobilized and two-thirds of continental France is occupied by German forces. Paris, in a physical sense, remains, however, and fewer Frenchmen are maimed, gassed and killed this time. There is probably less wastage and ruin in Continental France than in World War I, but allowance must be made for German depredations, appropriations and removals. For these we have no objective measurements. As these lines are written, the French navy and colonies are still beyond German control. In the unoccupied zone, whose population is less than three-eighths the total of continental prewar France, certain older institutions of government and governmental practices still exist, but this area of not unrestricted French governmental experimentation is subject to elimination by force at the moment that such a move would serve Hitler's purposes. Moreover, the German Armistice Commission at Wiesbaden enforces the provisions of the Franco-German armistice of June 22, 1940. The degree to which France cooperates in enforcement is determined by the German authorities, and these authorities have the right to terminate the armistice if France does not live up to her obligations.

One can scarcely be sanguine about the Vichy régime in spite of the constitutionality of the moves whereby Pétain's powers were acquired in July, 1940, when the National Assembly, sitting at Vichy, voted 569 to 80, to grant "all powers" to Marshal Pétain.[5] The roots of his régime are supported by thin soil, the confused sands of a crisis precipitated by disastrous military defeat, streams of refugees and rapid German occupation. Its personnel is Rightist only to the extent that it is not reactionary. The resources at its command are meager, both materially and morally. Whatever may be the symbolic value of Pétain, he is scarcely, at 84, a good actuarial risk. It is interesting to find that the closing words of Pétain's proposal for constitutional change contain a familiar French objective—that of directing the country "towards a new destiny, that of a France imperishable in its continuation of a sacred and millenial task." The implication of the "continuation of a sacred and millenial task" was given clear statement by Bernard Grasset in his "Open Letter to Friedrich Sieburg" in 1932, when he wrote:

Our attachment to the past, by which you have been so much struck, has no other origin than the feeling that everything is linked together and that nothing can be produced except from what already exists. Far from contrasting the past and the future, far from admitting that the survival of the past may act in us as a hindrance to the future, it is on the past that we base the future, and in its light that we judge every new value.[6]

"That nothing can be produced except from what already exists" needs to be remembered also by every reader of current French constitutional literature. There is as much evidence available to support the idea that the Pétain régime simply represents a swing to the political Right, combined with a more extreme form of parliamentary abdication than that developed during the last half-dozen years of the Third

Republic, than there is for the notion that France is now pos-
sessed of new and revolutionary institutions of government.
Pétain himself is a symbol of a glorious victory of the Third
Republic, and octogenarian Frenchmen do not begin anew.
The super opportunist, Laval, along with the other Hitlerized
Frenchmen, Doriot, de Brinon, and Bergery, is at Paris—not
at Vichy, and it will require treatises far better documented
than those that have appeared thus far to substantiate charges
that these men "sold out" France or that they have a sufficient
native following to be of import for the future.

For the "fleeting moment," Marshal Pétain is the Head of
the French State, vested with the governing power, which is
exercised upon the basis of his authority and signature. He is
likewise entrusted with the constituent power, with the proviso that a new constitutional document or documents must
be ratified by the Nation. Members of the family of nations,
with the notable exception of England, but including America and the Vatican, have extended recognition. Pétain is,
apparently, active in the formal exercise of both legislative
and executive powers. Legislation must be framed "in ministerial council," but the state head appoints and may remove
the ministers, subject in practice, it would seem, to the approval of the *Reichsführer*. The *affaire Laval* of last December may be interpreted to mean that Hitler cannot readily
force Pétain to keep or to reinstate a minister, but we cannot
be certain of the significance of this hand until we know the
eventual outcome of the game. Weygand, another superan-
nuated general, three years beyond three score and ten, working loyally in cooperation with Vichy, rules French Africa.

We are not without indication of the reaction of the French
themselves to the Pétain régime. One reaction was evidenced,
early in December, 1940—not by any direct expression of
French citizens, since they currently have no methods resem-

bling electoral campaigns through which to voice their pref-erences—but by the provisions of the new municipal law which abolishes the popular election of councils in towns and cities save those with populations under 2,000. Pétain's own explanation for the new arrangement was that there was "too much politics" in these councils. But "politics" exists in any group of Frenchmen, even when all members have the same political party grouping. Pétain's appointive municipal coun-cillors will apparently maneuver within the confines of a right-of-the-Center orientation of party attitudes. Since most of the prefects and colonial governors have also been replaced it appears certain that these groups of influential officeholders will have essentially the same political views as the members of Pétain's cabinet.

Pétain's original legal arrangements contained a disquieting possibility; Article 1 of the Constitutional Act, No. 4 of July 10, 1940, read:

If, for whatever reason, before ratification by the Nation, of the New Constitution, we [Pétain] shall be prevented from exer-cising the function of Head of the State, M. Pierre Laval, Vice-President of the Council of Ministers shall automatically assume it.

With the dismissal of Laval in December, 1940, this definite constitutional provision for succession ended also, but only for two months. When Admiral Darlan was given the key cabinet position in February, 1941, he was designated as first in the line of succession. In case of his own inability to serve, the choice of Pétain's successor reverts to the Council of Min-isters. The provisions of French law, however, must be un-derstood in the light of constant German interest and frequent interference.

Unnecessary stress need not be placed upon the matter of

the present possession of "sovereignty" in France or upon the Rightist orientation of internal politics. After World War I, Sisley Huddleston wrote a book to describe *France and the French*. In that little volume he alluded to the standing joke of the French people—the exclamation of Molière's quack doctor, upon deciding that, in the future, the heart should be on the right side of the body: *"Nous avons changé tout cela!"* During the period of the war and German occupation there may be many exclamations by persons labeled "heads of the state," "premiers," "vice-premiers," or "ministers" to the effect that "I (or we) have changed all that!" But the French masses will probably continue to be confident and conscious of regular political heartbeats on the Left. The function of the Left in French politics, broadly stated, has been to shape governmental policy in terms of the personal interests and codes of values of the average "small" Frenchman. But practically all Frenchmen, regardless of domestic politics, possess the sagacious and stubborn *esprit de corps*, as against foreign nations, that was manifest in the message posted by French troops on the French side of the Italian frontier early in December: "Notice to the Greeks—this is the French frontier." This *esprit de résistance* need not be conjured up from wishful thinking. Historically, the French have always been most united when opposed to outside forces, influences, pressures or ideas. Take those, for example, of the Papacy, of Marxian Socialism, of the English, of the Germans, or of "Americanization." Even the Pétain government seems to resist Nazi wishes and demands by means of delays and halfhearted execution of Hitler's directions. There is, as a case in point, the matter of the Riom trials of "leaders responsible for the war." The Supreme Court of Justice created to "try" these men held its first session early in August, 1940. But even an extraordinary court could not try them on ordinary criminal charges—that is, with the prospect of securing convictions. So the search for extraordinary charges has proceeded, but so far as can be learned, none has been found. If Daladier, Blum, Gamelin, and Reynaud are convicted on an irregular charge, there will be only criticism throughout France for those who allowed the iniquity to succeed. In the event that any of these men were to be executed, criticism would change to revulsion. It is reported that one of the former Riom judges, Professor Ripert, dean of the Paris Law Faculty, told the then current Minister of Justice, Alibert, "If you wish to take revenge upon political opponents you will have to find other men for the purpose. I will not now besmirch my gray hair." Stories of exhibitions of *l'esprit de résistance* by the Paris populace, during the trying winter of 1940-1941, are already legion.[7]

To turn to the institutional scheme of French government during the last year, and to future prospects. What of the electorate? The last Chamber, elected in 1936, prolonged its life because of the war. Universal manhood suffrage has existed in France for almost 100 years. Can that suffrage be denied, or be drastically curtailed in significance, in any new and permanent constitutional arrangements? Even the totalitarian régimes, Italy excepted, maintained suffrage and actual voting. It was through the exercise of suffrage in the Third Republic that men rose, or were raised, to political eminence. The Constitutional Law of July 10, 1940, mentions the "Assemblies" which the proposed new constitutional document was to create, and Constitutional Act No. 3 of the same date stipulates that the present Senate and Chamber of Deputies "shall continue to exist until the Assemblies anticipated by the Constitutional Law of July 10, 1940, have been formed." It is impossible to demonstrate that the French will choose the "assemblies" either directly or indirectly through man-

hood, or perhaps, universal suffrage, but it is even more difficult to conceive of a different procedure, especially since the
French, if and when they vote on the proposed new constitutional laws, would inevitably have to pass upon the question of the elimination of future voting.

Immediate prospects, under Pétain, are not reassuring. In
his speech to the nation October 10, 1940, he said that the exercise of the suffrage every four years gave the people the
impression that they were free citizens in a free state, whereas
for the last twenty years they had been successively and
sometimes simultaneously subservient to economic interests
or crews of politico-labor combinations professing to represent the working classes. Here Pétain's government carried
water on both the Right and Left shoulders, and we find it
there again in the municipal reform measure of December
11, which eliminated popular elections in 2,722 cities with
over 2,000 inhabitants, but preserved the method of popular
choice in 35,292 small communes. The small communes are
the bulwarks of French conservatism and the centers of
Rightist political strength.

Still another development must be mentioned. Late in
January, 1941, news dispatches from Vichy gave account of
the creation of a National Council—a provisional consultative assembly to serve as a mouthpiece of French public opinion. The personnel of this new agency, appointed by Pétain,
ran to a total of 188, of whom 92, slightly less than a majority,
were politicians of the Third Republic. But none of them,
apparently, was a Senator or a Deputy. There are elements
of compromise in this new creation but the fulcrum is unquestionably on the Right. The obvious purpose of Pétain
was to use the politicians in the National Council as a propaganda liaison with the masses, without, at the same time, permitting the political Left to state a majority viewpoint to him

in return. It should also be noted that the National Council is to be consulted only on questions submitted to it by Pétain. Unlike Louis XVI, Pétain does not ask for *Cahiers!*

In résumé, it can be said that the exercise of the suffrage is now restricted to the election of municipal councillors in small towns. Although membership in the Chamber of Deputies, elected in 1936, and in the Senate of 1940 has not expired, it is of no legal significance, since the powers of these two chambers have been removed to the office of Head of the State.

The elimination of the chambers from the institutional picture removes the opportunity for the expression of public opinion through elections, the traditional avenue for the recruitment of national political personnel through elections, and effective institutions for popular control over the central government. The National Council may render valuable legislative advice to Pétain, but he is under no obligation either to ask or to accept such advice. For the immediate present, therefore, the French system of government is unparliamentary. It is also non-parliamentary, for not more than one possible exponent of parliamentary government can be located in Pétain's present council of ministers.

There are some parallels in the executive power of Pétain, under Constitutional Act No. 2 of July 10, 1940, and those of the President of the Republic in the Constitutional Law of February 25, 1875. But the requirements of the 1875 law that "every act of the President shall be countersigned by a minister" and that "ministers shall be collectively responsible to the chambers for the general policy of the government and individually for their personal acts," are entirely absent from Pétain's current constitution. Under it, according to the provisions of Constitutional Act No. 2 of July 10, 1940, Pétain promulgates laws and sees that they are executed;

appoints to all civil and military positions unless other provision is made by law; commands the armed forces; exercises the power of pardon and amnesty; and negotiates and ratifies treaties. He may declare a state of siege in one or more parts of the country, and may also declare war. The envoys and ambassadors of foreign powers are accredited to him.

It may therefore be assumed, on the basis of provisions of current constitutional laws and acts, that there is now a strong executive power, but it would be rash to conclude that such power is actually exercised in arbitrary fashion by Pétain himself. Both the legislative and executive powers are exercised in terms of the advice Pétain receives from his coterie of ministers. The negotiations over Laval's return to power, for example, appear not to have involved the replacement of Pétain, but Laval's precise status in the Council of Ministers. Meanwhile, it is interesting to note that "the dance of portfolios" has not ended with the Third Republic. For example, there have been four Ministers of Foreign Affairs in the eight-month period from June, 1940, to February, 1941—Baudoin, Laval, Flandin and Darlan. These changes in the ministry of Foreign Affairs are not exceptional, but they seem to suggest that French individualism is even more basic than parliamentarism as a promoter of cabinet shifts.

The attention of American students of French government was keenly aroused in one of the cabinet shifts late in January, 1941, by the appointment of Joseph-Barthélemy, to succeed Dean Alibert as Minister of Justice. That appointment is another indication that the "French Counter-revolution," noted by Professor Gooch [8] and others, must be observed with due attention to the French maxim *Plus ça change, plus c'est la même chose*, for Joseph-Barthélemy is the former Paris professor from whose works many American students gained the greater part of their knowledge of French constitutional law, and Joseph-Barthélemy envisaged that law in terms of a unique French history extending from a period beginning much earlier than the Third Republic. It is rather difficult to picture him as the inventor of revolutionary changes in the *Code pénal* or in criminal procedure.

Restriction of the activities of the electorate, elimination of independent national legislative institutions, and hence of popular control over governmental policy hardly constitute a "counter-revolution" encompassing the entire system of French governmental institutions, particularly since these changes have not been accomplished through Pétain's leadership of a supporting political party, much less one with counter-revolutionary doctrine, organized in totalitarian fashion and employing totalitarian methods. If Pétain has dissolved the General Confederation of Workers, he has also dissolved the General Confederation of Employers, and both organizations fell under the ban on the same day, November 12, 1940. Less than a month later, early in December, 1940, a law for the *organization* of French peasants was put in effect. Whether the method employed be dissolution or organization, the end in view would appear to be increased governmental control over these three important branches of the forces of production. The purpose for which control is to be exercised appears to be ambiguous, but observers across the Atlantic cannot envisage the pressing nature of many problems which demand immediate solutions in the form of temporary measures.

Other institutions of French government, such as the law codes and courts, administrative organization both national and local, and a host of governmental practices, remain largely unaffected. It is true, as mentioned above, that a special court, the Supreme Court of Justice, has been instituted by Pétain, and that a decree issued in January, 1941, vests in the Head of the State the authority to prosecute and punish misdeeds of past, present, and future French officeholders. But it is also true (February, 1941) that under these "reforms" no prosecutions have been instituted and no persons have even been placed on trial. Some changes of minor import have been made in administrative organization, in ministerial titles, and in civil service recruitment and tenure. But none of these seems to be in terms of an ascertainable new political theory.

If the institutions and organization of Pétain's régime, his changes in national and local directing personnel, and his legislative policy have progressed on the basis of any coherent body of social theory, that theory is French, even though reactionary.

The foregoing description and speculation lead to two knotty problems regarding French government that have been raised by military defeat and internal changes since June, 1940. The first problem, that of the effects upon French government of German occupation, and the probable duration of the occupation, is one to which no reasoned solution appears possible at the moment. German exactions for occupational expenses alone have already amounted to more than the total of French annual budgets of prewar years. There are several offsets to this burden which cannot be described here. It must suffice simply to mention that France has been freed from making the heavy outlays necessary to wage war. The deeply-ingrained French habit of resistance will, unquestionably, find means and measure for avoiding full compliance with German demands and exactions. If German occupation were to continue for a generation, it might probably result in a French reassessment of values. But it might possibly also lead to a German revaluation of hitherto existing German values. The solution of the problem of German occupation, for the immediate future, is one to which the Vichy régime can make little contribution.

The second problem, raised by internal developments since June, 1940, is an old and persistent problem of the French constitution. It relates to the cooperation, and the terms upon which cooperation can be arranged, among (1) the electorate and political parties, (2) the policy-forming or legislative institutions, and (3) the executive. Temporarily, Pétain has eliminated parts (1) and (2) from the problem. Professor Gooch has systematized the temporary and practical solutions arrived at in the history of various régimes since the French Revolution in his theory of cycles and periods.[9] The first cycle extends from 1789 to 1848; the second, from 1848 to 1940. Within each of these cycles three periods are discernible: those of Assembly Omnipotence, Executive Dictatorship, and Parliamentary Government. In attempting to apply this interpretation to the present situation in France, we might say that a third cycle starts in 1940, with the second period of previous cycles, Executive Dictatorship, as the initial stage. But Professor Gooch does not attempt to project into the future what has happened in the past, and it seems preferable to use the cyclical-period theory as a reference to past developments rather than to employ it as a prophecy for the future.

Here are the terms of the present problem. Before the military defeat, the trend in French government was toward an energized executive. Substantial precedents for such a development had been set over a period of fifteen years before the war during which the Chambers through "Decree Laws" simply granted the cabinet the authority necessary to solve serious problems of public policy. The Doumergue proposals of 1934 were certainly calculated to strengthen the executive, and they received considerable support in public opinion and by publicists. Furthermore, during 1936 and part of 1937 there appeared to be a sufficient coalescence among party groups in and outside the Chamber to afford the necessary political party basis for a strong executive power in government. Thus the executive power vested in the present Head of the State might be regarded as a war-spurred modification initially induced by an internal trend. Yet the complete absorption of constituent and legislative powers by that executive is without precedent in the form of immediate internal developments, and it is not based upon political party consolidation, organization, or an appealing revolutionary ideology. The régime has not embraced the cause of monarchy and its affiliations with French fascist leagues appear to be as tenuous as affiliations among the leagues themselves. The outstanding feature of the Third Republic, rather complete dominance in government by the Chamber of Deputies, might be expected to pass through the loss of prestige occasioned by loss of the war. But the complete elimination of parliament is drastic beyond expectation, particularly because it removes all effective means for popular control over French government and totally denies, for central governmental purposes, the expression of the 100-year-old right and practice of universal manhood suffrage.

In June, 1928, Jean Martet posed for Clemenceau the question as to how French democratic experience would end. "I know nothing of that," was the reply. "Probably by a general."

In that event, observed Martet, "It will be necessary to start all over again." [10]

France now awaits that opportunity.

CHAPTER VIII

The Impact of World War II on the Balkans

BY JOSEPH S. ROUCEK

Hofstra College

B ALKAN politics can be understood only—as I have pointed out in my *Politics of the Balkans* [1]—in the light of "power politics," in terms of internal *Realpolitik*—direct action unashamed of its "illegal" or "undemocratic" nature. The Balkan states have developed political systems sharply at variance with both the principles and the operation of democratic government, although, riding on the wave of democratic enthusiasm, they applied to their postwar political institutions the veneer of high-flown Western principles of democracy and parliamentarism. But in spite of such flowery smoke screens, Balkan politics have been nothing else but personal régimes devoid of ideological content. Government and political power have had to be maintained primarily by force, particularly because the absence of a broad structure of public opinion providing political education for the peasant masses and the chaos of futile struggles in inefficient and troublesome representative assemblies have contributed to the need for a "strong hand."

In addition, the widening gap between the peasantry and the upper classes has resulted in hatred and bitterness, intensified by periodic excesses of the reign of terror which have been justified, in turn, by the revolutionary traditions. For

all practical purposes, and in spite of periodic pronounce-
ments of the Balkan rulers eulogizing parliamentary and
democratic institutions, government everywhere has been
carried on by the use of force, concentrated in the hands of
the monarch or a political leader-dictator. As political practices have been dominated by personalities, it has been
natural that subjective elements have come to be foremost considerations in political contests. This again has promoted violent methods—a respectable mode of political action in the
Balkans, rooted in the tradition of political murder, execution,
and exile of the Turkish days, when assassination of a Turkish master, an "infidel," by a Christian rebel was a religious as
well as a patriotic deed.

It is not surprising, therefore, that World War II has hardly
had any effect at all on the fundamentals of Balkan governments and politics. For the Balkan second-rate dictatorships
have practiced for a long time the kind of politics which only
during recent years have become a commonplace in Germany, Italy, and Russia, and which place all aspects of life
on a war footing. But now the Balkan dictatorships have been
proved to be just "babes in the woods" when compared to
Hitler and his satellites.

The present war has evidenced only the acceleration of the
use of naked force in Balkan politics, demonstrating, at the
same time, to what extent the power relationships have been
hidden there under constitutional and ideological smoke
screens. People talk of walking on top of a volcano, but in
southeastern Europe that phrase has real meaning. In the
Balkans the government holds on by a thread; everywhere
there is the seething and strain of the forces underneath.
Partly this is the pounding weight and drive of Germany,
pushing and crowding these little countries out, draining
their lifeblood. It is economic stress, hunger, hopelessness

and suspense, too. It is also just anger and hate, the same impulse to strike and to destroy, which is the motive force of the Nazi revolution. What we call Western civilization is spread very thin over the top of the Balkans, and the peasant masses have grown restless and bitter, ready to help any one pull down the structure that presses so heavily on their shoulders. Disorder and anarchy, a revolt without shape, theory or direction, a revulsion from all government, lie just under the top crust throughout the Balkans.

ROUMANIA—THE FIRST NAZI OBJECTIVE

Roumania has been destined to become the focal point of the revolutionary anarchy that may break out anywhere at any time. There was suppressed civil war in Carol's reign, fostering hates and discontents leading to assassination and counter-assassination, not because Carol was a bloodthirsty tyrant, but because Carol had to survive and hence had to dispose of the most dangerous contenders for power by the familiar Balkan technique. In addition to the usual opposition forces, Carol had to face the threats of the Iron Guard, Roumania's "Fifth Column," supported by Hitler. This problem he solved, temporarily, by having Codreanu, the Iron Guard's *Führer*, and his lieutenants shot on a lonely road outside Bucharest "while attempting to escape" one gray morning before 1938 had come to a close. Carol, in fact, must be credited with maintaining his government against his internal foes rather successfully; he failed only when Hitler decided that Carol had to be replaced and started to dynamite his régime by forcing him to give up a part of Transylvania to Roumania's ancient foe, Hungary. This territorial cession increased the hostility of so many Roumanians that Carol went out according to Hitler's schedule.

As in the case of the Protectorate of Bohemia-Moravia, Hitler preferred to maintain the semblance of Roumania's independence. Although the pattern of fascism is everywhere the same, the new Roumanian government seems to have taken vanquished France rather than Germany or Italy as its model. As in France, the head of the state, General Antonescu, is a non-party military leader. The cabinet, composed primarily of leaders of the Iron Guard, has been officially described as being made up of "men with unsmirched pasts." The new régime is supposedly based on "faith, justice, discipline, hard work, education, silence, and national solidarity." As a step toward this last objective, Jews were subjected to new restrictions. To complete the parallel with France, a public trial was planned for Carol who was held responsible for the loss of Transylvania.

The reign of terror, which subsequently claimed innumerable victims besides the officials of King Carol's government, resembled the periodic liquidations in Russia or Hitler's "blood purge" in Germany. The Iron Guard, a movement of revolt that has been fostered by the Nazis, but that grew out of internal conditions like all such weedy growths springing up in the sour soil of Europe's youth movements, was surprisingly widespread in the army, in the universities, in the factories, in the poorest villages. To most of the young Roumanians, living in a country striving so hard to be "modern," the movement was associated with machines, with the up-to-dateness of mechanical civilization. But, strange to say, this is part of the appeal of German-inspired movements to the youth of these backward countries, and the irony of this attraction is that the Germans are determined to throttle industrial development and force all the young in the Balkans back to the farms to produce food for Germany.

At any rate, originally a revolt against bad government, then

used by the Nazis to disrupt and divide the nation, the Iron
Guard went out of hand at the very end of November, 1940.
Split into fragments and driven by the hate it generated, it
proceeded to terrorize and to kill. It was doing the work of
the Nazis in making any but a completely Nazi régime impossible.

The significance of the recent tragic events in Roumania
is that they are symptomatic. Ill-governed as it was, until
the emergence of the Iron Guard it was not a country given
to systematic disorder. The murder of Premier Duca a few
years ago was its first political assassination in modern times
—although certainly not the first political murder in the Balkans. The Roumanian peasants are an industrious and gentle
people, beneficiaries of a land program much in advance of
that of their neighbors. The worst lawlessness they have ever
experienced coincided with the imposition of "German
Order," and if this is a paradox it is also a portent of the
difficulties ahead, not for the Germans alone but for all of
Europe. "Nothing is so contagious as violence. Nothing is
so easy to destroy and so hard to re-establish as the reign of
law. The codes by which society functions and protects
itself are the painful growth of centuries of discipline, and
when Hitler lightly scuttled the common law of Europe, he
opened the gates to the savagery that tears down all legality.
If he is producing the unit that will finally destroy him, he
is also undermining the foundations on which even his order
must be built." [2]

TURKEY IN INTERNATIONAL POLITICS

Turkish friendship was at stake in the present conflict between the Axis and Great Britain at the turn of 1941. For
some time before the war started, it appeared as though Ger-

many would be the victor in this game of *Realpolitik*, for the German government granted Turkey a special credit of RM.150,000,000. German Krupp and then Czechoslovak (now Nazi) Skoda armament works shared contracts for the refortification of the Dardanelles, and Krupp negotiated several contracts for the construction of barracks and shipyards in Turkey, and began construction of submarines for the Turkish navy, not only in German but also in Turkish shipyards.

But Great Britain was not slow to react to the growing German ascendancy in Turkey. Credits of varying amounts were arranged; British shipyards, thus aided, were able to secure contracts for the construction of a dozen naval vessels. Finally Vickers, the British armaments colossus, it is believed, won back from Krupp a major part of the contracts for the refortification of the Dardanelles. In addition, during the summer of 1939, France removed one of the major sources of Turkey's irritation by ceding to Ankara the Sanjak of Alexandretta, or Hatay Republic, formerly part of French Syria.

With the coming of war, political developments in Europe, the might of the British pound, and the Turkish fear of the old bogey, "Berlin-to-Baghdad," combined to give Britain one of her few victories during 1939 or 1940. Great Britain followed up the mutual assistance pact with Turkey by granting the Turks a credit of £43,500,000; of this amount £25,000,000 was earmarked for war materials.[3]

In this long melodrama of diplomatic intrigue, Turkey has energetically followed an independent policy. She can act somewhat more freely than her other Balkan neighbors because of her distance from Germany, the difficulty of foreign invasion, and her advantageous geographic position. By concluding the alliance with Great Britain and France in May, 1939, Turkey had checkmated Russian expansion to the south, toned down, for a time at least, Italian arrogance in the Mediterranean, and opened for Great Britain a foothold for a Balkan advance.

In 1936, Turkey was empowered to begin once again the fortification of the very important Dardanelles. This meant that Turkey was once more becoming a major power in southeastern Europe and the Near East. Control of the Dardanelles has always implied the ability to bottle up Russia in the Black Sea.[4] Thus, the geographical forces in European history are again reasserting themselves. At the end of the last war Turkey was virtually driven out of Europe by the Western powers. The Turks shifted their capital to Ankara, on the Asiatic peninsula. But as Istanbul and the Straits still remained in Turkish hands, it was inevitable that any progression of events during the present war would once again place the Straits in a prominent position as far as military strategy is concerned.

The nervousness now apparent in Turkey has been occasioned by the aggressive action of the Axis powers, for the Dardanelles figure importantly in German and Italian plans. It is for this reason that Turkish commitments, past and present, have been and are followed with intense interest by the Wilhelmstrasse and the Palazzo Venetia.

Material signs of Turkish resistance to Germany became quite clear on October 12, when the Turkish ambassador notified Hitler that any Axis move against the Near East would be resisted.[5] However, diplomatic action, to April, 1941, has been the only sign of activity between Turkey and the Axis.

Turkey, no matter how loud it raises its voice, is still fearful of the Axis on the one hand, and of Russia on the other. The only softening influence is the fact that Russia might become a Turkish ally if Germany offers too much of a threat to the Dardanelles. In any case, the way Turkey goes will be of importance to other Balkan nations, if there are enough free ones around by the time Turkey is aroused.

The ablest summation of Turkish activity was given on November 1, 1940, by Turkish President Ismet Inonu before a meeting of the National Assembly in Ankara. Stated the Turkish executive:

. . . developments in the 14 months of war in Europe has [sic] caused no change in the foreign policy of the Turkish republic, and no change in its attitude of non-belligerency is contemplated. . . . Turkey's relations of confidence with the Soviet Union . . . after experiencing difficulties which cannot be attributed to either of us, have returned to normal friendship.

He continued:

Russian-Turkish relations are a fact of intrinsic value, and our two countries should perpetuate this fact indefinitely and independently of all other influences.

In regard to England and Greece, the Turkish President's words were just as elusive. "At a time when England carries on a heroic struggle for her existence under difficult conditions, it is my duty to proclaim that the bonds of alliance which unite us to her are solid and unbreakable." Concerning the war in Greece, he said:

Our neighbor and friend, Greece, whose territory lies in that zone whose security and tranquillity are of primary importance to us, unfortunately finds herself forced to enter the war. Together with our ally, Great Britain, we now are studying and trying to envisage the results of the situation.[6]

In summing up the Turkish problems of the present war, it is sufficient to say that if the Allies win in the Balkans, Turkey will once again become a great Balkan and Mediterranean power. Furthermore, Istanbul will regain its place as one of the great trading centers of the world.

BULGARIA—THE *BÊTE NOIR* OF THE BALKAN ENTENTE

The principal question at any conclave of the Balkan Entente was usually that of Bulgaria. Although this is the only country on the Peninsula which is purely Balkan, and although its central mountain range gave its name to the entire area, it was not a member of the Balkan Entente. The reason, until recently, was that Bulgaria was the only European state which has been traditionally revisionist since the last war, and which received no compensation for its claims until the virtual dismemberment of Roumania at the insistence of Germany in August, 1940. Bulgaria said that it would never join the Entente until it was recompensed, at least in part, and this started a long chain of complications. For example, the two most urgent demands of the Bulgarians were for the southern portion of the Roumanian Dobruja province, which, since August, 1940, has been obtained, and for an outlet to the Aegean Sea through Greek territory. Now that Germany is the virtual ruler of the Balkans, Bulgaria has its Dobruja, but there are not enough free nations remaining to make an entente.

When, in 1935, the Bulgarian army abolished the parliament and established Boris, the king, as a figurehead of the military dictatorship, Boris turned right about and secured for himself the control of power. Within a year after coming to power, the dictatorship was exclusively in his hands, and the army was very much in the background. But while until recently Boris had reason to feel secure, at the present time his security rests upon his ability to placate the Germans.

During the autumn of 1940 Boris received a call from the Nazis and journeyed to Berlin for a conference with the *Führer*. The world believed for a time that Bulgaria would at once become a signatory to the Anti-Comintern Pact, but evidently the Russian Bear intervened, and Boris was allowed to depart with his country still independent. Then, early in 1941, Bulgaria finally bowed to German demands, adhered to the Axis, and agreed that Nazi troops might enter the country. In April, her territory became a spearhead of the Nazi drive into Yugoslavia.

RECENT POLITICAL EVENTS IN ALBANIA

The tension which gripped the eastern Adriatic following Italy's invasion and annexation of the little mountain kingdom of Albania, in April, 1939, was occasioned by the fact that Mussolini's "grab" upset the delicate balance in the Balkans.

Three days before the Italian attack on Albania, Italian Foreign Minister Ciano assured British Ambassador Lord Perth that Italy did not intend to take "drastic action" in Albania. Then, on Good Friday, Italian warships raced across the Adriatic and the occupation was under way. The official reasons given for Italy's aggressive move were: King Zog had shown ingratitude towards Italy; King Zog had been hoarding Italian loans which were supposed to have been used for developing the country; Albanian "patriots" had pleaded with Mussolini to come over and straighten things out; and finally, Rome had a sacred right to Albania because ancient Roman legions had conquered Albania in 229 B.C.[7]

Before the start of the present conflict with Greece, Italy had begun to reorganize Albania on Fascist lines, and with greater success than had attended Germany's efforts in Czechoslovakia, which had fallen a month before Albania. By means of bribery, the Italians bought the friendship of the Albanians—or so it was thought at the time. The practice began with Ciano going through the Albanian coastal towns and spreading Italian treasury notes among the simple peasants.

However, it was proved during the campaign against Greece, in the spring of 1941, that the acceptance of Italian money did not mean that the Albanians were really accepting the Italian order. Most of the people of this little land are mountaineers who resent dictation of any sort, domestic or foreign. In the Greek campaign the Albanians have acted as an effective "fifth column" for the Greeks.

The only tie between Italy and Albania is the crown, as Victor Emmanuel is the king of both, and this in theory only. However, Albania is tied both economically and politically to Italy because of various machinations of Mussolini during the decades after the first World War.[8]

The civil and political code which governed Albania from the time of the Italian conquest to the time of the Greek counter-invasion virtually eliminated the residue of independence which had been Albania's under Zog. The new code provided that the government would be monarchical, the throne resting with Victor Emmanuel and his heirs. All legislative, executive and judicial power resides nominally in the King of Italy. The Albanian legislative chamber was given the resounding title of "Superior Fascist Corporative Council." This body is theoretically convoked by the King and is adjourned by his orders; the council's president and vice-president are named by the King and nothing can go before the council without the King's consent. Voting has to be open and laws have to be sanctioned by the King, who may veto them or send them back for rediscussion.

Recent Political Events in Yugoslavia

From the very formation of Yugoslavia, as an aftermath of World War I, its politics have revolved around centralization, and its alternative, federalism—the Serbs fostering the notion of "Greater Serbia," and the Croats advocating regionalism. After many alarming domestic situations, the government of Yugoslavia was finally molded into one of modified dictatorship.

Yugoslav politics have been characterized by attempts to normalize political conditions and to attain a *modus vivendi* with the Croats. After Versailles, the Croats had entered into the new Kingdom with great enthusiasm; but they were sure that they did not want the new state to become a mere extension of Serbia. The adoption of the Vidovdan constitution without Croat consent added fuel to the incipient feud. Besides the constitutional question, there were issues involving "states rights," religious differences, cultural traditions and economic standards. Hence, it can be seen that the Croat problem was at best a complicated one.

The growing danger of Yugoslavia's international position helped to bring on the historic accord between the Serbs and the Croats on August 26, 1939, after years of bitter controversy. An autonomous Croatia, comprising 26½ per cent of Yugoslavia's territory and 28½ per cent of her population, was set up. A cabinet of "national union" was formed, with Serbian leader Dragisha Cvetkovich as Premier and Croatian leader Dr. Vladimir Matchek as Vice Premier. But it should be noted that even the far-reaching concessions granted did not fulfill all Croat aspirations. Moreover, powerful Serb elements remained firmly opposed to Croat autonomy. With Europe whirling dizzily toward war, both the Rome-Berlin and Paris-London coalitions brought increased pressure upon

Yugoslavia to secure its collaboration during the spring and summer of 1939. Prince Paul, regent for the young King Peter, maneuvered between Italy and Germany after the outbreak of World War II, since Yugoslavia's geographic position made resistance to concentrated pressure difficult. With Nazi troops in Roumania and Bulgaria in March, 1941, Hitler increased his pressure on the Yugoslav government for unconditional entry into the Axis,[9] aiming to use the Morava and Vardar river corridor so that he could assault British and Greeks on the latter's frontier. After several ministerial reorganizations, due to the popular outburst against any such cooperation with Hitler, a cabinet was formed which approved of Axis cooperation; on March 25, Premier Cvetkovitch and Foreign Minister Markovitch affixed Yugoslavia's signature to the Tripartite Pact. Nothing since the fall of France took Europe so completely by surprise as the events which occurred in Yugoslavia with such amazing rapidity thereafter. In the small hours of the morning, on March 27, while all Belgrade slept, tanks and gun carriages rumbled over cobbled squares and streets. Soldiers were singing in the streets. Almost before anyone realized what was happening, the key buildings were surrounded, Prince Paul was on his way into exile, and General Dushan Simovitch had formed a new government under the direction of the boy king, Peter II. In many ways the *coup* was a curious affair. It was not a Yugoslav *coup*, in the broader sense of the word, since the uprising came chiefly from the Serbs (who number about 6,500,000 in a population of 15,703,000). The Croats (numbering about 2,500,000) and the Slovenes (1,500,000) took no part. Dr. Matchek remained nominally in the new cabinet as Vice Premier, but he did not return to Belgrade after the overturn occurred.

At first, Germany and Italy took the position that the *coup* was an internal affair which did not in any way affect Yugoslavia's alignment with the Axis. Both Hitler and Mussolini had very good reasons for desiring to avoid fighting Yugoslavia. This land had been the chief source of bauxite for both the Axis partners. Then the Yugoslavs had been good bargainers, who had not accepted harmonicas, cameras, and handkerchiefs in exchange for their goods, but received guns, motor trucks, and munitions. Moves were made by Berlin and Rome to overcome the Yugoslav will to resistance. Berlin hoped that Yugoslav minorities, especially the Catholic Croats, living in the nation's exposed valleys, might refuse to support the Simovitch government. The Italians, fearful that in the event of conflict Yugoslav forces might march southward into shaken Albania, worked to restore good feeling between Belgrade and Berlin.

As feverish days sped by, the German and Italian moves failed. Croat leaders, though expressing hope for peace, pledged themselves to stand by the Simovitch Cabinet. The German press began screaming such headlines as "The Serbs want to wade in German blood!" In April, 1941—in the week that marked the first anniversary of the invasion of Scandinavia—Hitler launched another supreme bid for victory. The *Panzer* divisions and the planes that smashed into Greece and Yugoslavia employed the tactics first shown to the world on the plains of Poland—tactics that conquered Poland in eighteen days. In the Balkans, the Nazis, again using the *Blitzkrieg* technique, adapted to a mountainous terrain, launched a paralyzing blow from the air, chiefly against airports and communication lines. Then, while the Yugoslavs and Greeks were still stunned, they were stabbed through in half dozen places at once by swift, hard-hitting mechanized columns. Within eight days of the start of this Balkan *Blitzkrieg*, the Yugoslavs had been so badly disorganized that partitioning of their land

had already begun. In the north, Hitler set up a separate Croat
state, headed by two or three former terrorists, including Dr.
Ante Pavelitch and General Sladko Kvaternik—the former,
the leader of the terroristic *Ustashi*, a band of rapacious Croat
schemers who for years had hated the Serbs, Jews and Croatia's own peasants and plotted with Italian, Hungarian and
German money to split Yugoslavia, and who engineered the
assassination of King Alexander I in Marseilles in 1934. This
government was allegedly backed by Matchek. Italy claimed
Dalmatia, while Bulgaria and Roumania were exerting claims
to eastern sections of the country, and Hungary invaded the
northeast triangle of Yugoslavia and claimed as her own that
district, which she lost by the Treaty of Trianon in 1919. On
April 18, 1941, an armistice between the Yugoslavs and the
Nazis was announced.

RECENT POLITICAL EVENTS IN GREECE

The recent changes in the political affairs of Greece are due
primarily to the war and to the hatred of the Axis which
was evinced by the late Dictator-Premier John Metaxas.
However, about six months previous to the invasion it was
believed by many people that he was going to "sell out" to
the Italians. The British, upon hearing this news, began to
apply pressure upon Metaxas through King George II. To
back up their threats, the British promised in the event of
a "sell-out" to Italy to secure for themselves air bases on
Greek Islands in the Mediterranean and Aegean. This move
forced Metaxas' hand, and he aligned himself with Britain.
Germany and Italy, on the other hand, threatened to put a
new king on the throne, namely, Prince Paul, brother of the
present king.[10]

A military strategist at heart, with an army built on the

Prussian model and a large police force, Metaxas was ready when the Italians invaded Greece from Albania soon after their ultimatum of October 28th had been rejected by Athens. Great Britain assured Greece that she would give all possible aid and sent expeditionary forces to Salonika. Italy's objective was control of Salonika, the mouth of the Vardar River and Yugoslavia's gateway to the south, as well as the Balkan's chief communication center. The Greek Army with the aid of Royal Air Force bombers took the initiative on the 100-mile battlefront from the Yugoslav border to the Ionian Sea and drove the Italians back. Doritza, Argyrokastrion, Porto Edda and other Albanian towns were captured while Mussolini explained to the Italian people that the Greek terrain was not adapted to a "lightning war" but that Italians would eventually triumph. A change in the Greek government occurred on January 29, 1941, with the death of Premier General John Metaxas following a throat operation. Alexander Korizis, dignified governor of the National Bank was chosen as successor.[11] Little advance by either side was made during February because of unfavorable weather conditions. Mussolini tried to raise the flagging spirits of his army by promising a new offensive in the spring. German occupation of Italy, to aid and direct the latter's campaign fiascos in Greece and Africa, was recognized as the guarantee for this declaration. During the Yugoslavian crisis Germany struck simultaneously at Yugoslavia and Greece with tanks, infantry, dive bombers and parachute troops. Although Greek troops fought valiantly at Salonika and the Rupel pass, Nazi troops breaking in from the Vardar valley threatened their rear and forced them to abandon the Metaxas line. Possession of Salonika gave the Nazis their first outlet on the Mediterranean in April, 1941. Nazis later drove into Greece from Yugoslavia and overran the entire country.

Conclusion

In summing up the influence of World War II on the Balkan type of politics, it may be said that the Balkan governments have been wide open to totalitarian penetration by the very character of their politics based on the use of force. Only, unfortunately for the Balkans, the proverbial "Balkanization of Europe" is being reversed into the "Europeanization of the Balkans."

CHAPTER IX

The Effects of the War on the Governments of Norway and Sweden

BY A. G. RONHOVDE
Rutgers University

NORWAY

THE internal government of Norway is undergoing a series of changes that reflect, not merely a military conquest, but the introduction of a new social and political philosophy. The introduction of the one-party political system on the German model and the establishment of a Norwegian *Arbeitsdienst* (Compulsory Labor Service), a similar importation, are examples of the fundamental change. How genuine and how enduring these changes may prove is a matter which can only be tested in the course of future history.

NORWEGIAN GOVERNMENT BEFORE THE INVASION

From September, 1939 up to April 9, 1940, the Norwegian government continued under the essential forms and procedure of its constitutional monarchy dating from the Constitution of 1814. The outbreak of the War did not cause any serious changes in the parliamentary system. Unlike Sweden, Norway did not even organize a government of national union, but continued under the Labor cabinet of Premier Nygaardsvold. This cabinet (*Statsraad*) represented the largest party in the parliament (*Storting*), but was a minority government, since the Labor party had but seventy of the hundred and fifty seats in that body. On several occasions the formation of a coalition government was suggested by other parties. All such requests were refused.[1] Parliamentary elections were not scheduled before 1940, and the smaller parties were not willing to combine in a vote of no confidence. Major Quisling's *Nasjonal Samling* party was not represented, nor had the Communists been able to secure any seats in the *Storting*.

The changes that were made during the first months of the war were chiefly administrative.[2] New agencies were set up to direct the formulation and administration of new rules governing crisis problems of food supply, shipping, fuel supply, evacuation of the larger cities in case of emergency, and the like. A number of personnel changes in the departments were also made for reasons of administrative strength and efficiency. The *Storting* was called in special session at the outbreak of the war in September, 1939, and remained in almost constant session until the time of the invasion. It continued to function in its customary manner, exercising its normal powers of formulation of policy and control of the administration. It was consulted on questions of foreign, as well as on domestic, policies. Some of the sessions on foreign affairs were held behind closed doors. There was no grant of dictatorial powers to the cabinet, and criticism of the government's program was both vigorous in spirit and generous in amount. Norway was still a democracy.

THE INVASION AND RESULTING CONTEST FOR GOVERNMENT CONTROL

On the morning of April 9, 1940, the German invasion began. The Norwegian cabinet had spent the day before in drafting a vigorous protest to the British and French governments because of their mining of Norwegian territorial waters. After having refused the German government's offer of "protection" for the period of the War, the Norwegian King, cabinet, and parliament, decided to move to Hamar, an inland town north of Oslo.[3] On this as well as subsequent occasions care was taken to follow the constitutional procedures governing time and place of government meetings. At Hamar the *Storting* reassembled and quickly adopted a resolution giving the government full powers "to take every step and make any decision found necessary under actual conditions." The Prime Minister suggested the formation of a new cabinet based on all parties, and tendered his personal resignation. It was decided, however, by the King and his party advisers that a change should not be made, but that the cabinet should be strengthened by the appointment of two members from each of the other three parties to consult with it. The *Storting* also approved unanimously a resolution empowering the King and his Council to govern the country from a place outside of Norway if that should become advisable.[4] This last resolution proved to be of significance, since according to Article 11 of the Constitution the King may spend only six months out of the country without the consent of the *Storting*, but with the parliament's consent he may prolong such stay. When, therefore, on June 27th the Bureau of the *Storting* in occupied Oslo addressed a letter to King Haakon in London, suggesting that since he was no longer in Norway he could no longer continue his constitutional functions, the King replied that he was, on the contrary, acting in complete accordance with his constitutional rights in continuing his offices from abroad.[5]

During the period April 9 to June 7, while the military resistance still continued, there were, naturally, two different

governing systems in operation; one for the occupied and one
for the unoccupied areas. The King and his government
moved from place to place and organized civil as well as military government in the territory under control. On June 7
the King and his ministers left Norway and took up their
residence in London. From there they have continued to
function in the control of all Norwegian subjects, property,
and interests not under German military control. The Nygaardsvold government has refused to recognize the constitutional authority of any parliament or other agency set up
in occupied Norway. It has denied requests to resign or abdicate, and contends that according to Article 85 of the Constitution no parliament sitting in foreign-occupied Norway
has any authority. It also contends that any parliamentary
election held in such territory would, according to Article
50, be invalid. In conclusion, therefore, it holds that the present government in Norway has no constitutional authority,
nor can any new constitutional government be set up as long
as the country is occupied by an invader.

GOVERNMENT IN OCCUPIED NORWAY

In the meantime a number of important political changes
have occurred in Norway itself. On April 9 Major Vidkun
Quisling announced the formation of a new cabinet that
would cooperate with the German authorities. King Haakon
refused to appoint a Quisling cabinet; several men designated
refused to serve; and popular opposition in Oslo soon forced
Quisling to withdraw.[6]

A temporary Administrative Council was then set up by
the Norwegian Supreme Court to take over the function
of local administration in the occupied area. This council
acted, of course, under the supervision of the German mili-

tary command. The Supreme Court emphasized that the new council was in no sense a government; it was merely a provisional agency to maintain order in the occupied areas.[7] King Haakon refused to accept any responsibility for its actions.[8]

In June a meeting of *Storting* members remaining in Norway was held at Oslo, and it was the Bureau of this group that invited King Haakon and his government to abdicate.[9] Meanwhile, on April 24th, a German High Commissioner, Herr Terhoven, was sent to Norway to direct the civil administration on behalf of the German government. The Administrative Council, appointed in April, continued its functions under the supervision of the German High Commissioner, while plans for the future were being made by the members of the *Storting* sitting with representatives of the Norwegian trade organizations and the members of the council itself.[10] The reorganization was declared on September 25, 1940, when the "New Order" was finally announced. This action has been summarized in a German publication as follows:

In the north of Europe the New Order is consolidating itself under the leadership of that much-maligned Norwegian patriot, V. Quisling. In the German periodical, *Reich*, Quisling explains the overthrow on September 25, 1940, "of the plutocratic and Marxistic system in Norway" and "the dethronement of the fugitive King." The old political parties were dissolved and a *Nasjonal Samling* established as the only legal party.

The Commissar of the Reich continues to exercise supreme power, but an increasing measure of executive and legal functions is being transferred to the chiefs of the new State departments or ministries. The new government and the German officials collaborate harmoniously.

"A National Socialist Revolution has taken place which, with irresistible strength, pervades every sphere of social life and of the state. With this event," Quisling exclaims, "Norway enters the New Order in Europe. The new World-Axis Rome-Berlin (*sic*) now extends to Oslo." [11]

The "National Socialist Revolution" in Norway has in fact developed in a systematic way. During the first days of the German occupation efforts were made to bring about the revolution by constitutional means, as it was done in Denmark. When the King and his government refused to cooperate, the task was put into other hands. While the German High Commissioner was given supreme power at the outset, it was not until September, 1940, that the King was formally declared deposed. In the meantime, the details of both local and central administration were largely left in the hands of Norwegian officials who were willing to cooperate. In September a new government under Major Quisling was appointed and a general reorganization in the national administration was carried through. On October 11, 1940, a new civil service law was promulgated. [12]

The new government is modeled on German lines, with political power concentrated in the hands of the only party permitted to exist, the *Nasjonal Samling*. This party, which had existed for some years before the invasion, has thus been given the power to develop its policies and program under German tutelage. Major Quisling had for a number of years been the leader of the party and had attempted to gain a foothold in the constitutional government of Norway. His following had been small, however, and his party's official newspaper, *Fritt Folk*, had enjoyed a very limited circulation. The party had not been taken seriously by most Norwegians and had never succeeded in electing a single member to the *Storting*.

The outlines of the cultural and economic revolution taking place have already been rather clearly indicated. Less than a month after the Quisling government was appointed a Compulsory Labor Service law was promulgated, establishing the Norwegian version of the German *Arbeitsdienst*. This law has implications far beyond the immediate organization of a labor service; for it is through such organizations that education and propaganda in National Socialist philosophy can be most effectively carried out. An extensive work program has already been announced aiming at the construction of numerous roads, bridges, and other public works.[13]

The Norwegian press and radio were effectively coordinated soon after the occupation. Existing newspapers were not suspended, but only such articles could be printed as were approved by the German censor. The result was a serious change in the content, if not the format, of the leading newspapers. The government-operated radio (*Rikskringkasting*) was also placed under German censorship and control.

Economically Norway has been linked to the Reich through a series of decrees and arrangements regarding foreign trade, monetary exchange, export and import regulations, currency circulation, and the like.[14] The circulation of German currency in Norway was authorized on the day following the invasion. In the summer of 1940 an attempt was made to restore normal trade relations with the other Scandinavian countries through special clearing and trade agreements. Norwegian exports to Sweden alone during the second half of 1940 reached a total of 34,000,000 Swedish kronor.[15]

In summary, it may be said that the government in Norway has been left largely in the hands of Norwegians themselves, subject always to the proviso that the policies pursued are consistent with the aims and policies of the German government as expressed through the High Commissioner. A revolution, both political and social, is being forced.

SWEDEN

In Sweden the effects of the European wars have as yet been neither revolutionary nor catastrophic. The fact that the three other (four, if we include Iceland) states in the Nordic bloc have been invaded or occupied during the first year of the War has had serious, but not violent, effects on the Swedish government. In spite of the modifications, changes, and additions in governmental machinery, methods, and procedures, the outstanding fact is that Sweden has retained its constitutional monarchy in its parliamentary form. Swedish democracy has been strengthened rather than weakened.

PARLIAMENTARY GOVERNMENT CONTINUED

In the period since September 8, 1939, the *Riksdag* has been in almost constant session. Normally it convenes in regular session early in January and sits through June. Following the outbreak of the war, however, a special session convened on September 8, 1939, and continued through to January 9, 1940. The regular session thereupon began on January 10 and continued to July 31. A second special session thereupon began August 1 and continued until the opening of the regular January session in 1941. The *Riksdag* has not only been in session, but it has continued to exercise its normal functions with independence and vigor. Aside from its duties in connection with the formulation of national policies and legislation, it has continued to carry on its powers of control through interpellations, investigations, supervision, and review of executive policies and acts. Even in the field of foreign affairs the *Riksdag* has retained its essential functions of advice and criticism.

In fact, one of the effects of the crisis period has been the increased activity of the special commission which was set up after the last war to exercise some control over foreign policy. This commission consists of the leaders of the various parties in the *Riksdag*, as well as other members designated by the *Riksdag*. The function of the commission is to secure greater parliamentary control over foreign affairs, at the same time keeping the conduct sufficiently secret to prevent the embarrassment which might result from too much publicity during a stage of policy formulation. From November, 1939, to June, 1940, this commission met sixteen times; no less than five of these in the critical month of April. Normally it meets on an average less than six times a year. In addition to the meetings of this commission there were also a number of secret meetings of the *Riksdag* in which the Foreign Minister and Prime Minister gave information which, at that time, could not be given publicly.[16]

PARLIAMENTARY ELECTIONS OF 1940

Indicative also of the strength of parliamentary government in Sweden was the decision to hold the regular *Riksdag* elections on September 14 and 15, 1940. Although the election was sufficiently non-competitive to be called a "gentlemen's election," the several parties had their candidates in the field and the vote resulted in a slight shift in party strength in both chambers.[17] The press indicated that there was a real campaign and that issues were openly debated and contested. There was a 70 per cent vote cast, the second highest since the introduction of woman suffrage. Considering the hundreds of thou-. sands of men in uniform and the many people working in defense industries away from home, this figure was really remarkable. The government had extended the absentee-voting privileges to meet the situation. This undoubtedly helped to swell the percentage of votes cast.[18]

FORMATION OF COALITION CABINET

The wars in Sweden's back and front yards have, nevertheless, caused several important innovations and changes in its governmental machinery and methods of action. Foremost among these must be mentioned the establishment of the Government of National Union, in December, 1939. In September, 1939, Prime Minister Per Albin Hansson had consulted the opposition leaders and offered to share executive responsibility with them. At that time they declined, but shortly after the outbreak of the war in Finland the cabinet was reconstituted so as to contain members of all four anti-totalitarian parties in the *Riksdag*. Mr. Hansson continued as Prime Minister, but Foreign Minister Rickard Sandler was replaced by the career-diplomat Christian Günther. Some Social Democrats from the former cabinet were dropped and the two leaders of the Conservative party in the *Riksdag* and the two from the People's Party were brought in. The reconstructed cabinet contained four Social Democrats, two Agrarians, two Conservatives, two members of the People's Party, and three men without strong party coloring.[19]

The elections in September, 1940, gave the Social Democrats a clear majority in the Second Chamber and an even half in the First Chamber, but the cabinet was not further reconstructed. At the Social Democratic Party Congress in June, 1940, Mr. Hansson suggested that a government of national union might be continued even after the present critical period is over.[20] This spirit of political unity is in marked contrast to the situation in the last world war when the country was torn by violent political dissensions.

CRISIS DELEGATION OF POWER

In the face of the serious international and domestic situation the *Riksdag* has voted a number of extraordinary powers to the government, but these are exercised by a cabinet representing the several parties and are under constant scrutiny by the *Riksdag* itself. The special powers relate particularly to matters of national defense, labor, trade, foreign exchange, and public information. Acting under these powers the government has taken several drastic steps in the military, economic, and monetary fields.

NEW ADMINISTRATIVE AGENCIES

For the administration of the many crisis activities of the government there have been established a number of new administrative agencies, under cabinet and parliamentary control. A number of these were placed in the regular departments, but a large number of them were placed in a new Department of National Economy created on October 8, 1939. In addition to many minor ones there were set up altogether some 25 major organs of this kind. Among the many fields administered by these new agencies may be mentioned: wartime labor market, food supply, price control, trade licenses, maritime trade, gasoline, oil, wood and coal supply, state insurance, and public information.[21] In addition to the central organs there were also created numerous provincial and communal agencies to handle special local problems.

THE PRESS AND PUBLIC INFORMATION

Among the many special problems of crisis government has been that of maintaining the traditional freedom of the press and of public expression without endangering the unity, neutrality, and safety of the state. In this field the Bureau of Public Information has been of fundamental importance. The government has denied that "a single newspaper in Sweden has been suppressed or forbidden to appear for the simple reason that under Swedish constitutional law neither the government nor the courts have the right to issue such a decree." According to the law the author of a book or newspaper that has been printed and placed in circulation can be summoned before a court if the contents violate the law. Jury trial is guaranteed in such cases. Twenty-seven such trials were held in 1939 involving charges of issuing defamatory attacks or violent outbreaks against a foreign power. Thirteen cases resulted in acquittal. Two editors of Communist newspapers were sentenced to five months in prison. In the other cases fines or short jail sentences were imposed. Confiscations without trial were made against 18 single issues of newspapers and 12 books or pamphlets. More than half of the court cases and confiscations involved Communist attacks on Finland during the Russo-Finnish war. In January, 1940, the Bureau of Public Information was set up to cooperate with the free organizations of the press itself in order to promote discretion in the handling of information about military matters, shipping, munitions works and other matters of vital importance to the state. Its functions are purely advisory.[22] In summary, it may be said that there has been a minimum of governmental control and suppression, considering the extreme delicacy of Sweden's political and military position during this period.

NEUTRALITY AND INDEPENDENCE

The wars in Finland and later in Norway placed a serious strain on the government's policy of peace and neutrality.

In both cases the policy was, however, successfully maintained. Although there was some internal criticism of the government's cautious policy during the Finnish war, there was a strong tendency to acquiesce once the true situation was understood. The war in Norway presented a different problem. Since it was regarded essentially as a clash between Germany and the Allies, the strictest neutrality policy was followed. Requests for exports or transshipment of war materials to either side were refused, despite pressure. When the military operations in the Narvik area came disturbingly close to the Swedish border, the Swedish government sought the consent of both parties in the war to a pacification of northern Norway through a provisional occupation of the Narvik area by Swedish troops. This plan collapsed with the withdrawal of Allied forces and the cessation of hostilities on June 10, 1940.[23]

A month later, on July 8, an agreement was reached by the Swedish and German governments whereby permission was given to the German government to send war materials and troops through Sweden on the way to or from Norway. In some circles this agreement was interpreted as an abandonment of the neutrality policy and as an indication that Swedish independence was no longer a reality. The Prime Minister and the Foreign Minister both vigorously rejected this interpretation, and pointed out that the circumstances and conditions of the agreement gave no warrant for such conclusions.[24] It was pointed out that, as long as the fighting was going on in Norway, the Swedish government had been unwilling to take part in anything that would have increased the difficulty of the Norwegian people in their struggle for independence, but once the fighting was stopped, there was no further reason for maintaining the bar against transshipments and transit to or from the neighboring country. The

ministers also emphasized the very strict safeguards set up
in the case of German troop transit through Sweden. Permits
were granted only under carefully specified conditions to
German troops on leave, who must travel without arms or
weapons and in special cars or trains. According to Mr.
Günther no demands for transit of war materials have been
made.[25]

Early in July, 1940, a new trade treaty with Germany was
signed. This treaty, it was explained, was made to adjust the
Swedish trade to the new situation as a result of the extension
of the blockade to Sweden after the beginning of the Norwegian campaign.[26] The difficult economic problem created
by the shutting off of Swedish trade to the West was also
met by trade negotiations with the U.S.S.R. and Italy, as well
as with Norway and Denmark. Sweden's import and export
needs have thus been partially cared for, but the government
has also emphasized that in the long run Sweden cannot live
without sea traffic westward.[27]

Suggestions emanating from Germany that Sweden should
be made a part of a permanent Germanic-Nordic federal
union have been clearly and energetically opposed by Swedish
public opinion.[28] The surest indication of the government's
intentions of retaining Sweden's independence is to be found
in the very costly, but vigorously continued, military preparations for defense. In the budget year 1939-40 almost two
billion kronor were spent on national defense, and since then
the rate of expenditure has increased. The tremendous popular response to the appeal for contributions to the defense
loan in 1940 and again in 1941 indicates in no uncertain terms
the determination of the Swedish people to retain their
national independence and freedom. For that independence
they have indicated that they would fight rather than submit.

Sweden's position is not enviable, but as long as the spirit of national unity remains high, the Swedish people are hopeful that their nation may escape the ultimate catastrophe of war itself. It is this spirit of intense national unity that has in large part been responsible for the continuation of both the internal democracy and the external independence of the Swedish nation.

Notes

CHAPTER I (ENGLAND, I)

1. The chief sources of information for this study have been English publications available in the United States. For the day-to-day record of facts and intentions I have relied upon the daily *Manchester Guardian* and the official *Debates* of the House of Lords and House of Commons. Of exceptional value are the *Economist*, the *Spectator*, the *New Statesman and Nation* (all weeklies), and the *Political Quarterly*. All the information contained in the study can be traced to one of these sources or to sources specially referred to in the footnotes.

Most of the works published in England dealing with the war are concerned with policy rather than with the working of the government.

2. The best summary of the emergency legislation passed in 1939 is found in the section under that heading in the *Annual Survey of English Law: 1939* (London, 1940), published by the Department of Law of the London School of Economics and Political Science. This section is written by Mr. W. Ivor Jennings, who has made himself the leading authority on English constitutional law. Most emergency laws were passed in 1939. For subsequent laws reliance has been placed largely upon the House of Commons reports and the official announcements recorded in the *Manchester Guardian* and the *Economist*. Many, though not all, of the orders and regulations under the Defense acts are published as *Defense Regulations*.

3. The Registrar-General as quoted in the *Manchester Guardian* of September 18, 1939.

4. All regulation of aliens has for many years been made by order under the provisions of the Alien Acts.

5. *Cf.* Jennings, *op. cit.,* p. 34.

6. Ordinarily the Secretary of State for Home Affairs, but any Secretary of State may exercise the powers of any other Secretary of State.

7. New offenses suggested probably to be created under the Act are "looting" and "forcing a picket," both to be punishable by death. W. Ivor Jennings "Parliament in Wartime," *Political Quarterly*, Vol. 11, pp. 358-361 (Oct.-Dec., 1940), gives the parliamentary history of this act.

8. Land can be taken over and used, but its ownership cannot be acquired because such ownership would lapse when the Act expired. (The Act was limited to one year with a proviso that it might be extended by parliamentary resolution, which has been done.) The borrowing of money

and the levying of taxes are still impossible without express parliamentary sanction. See W. Ivor Jennings, "The Rule of Law in Total War," *Yale Law Journal*, Vol. 50, pp. 365-386 (January, 1941).

9. By an Order in Council of November 23, 1939.

10. Jennings, "The Rule of Law in Total War," cited above.

11. Critical discussions of the Defense Acts in relation to civil liberties are to be found in *idem.*, and in Ronald Kidd, *British Liberty in Danger* (London, 1940). Mr. Kidd is the secretary of the Council of Civil Liberties. Mr. Jennings finds that the Acts as administered are not restrictive of liberty; Mr. Kidd gives specific examples of restrictive action.

12. After the bombing was under way it was supplemented in the autumn of 1940 by fire-watchers, etc., and the government took power, in January, 1941, to make fire-fighting compulsory.

13. One of the most balanced surveys of the problem is Kingsley Martin, "Reflections on Air Raids," *Political Quarterly*, Vol. 12, pp. 66-80 (January-March, 1941).

14. Many banks and other private enterprises had provided themselves with alternative headquarters in rural villages and cathedral cities. Such unoccupied Londoners as were free to do so had acquired alternative homes outside London.

15. There were other signs that in certain ways the war had been over-provided for. The "blackout" was at first so intense as to cause great inconvenience and many traffic deaths. The rules for rationing of petrol, gas, and electricity produced an undesirable and unnecessary underconsumption. Billingsgate fish market was removed to Sheffield, with the result that fish disappeared from the London bill of fare. Later it was returned to Billingsgate. One dignified Oxford College housed for a time two irreconcilable government commissions and was known as "fish and chips." Many civil servants were forced to leave the seacoast of Bohemia for the less familiar coasts of North Wales. The University of London was cut in pieces and distributed about the country. Physicians were enrolled to attend casualties who did not appear, and their civilian patients went uncared for. Sir E. Graham-Little, a physician, M.P. for London University, later referred to the situation as having all the characteristics of a panic. 359 H. C. Deb., 5s., 637-638.

Unemployment increased at once, but men out-of-work who belonged to scheduled occupations were forbidden to join the army.

Gradually, in the course of several months, the most serious dislocations were relieved.

16. 359 H. C. Deb., 5s., 699.

17. For a comprehensive statement of the proper wartime functions of the service departments and of the Committee, see Major-General Sir Frederick Maurice, *Haldane 1915-1928* (Toronto, 1939), Ch. IV.

18. *Annual Survey of English Law, 1939*, pp. 41-42.

19. *Ibid.*, p. 48. It is not difficult to understand why wartime socialization should be resisted in England. "In this country now, the private interest

is very deeply rooted; and many of the biggest private interests are terrified that the communal public ethic should become so strong and collectivized that people would not naturally return to the private after the war." "Mass Observation," as quoted in *Political Quarterly*, Vol. 11, pp. 256-257 (April, 1940). "Mass Observation" goes on to point out that the conflict between the public and the private "ethic" produces tensions in England, in contrast to Germany and Russia where the public and private interests are much more closely allied than in the British system. Perhaps "Mass Observation" has here hit on the prime dilemma of a war fought by a capitalistic democracy.

20. The great exception was the railroads. See below, p. 61.

21. "The noble army of controllers was recruited from organized industry; the rings, from being tolerated, became endowed with all the power of the State . . . The result has been what we see—a startling inadequacy of production." *Economist*, Vol. 138, p. 1033 (June 15, 1940). *Cf.* "Finance and Business," *Manchester Guardian*, August 3, 1940.

22. His place was filled in March, 1940, by Mr. Robert S. Hudson.

23. The arrangement was outlined by Mr. Attlee for the government on June 4, 1940 (361 H. C. Deb., 5s., 769-770) and explained by Mr. Greenwood on August 7 (364 H. C. Deb., 5s., 241-260).

24. *Cf.* the *Economist* of November 23, 1940, for an analysis of the situation.

25. Strikes had been outlawed by order in the summer. But a long dispute with the engineers brought the problems forward.

26. Incidental to the plans for compulsion, the *Daily Worker*, which opposed, was suppressed on January 22. Few members of the Labor party showed enthusiasm for the plans in the House of Commons discussion.

27. The best, though not the frankest, comment was these words of the *Economist*, Vol. 139, p. 420 (October 5, 1940): "The Prime Minister does not seem to have made up his mind between the two conflicting theories. According to one of them the War Cabinet is a supernumerary council of advisors to those who are really doing the work, made up in the main of men whose party eminence is not matched by technical competence. According to the other theory, membership in the War Cabinet is an honorific rank by which those Departmental Ministers who have been most successful can be rewarded. The third theory, that the War Cabinet should be made up of the ablest men available, who should be entirely relieved of departmental responsibilities, finds no countenance at all. The members of the War Cabinet fall into two groups, one able and over-burdened, the other free to think but mediocre . . . As it is, it is a parody of government."

28. Sir John Anderson, a distinguished ex-Indian civil servant, had been entrusted with civil defense arrangements since October, 1938.

29. It is significant that the new government made a mild gesture in the direction of conciliating Russia by sending as ambassador Sir Stafford Cripps, M.P., who had been expelled from the Labor party for sponsoring a "united front" policy.

30. The organization set up under Mr. Churchill's war cabinet in May, 1940, was explained in an official statement to be as follows:

Defense is in charge of the Prime Minister as Minister of Defense. He presides over a committee of the three defense ministers with the Chiefs of Staff as advisors.

Foreign Policy is in charge of the Foreign Secretary who reports directly to the war cabinet.

Economic and Home Affairs were entrusted to a number of committees:
(1) Production Council.
(2) Economic Policy Committee.
(3) Food Policy Committee.
(These are discussed above under Production, p. 15).
(4) Home Policy Committee (chairman, the Lord Privy Seal) in charge of the home front, the Social Services, and draft legislation and regulations.
(5) Civil Defense Committee (chairman, the Home Secretary).
All five committees are coordinated by the Lord President's Committee. Statement of Mr. Attlee, leader of the House of Commons, 361 H. C. Deb. 5s., 769-770 (June 4, 1940).

31. On April 10, 1940, the House of Commons discussed the lack of system in civil service appointments and appealed unsuccessfully to the Treasury to restore the examination system. 359 H. C. Deb., 5s., 619-672.

32. Under the Regional Commissioners Act, 1939. See Mr. Jennings' comment, *Annual Survey of English Law, 1939,* p. 58.

33. See the list in 361 H. C. Deb., 5s., 1391.

34. Sir John Anderson outlined the organization. 361 H. C. Deb., 5s., 1284-1285 (June 12, 1940).

35. *Economist,* Vol. 139, p. 239 (August 24, 1940).

36. *Idem.*

37. The problem of the London area is the most serious, since the Metropolis contains many separate local governments. Mr. Morrison, as former leader of the London County Council, is particularly familiar with this situation. The *Spectator* on October 11, 1940, demanded full-fledged regional government for London.

38. Next to the Official Debates, the best source of information as to Parliament is the daily reports in the *Manchester Guardian.* W. Ivor Jennings' "Parliament in Wartime" is a brilliant analytical and critical survey. *Political Quarterly,* Vol. 11, pp. 183-195, 232-247, 351-367 and Vol. 12, pp. 53-65 (April, 1940 to March, 1941).

39. By some Conservatives, the party truce was supposed to extend to the prohibition of ordinary party propaganda; but members of the minority parties insisted on a limited right of speaking and campaigning for their own programs.

An interesting example of the working of the party truce may be seen in the refusal of the Ministry of Information to allow Miss Margaret Bondfield, a former Labor minister, to speak under its auspices in Newcastle for the reason that one Conservative M. P. from Newcastle objected. The Ministry stated that "one of the principal objects of meetings arranged under the auspices of the Ministry of Information is to keep the party truce." When the local committees of the ministry objected to the ruling, the ministry yielded. *Manchester Guardian*, December 4 and 14, 1940.

40. The general election of 1935 had been a second "national" election. In 1935 the Conservative party and its allies had cast approximately 12⅓ million votes. The Labor and Liberal parties and the other fragmented oppositions had cast approximately 10⅓ million votes. Yet the Conservative party and its allies won 433 seats in a House of Commons of 615, and the opposition won only 182 seats. By-elections between 1935 and 1939 had done little to change the figures. See *Constitutional Yearbook: 1936*, pp. 277 and 191.

41. See E. P. Chase, "House of Lords Reform since 1911," *Political Science Quarterly*, Vol. 44, pp. 569-590 (Dec., 1929).

42. No qualitative judgment is entirely fair. But such statements as that of the aged but still influential Lord Newton reveal a characteristic attitude. Said he: "There is an extraordinary delusion in peoples' minds, fostered by our propagandists, that we are fighting this war solely on behalf of democratic institutions, and that Hitler is naturally at war with us for that reason . . . I maintain that Hitler is no enemy to democratic principles . . . Democracy, however, has nothing to do with the question at all." 116 H. L. Deb., 5s., 863-864 (July 10, 1940).

43. Earl Winterton on July 30, 1940, complained that in the whole of the last war there had only been seven secret sessions, whereas there had already been five in this. Commander Wedgwood remarked that the House had discovered historically that it was to its own interest for debates to be held in public. 363 H. C. Deb., 5s., 1193-1206.

The danger of secret sessions is that members of the House will be satisfied that they understand the situation and will forget that the government is responsible to them as representatives of the people and not to them as individual masters. A further disadvantage is that the House loses publicity and consequently ceases to lead popular opinion.

W. Ivor Jennings, in "Parliament and Wartime," III and IV, discusses secret sessions, with emphasis on their dangers.

44. *Cf.* many of the suggestions made before the Select Committee on Procedure in Public Business. *Special Report* 161 of 1931.

45. Mr. Kenneth Pickthorn, a Conservative supporter of the government, remarked on July 31, 1940: "To some of us, it seems that the real danger in which our general liberties are involved at present is that the Executive now controls some ninety-nine one-hundredths of this House." 363 H. C. Deb., 5s., 1323.

46. The composition of Mr. Churchill's government is described above, in the section on Ministerial Changes.

The reasons for the ignorance of Mr. Chamberlain's government, which was largely responsible for its fall, are interesting and perhaps significant.

There appears to have been a general complacency among those in high office, so that success was assumed and failure unthinkable. There was a lack of liaison between men in the field and men in Whitehall. And between the government and the people was interposed a stupidly managed censorship and a Ministry of Information which encouraged the press in its rosy visions. The belief that the Norwegian expedition was a success was universal in the press, up to the moment when its failure was egregious. Such a situation could have resulted only from universal misinformation. Since the change of government the censorship has been at least as strict, as touching matters of strategy, but there has been much more frankness in letting the press know what is actually occurring. The newspapers may be reticent, but they are informed.

47. The House of Commons debates on May 7 and 8, among the crucial debates in English parliamentary history, are in 360 H. C. Deb., 5s., 1073-1196 and 1251-1366. In the division which came at the end, the government was supported by a majority of 281-200.

48. I am obliged for some suggestions in this analysis to Professor H. J. Laski's article, "The War Cabinet and Parliament," *New Statesmen and Nation,* Vol. 20, pp. 612 ff. (December 14, 1940); and also to H. Boardman, "Parliament, Mr. Churchill and the Future" *Nineteenth Century,* Vol. 129, pp. 12-17 (January, 1941), as representing an ultra-conservative view.

See also Jennings, "Parliament in Wartime," IV. Writing about December 1, 1940, he says (p. 64): "The impression cannot be avoided that the House of Commons has lost ground as a democratic instrument during the past three months." See also the comment in the *Manchester Guardian's* "London Notes," November 4, 1940.

49. The removal of Sir John Anderson from the post of Home Secretary is perhaps the greatest example of the power of the House. Sir John had been brought into office by Mr. Chamberlain as an ex-civil servant, but his methods seemed to the House more suited to an Indian than an English administrator. In his subsequent post of Lord President of the Council his great administrative ability can be used in fields where he is not brought into contact with the representatives of the people.

50. "If we are to win the battle of democracy on the home front we have to study not only the preservation of the representative system but also its improvement so that it may be more truly representative, and Parliamentary life more free." The *Spectator,* November 29, 1940.

51. See its program in the *Manchester Guardian,* January 12, 1941; *Cf.* also "Critic," *New Statesman and Nation,* Vol. 21, p. 53 (January 18, 1941). "The electoral truce, the absorption of the Labor party leaders in the government, and the concentration of their energies in the terrific administrative problems of the war leaves a gap wide open for alternative leadership. The Communist party means to fill that gap."

52. The resolutions of the Conference are printed in full in the *Christian Century* (Chicago), Vol. 58, pp. 253ff. (February 19, 1941).

Chapter II (England, II)

1. *Spectator* (London), February 16, 1940.
2. *Ibid.,* September 6, 1940.
3. Some details of economic and fiscal policy are to be found in D. H. Popper and J. C. de Wilde, *Wartime Economy of Britain and France* (New York, 1940).
4. *Federal Reserve Bulletin,* March, 1940, and following months. British-held Canadian securities had been similarly requisitioned in October, 1939.
5. August, 1939, figures in *Federal Reserve Bulletin,* January, 1941; January, 1941, figures in U. S. Treasury Statement, *New York Times,* January 16, 1941, p. 10.
6. Admirably analysed in *Federal Reserve Bulletin,* May, 1940.
7. *Cf.* A. D. K. Owen, "The Great Evacuation," *Political Quarterly,* Vol. 11, pp. 30ff. (January, 1940), with Kingsley Martin, "Reflections on Air Raids," *ibid.,* Vol. 12, pp. 66ff. (January, 1941). *Cf.* also W. H. Wickwar, *The Social Services* (London, 1936), p. 248.
8. H. L. Franklin, "British Food Control," *Foreign Agriculture* (U. S. Dept. Agriculture), December, 1939.
9. *New York Times,* Jan. 27, 1941, p. 24, citing *Board of Trade Index* (London). Alternatively, using the index of the London *Economist* (1927 base), wholesale commodity prices rose from 70 in August, 1939, to 90 in December, 1939, and to 101 in December, 1940.
10. *Cf.,* for the first World War, W. H. Wickwar, *Public Services* (London, 1938), pp. 68, 83.
11. U. S. Congress, 76th Session, *Senate Document No. 273* (Washington, 1940).
12. According to the antiquated Ministry of Labor index (1914 base) reprinted monthly in the *Federal Reserve Bulletin,* the cost of living rose from 155 on September 1, 1939, to 174 on January 1, 1940, to 187 in September, 1940, and to 196 on January 1, 1941. Part of this rise was due to increased taxes.
13. For further preparatory steps, see *New York Times,* January 7, March 17, and April 18, 1941.
14. Additional details may be found in F. Wunderlich, *British Labor and the War* (New York, 1941), and International Labor Office, *The Labor Situation in Great Britain* (Montreal, 1941).
15. W. Citrine, *The TUC in War-time* (London, 1940), p. 3.
16. These were worth approximately £200 each a year.
17. D. K. Price and J. L. Sundquist in *The British Defense Program and Local Government* (Chicago, 1940), quote much British municipal criticism of details.
18. J. D. Imrie, "The Impact of War on Local Finances," *Public Administration,* Vol. 18, pp. 18ff. (January, 1940).

Chapter III (Germany, I)

1. *Cf.* Fritz Morstein Marx, *Government in the Third Reich*, 2d ed. (New York, 1937), p. 181.

2. "Once more the regime must be credited with having found a simple and happy solution . . ." Karl Loewenstein, *Hitler's Germany* (New York, 1939), p. 174. On the application of the council formula as a general device of political leadership in the Third Reich, *cf.* Herbert Schneider, *Führer und Führerrat* (Gelnhausen, 1938).

3. *Cf.* Wolfgang von Gehlen, *Die Umwandlung in der Staatsleitung vom Kanzlersystem zum Führerprinzip* (Düsseldorf, 1939). Many an illuminating insight is also provided by Heinrich Triepel, *Die Hegemonie* (Stuttgart and Berlin, 1938). For a comparison with the constitutional dictatorship under the Weimar Republic, *cf.* Frederick M. Watkins, *The Failure of Constitutional Emergency Powers under the German Republic* (Cambridge, 1939).

4. These supervisory prerogatives are specific and defined by law. *Cf.* Fritz Morstein Marx, "Germany," in William Anderson, ed., *Local Government in Europe* (New York, 1939), pp. 223ff. An annotated translation of the German Municipal Act of 1935 is supplied *id.*, pp. 277ff.

5. For earlier developments, *cf.* Alfred V. Boerner, "Toward *Reichsreform*—The *Reichsgaue*," *American Political Science Review*, Vol. 33, pp. 853ff. (Oct., 1939).

6. *Erlass über Gliederung und Verwaltung der Ostgebiete* of October 8, 1939 (*Reichsgesetzblatt*, 1, p. 2042).

7. *Reichsgesetzblatt*, 1, pp. 52, 55.

8. *Cf.* Gustav Stolper, *German Economy 1870-1940* (New York, 1940); Henri Laufenburger, *L'Économie Allemande à l'Épreuve de la Guerre* (Paris, 1940); Otto D. Tolischus, *They Wanted War* (New York, 1940). *Cf.* also L. Fauvel, *Problèmes Économiques de la Guerre Totale* (Paris, 1940); A. C. Pigou, *The Political Economy of War* (London, 1940); John C. de Wilde and others, *Handbook of the War* (New York, 1940). In recent years there has been a steady flow of German writings dealing with the technical issues of "total preparedness," but definitive works are still to be written. On the organizational construction of the Third Reich, *cf.* Paul Meier-Benneckenstein, ed., *Das Dritte Reich im Aufbau*, Vols. I-III (Berlin, 1939).

9. For a Marxist interpretation, which makes Hitler appear to be a puppet of big business, *cf.* Hans Behrend, *The Real Rulers of Germany* (London, 1940). A good illustration of the extent to which the entrepreneur has been subjected to regulatory impositions is Karl Siegert, *Deutsches Wirtschaftsstrafrecht* (Berlin, 1939), an analysis of penal sanctions of government control running to nearly 600 pages. *Cf.* also Robert R. Kühlewein, "German Legislation from 1937 to 1939," *Tulane Law Review*, Vol. 14, pp. 593ff. (June, 1940).

10. *Cf.* L. Hamburger, *How Nazi Germany has Mobilized and Controlled Labor* (Washington, 1940); Robert Frase, "A Study of Labor Market Control," in Carl J. Friedrich and Edward S. Mason, eds., *Public Policy* (Cambridge, 1940), pp. 247ff.

11. Hardly considered necessary at the beginning, the system of war management evolved in the course of the first World War was in itself no minor feat. *Cf.* the volumes of the *Economic and Social History of the World War* (German Series) under the general editorship of James T. Shotwell, Carnegie Foundation for International Peace. While these studies, on the whole, deal only incidentally with the record of organizational and administrative achievement, they do contain rich materials on which to base a valid appraisal. *Cf.* also Erich Ludendorff, *The Nation at War* (London, 1936).

12. *Kriegswirtschaftsverordnung* of September 4, 1939 (*Reichsgesetzblatt*, 1, p. 1609).

13. *Cf.* in general Kenyon E. Poole, *German Financial Policies 1932-1939* (Cambridge, 1939). Significant as a German study published on the eve of war: Ad. Fleischer, *Kriegsfinanzierung unter Einschluss des totalen Krieges* (Berlin, 1939).

14. *Verordnung über die Wiedereinführung der Mehrarbeitszuschläge* of September 3, 1940 (*Reichsgesetzblatt*, 1, p. 1205).

15. *Verordnung über die Aufhebung der Mehreinkommensteuer* of August 21, 1940 (*Reichsgesetzblatt*, 1, p. 1129).

16. *Cf.* Taylor Cole, "Corporative Organization of the Third Reich," *Review of Politics*, Vol. 2, pp. 438 ff. (Oct., 1940).

17. *Cf.* in general Eberhard Barth, *Wesen und Aufgaben der Organisation der Gewerblichen Wirtschaft* (Hamburg, 1939).

18. *Frankfurter Zeitung*, September 10, 1939, nos. 461-462, p. 5.

19. *Cf.* Fritz Morstein Marx, "Totalitarian Politics," *Proceedings of the American Philosophical Society*, Vol. 82 (1940), pp. 1ff.

20. *Frankfurter Zeitung*, August 27, 1939, nos. 435-436, p. 15. Italics are the *Frankfurter's*.

21. *Id.*, p. 1.

22. *Cf.* Otto Dietrich, *A Revolution in Thought* (Berlin, 1939). The "we or they" alternative clearly overshadows the *Lebensraum* theme. On the latter, *cf.* Charles Kruszewski, "Germany's *Lebensraum*," *American Political Science Review*, Vol. 34, pp. 964 ff. (October, 1940). As to the policies of the Hitler régime, however, the drive for continental hegemony is a very real factor. There is something of a "hungry look" in much of the German literature too. One may think of writings such as Hans Ballreich, *Karpathenrussland* (Heidelberg, 1939); F. W. von Oertzen, *Baltenland* (Munich, 1939); Alex Schmidt, *Ukraine: Land der Zukunft* (Berlin, 1939); Ernst Berger, *Die verfassungsrechtliche Struktur Polens* (Breslau, 1939); Werner Best, *Die Verwaltung Polens vor und nach dem Zusammenbruch der polnischen Republik* (Berlin, 1940); Werner von Rheinbaben, *Um ein neues Europa* (Berlin, 1939); Paul and Justus Rohrbach, *Afrika heute und morgen* (Ber-

lin, 1939); Kurt Weege, *Panamerikanismus und Monroedoktrin* (Schönberg, 1939). *Cf.* also Kurt Bloch, *German Interests and Policies in the Far East* (New York, 1940). On German foreign policy, *cf.* Axel Freytagh-Loringhoven, *Deutschlands Aussenpolitik 1933-1939* (Berlin, 1939); Alfred Mensel, *Germany's Foreign Policy* (London, 1939).

23. Official emphasis on Versailles is not lacking. *Cf.* Fritz Berber, *Das Diktat von Versailles*, 2 vols. (Essen, 1939). A significant testimonial is Otto Braun, *Von Weimar zu Hitler* (New York, 1940). *Cf* also Edmond Vermeil, *L'Allemagne: Essai d'Explication* (Paris, 1940). German psychology never distinguished between the cost of war itself and the burdens of the peace of 1919. On the former, *cf.* James T. Shotwell, *What Germany Forgot* (New York, 1940).

24. *Frankfurter Zeitung*, September 10, 1939, nos. 461-462, p. 1.

25. *Cf.* for the earlier attitude, Oswald G. Villard, *Inside Germany* (London, 1939); Theodore L. Stoddard, *Into the Darkness* (New York, 1940); Nevile Henderson, *Failure of a Mission* (New York, 1940).

26. *Cf.* Kenneth Holland, *Youth in European Labor Camps* (Washington, 1939).

27. *Cf.* Gerhard Wehner, *Die rechtliche Stellung der Hitler Jugend* (Dresden, 1939).

28. A comparison is suggested by J. Demarquette, *Le Pacifisme des Jeunes* (Paris, 1940).

29. *Cf.* also Hans Gerth, "The Nazi Party: Its Leadership and Composition," *American Journal of Sociology*, Vol. 45, pp. 517ff. (January, 1940). On the administrative organization of the National Socialist Party in general, *cf.* Anton Lingg, *Die Verwaltung der Nationalsozialistischen Deutschen Arbeiterpartei* (Munich, 1939).

30. *Cf.* Morstein Marx, *loc. cit.* in note 19.

31. *Cf.* Fritz Morstein Marx, "Bureaucracy and Dictatorship," *Review of Politics*, Vol. 3, pp. 100ff. (January, 1941).

32. *Erlass* of March 17, 1940 (*Reichsgesetzblatt*, 1, p. 513).

33. *Anordnung über die Verwaltungsführung in den Landkreisen* of December 28, 1939 (*Reichsgesetzblatt*, 1, p. 45).

34. *Frankfurter Zeitung*, March 17, 1940, nos. 140-141 (*Beilage*, p. 2).

35. *Cf.* also Werner Sombart, *Weltanschauung, Science, and Economy* (New York, 1939).

36. *Cf.* H. Rosinsky, *The German Army* (New York, 1940).

37. An outstanding elaboration is to be found in a volume published recently by an officer of the German General Staff: Hermann Foertsch, *The Art of Modern Warfare* (New York, 1940). Closely similar conceptions have gone into the new *Infantry Field Manual F M 7-5*, ed. by Major General George A. Lynch, War Department (Washington, D. C., 1940).

38. *Cf.* Morstein Marx, *loc. cit.* in note 19, pp. 36ff.

39. See note 23.

40. There is less vigor today in religious persecution than was the case in the preceding period. *Cf.* for the latter Michael Power, *Religion in the*

Reich (London, 1939); Nathaniel Micklem, *National Socialism and the Roman Catholic Church* (New York, 1939).

CHAPTER IV (GERMANY, II)

1. *Völkischer Beobachter*, Dec. 11, 1940, pp. 1ff.

2. *Frankfurter Zeitung*, Dec. 13, 1940, p. 1.

3. *Völkerrechtliche Grossraumordnung mit Interventionsverbot für raumfremde Mächte* (Berlin, 1939). Note the discussions in Charles Kruszewski, "Germany's *Lebensraum*," *American Political Science Review*, Vol. 34, pp. 974-975 (Oct., 1940); Joseph Florin and John H. Herz, "Bolshevist and National Socialist Doctrines of International Law," *Social Research*, Vol. 7, pp. 15ff. (Feb., 1940).

4. Schmitt, *op. cit.*, pp. 69-70.

5. Carl Schmitt, "Der Reichsbegriff im Völkerrecht," *Deutsches Recht*, Vol. 9, pp. 341ff. (April, 1939).

6. *Frankfurter Zeitung*, Nov. 24, 1940, p. 4.

7. On the duty of German leadership *(Führung)*, as distinguished from British domination *(Herrschaft)* in Europe, see the comments in *ibid.*, Nov. 5, 1940, p. 2.

8. O. Tolischus, *They Wanted War* (New York, 1940), pp. 42-43.

9. The best account of these writings is to be found in Eduard Bristler (pseud.), *Die Völkerrechtslehre des Nationalsozialismus* (Zurich, 1938); John H. Herz, "The National Socialist Doctrine of International Law and the Problems of International Organization," *Political Science Quarterly*, Vol. 54, pp. 536ff. (Dec., 1939).

10. Carl Schmitt, *Die Wendung zum diskriminierenden Kriegsbegriff* (Munich, 1938).

11. G. A. Walz, *Inflation im Völkerrecht der Nachkriegszeit* (Berlin, 1939), esp. pp. 12ff. and 34ff.

12. *Völkischer Beobachter*, Sept. 17, 1939, p. 3.

13. *Ibid.*, Oct. 12, 1939, p. 1.

14. *Ibid.*, Nov. 30, 1939, p. 1.

15. *Ibid.*, Dec. 4, 1939, p. 1; *cf.* Werner Freiherr von Rheinbaben, "Aussenpolitische Kriegschronik," *Berliner Monatshefte*, Vol. 18, p. 52 (Jan., 1940).

16. *Das schwarze Korps*, Feb. 29, 1940, p. 1.

17. *Völkischer Beobachter*, Dec. 6, 1940, p. 4.

18. *The Round Table*, no. 121, p. 169 (Dec., 1940).

19. *Frankfurter Zeitung*, Nov. 24, 1940, p. 4.

20. See Erich Voegelin, "Extended Strategy," *The Journal of Politics*, Vol. 2, pp. 189ff. (May, 1940).

21. Alfred Vagts, "War and the Colleges," *Journal of the American Military Institute*, Vol. 4, pp. 67ff. (Summer, 1940).

22. Henry W. Spiegel, "Wehrwirtschaft: Economics of the Military State," *The American Economic Review*, Vol. 30, p. 722 (Dec., 1940), and the literature there cited.

23. The "full powers" granted under this plan were extended for four more years on Oct. 18, 1940. *Reichsgesetzblatt*, 1, p. 1395.

24. A. Hueck, *Deutsches Arbeitsrecht* (Berlin, 1938); A. Hueck, H. C. Nipperdey and R. Dietz, *Gesetz zur Ordnung der nationalen Arbeit* (3rd ed., Berlin, 1939); L. Hamburger, *How Nazi Germany Has Mobilized and Controlled Labor* (Washington, 1940).

25. The early developments are discussed in A. Nikisch, "Arbeitsrecht im Kriege," *Deutsches Recht*, Vol. 9, pp. 1869ff. (Oct., 1939); "Arbeitsrecht," *Soziale Praxis*, Vol. 48, col. 1101ff. (Sept., 1939); Timm, "Die Beschränkung des Arbeitsplatzwechsels in der Kriegswirtschaft," *Deutsches Arbeitsrecht*, Vol. 7, pp. 255ff., and 272ff. (Oct. and Nov., 1939); Günther Schelp, "Das Arbeitsrecht der Kriegswirtschaft," *ibid.*, Vol. 7, pp. 257ff. (Oct., 1939); Steinmann, "Die Gestaltung der Arbeitsbedingungen im Kriege," *Deutsche Verwaltung*, Vol. 16, pp. 621ff. (Dec. 25, 1939); *Weekly Report of the German Institute for Business Research*, Feb. 3, 1940. The numerous laws, decrees, etc., are cited in full in these articles.

26. *Reichsgesetzblatt*, 1, p. 2370; *cf.* Harlow J. Heneman, "German Labor Trustees," *Brooklyn Law Review*, Vol. 10, p. 47 (Oct., 1940).

27. Notice the carefully worded statement in the *Weekly Report of the German Institute for Business Research*, May 22, 1940, pp. 1-2.

28. *Reichsgesetzblatt*, 1, p. 1658.

29. Grau, "Die arbeitsrechtlichen Vorschriften in kommenden Strafrecht," *Deutsches Arbeitsrecht*, Vol. 5, pp. 65ff. (March, 1937).

30. *Reichsgesetzblatt*, 1, p. 243.

31. Quoted from Ernst Fraenkel, *The Dual State* (New York, 1941), p. 195.

32. *Ibid.*, p. 196.

33. *New York Times*, Feb. 14, 1940, p. 6.

34. Obviously, under the ration system, these wage and payment provisions have a limited meaning. For recent considerations of prices and wages, for whatever value they may have now in considering real wages, see *Wirtschaft und Statistik*, Oct. 1, 1940, pp. 439ff., and *The Economist*, Vol. 140, p. 799 (Dec. 28, 1940).

35. *Weekly Report of the German Institute for Business Research*, May 22, 1940, p. 2.

36. Emil Lederer, "Who Pays for German Armament?" *Social Research*, Vol. 5, pp. 70ff. (Feb., 1938).

37. *Reichsgesetzblatt*, 1, p. 1205.

38. *Frankfurter Zeitung*, Nov. 23, 1940, p. 2, summarizing a report of State Secretary Syrup. It was stated that there were only 32,000 unemployed, of which number only 2800 were "fully employable."

39. *Idem.*

40. *New York Times*, Sept. 15, 1940, p. 46.

41. *Völkischer Beobachter*, Dec. 8, 1940, p. 1; *cf.* "Wehrhafte Wohnungs-wirtschaft," *Soziale Praxis*, Vol. 49, col. 119ff. (Feb. 15, 1940).

42. *The Economist*, Dec. 28, 1940, p. 799; *cf.* Sitzler, "Deutschland beim Aufbau," *Soziale Praxis*, Vol. 49, col. 129 ff. (March 1, 1940).

43. *New York Times*, Feb. 10, 1941, p. 5.

44. See R. H. Wells, "The Financial Relations of Church and State in Germany 1919-1937," *Political Science Quarterly*, Vol. 53, pp. 36ff. (March, 1938).

45. *New York Times*, Oct. 30, 1939, p. 8, and Nov. 5, 1939, p. 39.

46. *Ibid.*, Nov. 9, 1939, p. 11.

47. *Völkischer Beobachter*, Dec. 24-26 (combined edition), 1939, p. 11; *New York Times*, Jan. 18, 1940, p. 9.

48. *Ibid.*, March 1, 1940, p. 9.

49. *Ibid.*, May 16, 1940, p. 7.

50. George La Piana, "Vatican-Axis Diplomacy," *Nation*, Vol. 151, p. 532 (Nov. 30, 1940).

51. Note Karl Loewenstein's reference to the treatment of the Jehovah's Witnesses in *Hitler's Germany* (New York, 1939), pp. 96-97, note 5.

52. On this point, see Hans Gerth, "The Nazi Party: Its Leadership and Composition," *The American Journal of Sociology*, Vol. 45, pp. 529ff. (Jan., 1940).

53. Heinrich Muth, "Die Verwaltungsgerichtsbarkeit und der Krieg," *Deutsches Recht*, Vol. 9, pp. 1874ff. (Oct., 1939).

54. *Cf.* Fraenkel, *op. cit.*, pp. 24ff.

55. (New York, 1940).

CHAPTER V (RUSSIA)

1. See V. M. Molotov, *Report on the Foreign Policy of the Soviet Union*, Seventh Session of the Supreme Soviet of the U.S.S.R., August 1, 1940. For English translation, see *Moscow News*, 1940, No. 31.

2. Karelian-Finnish Republic, admitted March 31, 1940; Moldavian Republic, admitted August 2, 1940; Lithuanian Republic, admitted August 3, 1940; Latvian Republic, admitted August 5, 1940; Esthonian Republic, admitted August 6, 1940. Article 13 of the Constitution of the U.S.S.R. was amended by the Supreme Soviet of the U.S.S.R. at its Seventh Session on August 7, 1940, to include the new Republics. See Stenographic Report of Seventh Session (in Russian), p. 189.

3. Commenced on November 30, 1939, and terminated by the Soviet-Finnish Peace Treaty dated March 12, 1940. For official Russian text, see *Ved. Verkh. Sov.*, *S.S.S.R.*, No. 14 (77), June 3, 1940, p. 3. By decree of July 16, 1940, a general amnesty was granted to persons who fought in the Finnish war and who had previously been sentenced to compulsory labor at their regular place of work. See *idem*, No. 25 (88), July 30, 1940, p. 1.

4. See "Political Report to Sixteenth Party Congress (1930)," published in J. Stalin, *Leninism* (New York, 1934), Vol. 2, p. 342.

5. See *Report on the Work of the Central Committee to the Eighteenth Congress of the C.P.S.U. (b),*" March 10, 1939, published in English translation in Moscow, 1939.

6. See *Constitution,* promulgated December 5, 1936, Chap. IX. For English translation, see Rappard *et al., Source Book on European Governments* (New York, 1937), p. v-107.

7. Official text of interview published in brochure form in Moscow, in Russian and English, 1936.

8. See Speech of M. M. Litvinov, delivered at the Extraordinary Eighth Congress of Soviets of the U.S.S.R., November 28, 1936, published in English in Moscow, 1937.

9. Voters marked their ballots in curtained booths in which secrecy was possible. Each booth was provided with a pencil.

10. For a history of Lenin's efforts, see W. Knorin, *The Communist Party of the Soviet Union, a Short History,* published in English translation in Moscow, 1935, p. 39, *et seq.*

11. Statistics taken from E. Yaroslavsky, *Bolshevik Verification and Purging of the Party Ranks* (Moscow, 1933), and reports at Party Congresses.

12. English translations of the stenographic record of the three trials have been published in 1936, 1937 and 1938 by the People's Commissariat of Justice, under the titles: "The Case of the Trotskyite-Zinovievite Terrorist Center; The Case of the Anti-Soviet Trotskyite Center; and The Case of the Anti-Soviet Bloc of Rights and Trotskyites."

13. The Report of Shcherbakov to the Supreme Soviet stated that 81 per centum of the delegates to the Soviet of the Union were Party members. The lower average for both houses of the Supreme Soviet is probably due to the fact that the regions of the national minorities who provide a large number of delegates in the Soviet of Nationalities are less politically advanced regions than the densely populated areas which provide the majority of delegates in the Soviet of the Union.

14. See *Sobr. Zak., S.S.S.R.,* 1937, Vol. 1, No. 31, Art. 126.

15. Decree of August 2, 1940. See *Ved. Verkh. Sov., S.S.S.R.,* No. 28 (91), August 22, 1940, p. 2.

16. For revised text of oath, see *idem,* No. 30 (93), Sept. 12, 1940, p. 3.

17. For criticism of this nature, see George Fielding Eliot, "The Russian Army," *The American Quarterly on the Soviet Union,* Vol. 1, No. 3, p. 19, (Oct., 1938).

18. For English translation of these rules, see *American Quarterly on the Soviet Union,* Vol. 2, No. 1 (April, 1939).

19. See *Izvestiya,* No. 21 (7093), January 27, 1940, and *idem,* No. 43 (7115), Feb. 22, 1940.

20. Decree of September 6, 1940, *Ved. Verkh. Sov., S.S.S.R.,* No. 31 (94), Sept. 17, 1940, p. 1.

21. See *Pravda*, No. 249 (8295), Sept. 7, 1940, p. 1.

22. See *Izvestiya*, April 18, 1940.

23. *Ved. Verkh. Sov., S.S.S.R.*, No. 20 (83), p. 1; approved by Supreme Soviet of the U.S.S.R. at its Seventh Session, August 7, 1940, see *idem*, No. 28 (91), August 22, 1940, p. 2.

24. See "Order of Council of People's Commissars," June 26, 1940, *idem*, No. 20 (83), p. 1. A corresponding increase in wages was required, however, in the few remaining enterprises operated as concessions by private capital. See decree of August 16, 1940, *idem*, No. 29 (92), p. 4.

25. See N. Shvernik, "The Transfer to the Eight Hour Workday and Seven Day Work Week and the Forbidding of Voluntary Departure of Workers and Clerks from Enterprises and Offices" (in Russian), *Bolshevik*, No. 11-12, p. 6 (July, 1940).

26. *Sobr. Post. i Rasp., S.S.S.R.*, 1939, No. 1, Art. 1.

27. See *Sovetskaya Yustitsiya*, No. 13 (1940).

28. Decree of August 10, 1940, *Ved. Verkh. Sov., S.S.S.R.*, No. 28 (91), August 22, 1940, p. 2.

29. See *Sovetskaya Yustitsiya*, No. 13 (1940).

30. The decree of July 29, 1940, provided for warnings, censures and dismissals of judges who permitted violation of labor discipline; see *Ved. Verkh. Sov., S.S.S.R.*, No. 28 (91), August 22, 1940, p. 4. See also report on events in People's Commissariat of Justice of the U.S.S.R., in which it is stated that one judge was sentenced on August 21, 1940, to one year of compulsory labor at reduced pay for criminally negligent relationship to the execution of a sentence imposed for absence from work. *Sovetskaya Yustitsiya*, No. 13, p. 9 (1940).

31. *Lex, cit. supra* note 23, sec. 3.

32. Decree of July 17, 1940, *Ved. Verkh. Sov., S.S.S.R.*, No. 25 (88), July 30, 1940, p. 1. Approved by Supreme Soviet at its Seventh Session, August 7, 1940, *idem*, No. 28 (91), August 22, 1940, p. 2.

33. Order dated August 15, 1940, No. 29 (15) V. See *Sovetskaya Yustitsiya*, No. 13, p. 6 (1940).

34. *Ved. Verkh. Sov., S.S.S.R.*, No. 42 (105), Oct. 26, 1940, p. 1.

35. The law of December 8, 1933, still in force, provides a penalty of not less than five years' deprivation of liberty for directors and administrative personnel of an enterprise in the event of a criminally negligent relationship to the tasks assigned to them. This law was carried into the Criminal Code of the R.S.F.S.R. as Article 128-a. No penalty at the time this law was enacted could exceed ten years.

36. Decree of July 10, 1940, *Ved. Verkh. Sov., S.S.S.R.*, No. 23 (86), July 20, 1940, p. 1. The penalty is imprisonment for from five to eight years. Decree approved by Supreme Soviet of the U.S.S.R. at its Seventh Session, August 7, 1940, *idem*, No. 28 (91), August 22, 1940, p. 1.

37. *Idem*, No. 37 (100), Oct. 9, 1940, p. 1.

38. Law of September 15, 1933, *Sobr. Zak., S.S.S.R.*, 1933, Vol. 1, No. 56, Art. 356.

39. Decree of May 7, 1940, *Ved. Verkh. Sov., S.S.S.R.*, No. 15 (78), June 11, 1940, p. 1; approved by Supreme Soviet at its Seventh Session, August 7, 1940, *idem*, No. 28 (91), August 22, 1940, p. 1.

40. One hectare is the equivalent of 2.47 acres.

41. See *Pravda*, May 28, 1939.

42. *Sobr. Post. i Rasp., S.S.S.R.*, 1940, No. 5, Art. 147.

43. *Sobr. Post. i Rasp., S.S.S.R.*, 1940, No. 9, Art. 236.

44. See S. Fainblit, "The Application of Soviet Legislation in the Western Districts of the Ukrainian S.S.R. and the White Russian S.S.R." (in Russian), *Sovetskaya Yustitsiya*, No. 14, p. 14 (1940). Information concerning these areas and appearing in this paper has been taken from this source.

45. See I. Trainin, "The Constitutions of the Baltic Soviet Socialist Republics" (in Russian), *Bolshevik*, No. 22 (Nov., 1940), p. 71. For a partial English translation, see *The American Review on the Soviet Union*, Vol. 4, No. 1, pp. 28-41 (April, 1941). Information concerning these areas and appearing in this paper has been taken from this source.

46. The Russian Socialist Federated Soviet Republic is usually referred to as R.S.F.S.R.

CHAPTER VI (ITALY)

1. For this background, see William Ebenstein, *Fascist Italy* (New York, 1939).

2. Mussolini, in an address delivered in Rome on September 23, 1939.

3. *Regime Fascista*, April 20, 1940.

4. This statement was made by Ettore Muti, at that time Secretary General of the Fascist party. In the Italian totalitarian system this position is second only to that of *il Duce* himself.

5. Mussolini, in his congratulatory telegram to Hitler, on May 22, 1939, on the occasion of the conclusion of the German-Italian military alliance.

6. Mussolini, in an address in Rome, on March 26, 1939, commemorating the twentieth anniversary of the founding of Fascism.

7. This is being written in the middle of April, 1941.

8. *Difesa Sociale*, Vol. 19, p. 230 (1940).

9. Mussolini, in his address of June 10, 1940.

10. See Ebenstein, *op. cit.*, pp. 186ff.

11. *Popolo di Roma*, December 11, 1940.

12. See F. Orestano, "Guerra di sistemi," *Nuova Antologia*, Vol. 75, pp. 105-115 (1940).

13. Consult Ebenstein, *op. cit.*, pp. 146ff.

14. See G. Palomba, "Le grandezze fondamentali dell'economia corporativa," *Giornale degli Economisti*, Vol. 2 (new series), pp. 168-181 (1940).

15. See the stimulating book of the same title by Peter F. Drucker (New York, 1939).

16. *Regime Fascista*, December 12, 1940.
17. *Popolo di Roma*, December 13, 1940.
18. *Lavoro Fascista*, December 11, 1940.
19. *New York Times*, January 10, 1941.
20. See Bruno Cappuccini, "La guerra totalitaria nel quadro politico," *Rassegna Italiana*, Vol. 23, pp. 267-278 (1940).

CHAPTER VII (FRANCE)

1. Georges Clemenceau, *Grandeur and Misery of Victory* (New York, 1930), pp. 384-385. (Quoted with the permission of the publishers, Harcourt, Brace & Co.)
2. Jean Martet, *Le Tigre* (Paris, 1930), p. 75.
3. André Morize, "Ten Lessons From the Fall of France," *St. Louis Post-Dispatch*, January 26, 1941.
4. R. K. Gooch, *The French Counter-Revolution of 1940. The Pétain Government and the Vichy Régime.* (New York, 1940), p. 1. Contains the texts of Pétain's initial constitutional laws and acts.
5. Karl Loewenstein, "The Demise of the French Constitution of 1875," *American Political Science Review*, Vol. 34, pp. 867ff. (October, 1940). A careful study of the transition from the Third Republic to the present régime.
6. Friedrich Sieburg, *Who Are These French?* (New York, 1932), pp. 276-277.
7. See, for example, the account in the *New York Times*, January 15, 1941.
8. *Op. cit.*
9. In James T. Shotwell, ed., *Governments of Continental Europe* (New York, 1940), pp. 70-75.
10. Jean Martet, *M. Clemenceau peint par lui-même* (Paris, 1929), p. 157.

CHAPTER VIII (THE BALKANS)

1. J. S. Roucek, *Politics of the Balkans* (New York, 1939).
2. Anne O'Hare McCormick, "Roumania is the Focal Point of Revolt Against Government," *New York Times*, November 30, 1940.
3. When the Nazis invaded Yugoslavia and Greece in April, 1941, Turkey remained neutral.
4. The aim of Russian foreign policy is to prevent the bottling up of the Black Sea by acquiring a "window on the west." Ever since the days of Peter the Great, Russia has been attempting this. By virtue of the Finnish

campaign of 1940 and the re-acquisition of Esthonia, Latvia and Lithuania, the Dardanelles, as a bogey to Russia, have become less important.

5. *New York Times*, October 12, 1940, p. 1.

6. For full text of this address, see the *New York Times*, November 2, 1940, p. 3.

7. For further information, see the *New York Times*, April 8, 1939, p. 1.

8. *Cf.* Roucek, *Politics of the Balkans*, pp. 84-98.

9. For the economic and other values of Yugoslavia to Germany, see J. S. Roucek, "The Balkans: Key to World War II," *World Affairs Interpreter*, Vol. 11, pp. 179-197 (July, 1940), and "World War II and the Balkans," *Social Education*, Vol. 5, pp. 187-189 (March, 1941).

10. For a full review of the events leading up to the Italian invasion of Greece, see "Land of Invasion," *Time*, November 4, 1940, pp. 24ff.

11. Korizis took his own life in April, 1941.

CHAPTER IX (NORWAY AND SWEDEN)

1. *Morgenbladet* (Oslo), March 15, 1940, p. 4.

2. The writer resided in Oslo from July 1, 1939, until the time of the invasion. Some of the statements in this chapter are, therefore, based on personal observation and on the use of unprinted materials.

3. The German government's demands on Norway were made in a memorandum, an English translation of which may be found in C. J. Hambro, *I Saw it Happen in Norway* (New York, 1940), Appendix, pp. 203-207. The memorandum and an official summary of the Norwegian government's deliberations leading to a rejection of its demands are contained in the *Ny Norsk Kvitbok, Opplysninger om det tyske overfallet paa Norge (April-July, 1940)*, pp. 2-6.

4. Hambro, *op. cit.*, pp. 29-30.

5. *Kvitbok, op. cit.*, pp. 26-29.

6. See Hambro, *op. cit.*, pp. 24-27, and Chapter IV entire.

7. *Kvitbok, op. cit.*, p. 9, letter from the Norwegian Minister in Stockholm to King Haakon.

8. *Ibid.*, p. 10, reply of the King to Minister Wollebak.

9. *Ibid.*, pp. 25-28.

10. *Ibid.*, p. 25.

11. *Facts in Review*, Vol. 2, No. 42, p. 511 (October 28, 1940).

12. Letter to the writer from the German Library of Information, New York. The text of the law was not yet available.

13. *Facts in Review*, Vol. 3, No. 4, p. 43 (February 3, 1941).

14. Foreign exchange regulations were issued July 7, 1940. The exchange rate was fixed at .60 RM per Krone, by order of April 10, 1940.

15. Gunnar Hägglöf, *Sweden's Foreign Trade Policy in War-Time* (mimeographed ms.), p. 7.

16. Notes received by the writer from Eric C. Bellquist. Professor Bellquist, a well-informed observer, was in Stockholm during the year 1939-40.

17. *The American Swedish Monthly*, October, 1940, p. 14.

18. Bellquist, *op. cit.*

19. *The American Swedish Monthly*, January, 1940, p. 20.

20. *Ibid.*, September, 1940, p. 18.

21. The new agencies are listed in *Sociala Meddelande, utgivna av K. Socialstyrelsen*, 1939, No. 9, pp. 625-631.

22. Wollmar Boström, Swedish Minister to the United States, *Sweden Makes Sacrifices to Preserve Neutrality* (mimeographed ms.), pp. 2-4.

23. Report of an address delivered by Osten Unden, former Minister of Foreign Affairs, at Katrineholm, December 15, 1940. (Mimeographed ms. issued by the Swedish Legation in Washington.)

24. *The American Swedish Monthly*, August, 1940, p. 22; and statement by Minister Boström, *American-Scandinavian Review*, Autumn, 1940, p. 242.

25. Speech before the *Riksdag*, August 16, 1940, quoted by Minister Boström in an interview with the Swedish-American Press; reprint by the *American-Scandinavian Review*, August 23, 1940.

26. Gunnar Hägglöf, *op. cit.*, and Marcus Wallenberg, Jr., in a speech delivered before the Swedish-American Chamber of Commerce, New York, December 17, 1940 (mimeographed ms.)

27. Hägglöf, *op. cit.*, p. 9. In the year 1938 these markets absorbed 70% of Sweden's total export. *Ibid.*, p. 3.

28. Wollmar Boström, press interview of August 23, 1940, reprint by the *American-Scandinavian Review*.

Index

A

Acland, Sir Richard, 41
Administrative Council (Norway), 208, 209
Africa, Italian Campaigns in, 39, 154, 164, 165, 166, 203
Agrarian Party (Sweden), 214
Agricultural Wages Board (England), 65
Agriculture, in England, 60, 72; U.S.S.R., 136-137, 142
Air-Raid Precautions Act (1937) (England), 8
Air-Raid Protection, 8-9, 18, 70
Albania, 145, 149, 153, 154, 197-198, 203
Alexander I, King, 202
Alexander, A. V., 20, 48
Alibert, 180, 183
Aliens Advisory Committees (England), 24
Aliens Order (England), 4
Alsace-Lorraine, 152
Amendola, 164
Amery, L. M. S., 21, 36
Anderson, Sir John, 9, 15, 18, 19, 21, 36
Ansaldo, 151
Anti-Comintern Pact, 124, 196-197, 200
Antonescu, General, 191
Arbeitsdienst (Compulsory Labor Service) (Norway), 206, 211
Archbishop of York, 41
Armed Forces (Conditions of Service) Act (1939) (England), 4

Asquith, Lord, 12
Attlee, Clement, 15, 17, 20, 31, 34
Austria, 80, 82, 104, 162

B

Badoglio, Marshal, 157, 166
Balbo, Italo, 158
Baldwin, Stanley, 12
Balfour, 12
Baltic Countries, 96, 138; See also Esthonia; Latvia; Lithuania
Baudoin, Paul, 183
Beaverbrook, Lord, 14, 18, 21, 48
Belgium, 117, 150
Bergery, Gaston, 177
Bessarabia, 120, 137
Beveridge, Sir William, 44
Bevin, Ernest, 14, 18, 21, 48, 66
Bianchi, Michele, 158
Blum, Léon, 180
Bohemia-Moravia, 191
Boris, King, 196, 197
Bosch, Karl, 87
Bouhler, Philip, 92
Brinon, Fernand de, 177
British Broadcasting Corp., 19, 33
British Employers' Confederation, 66
British Union of Fascists, 5-6
Brown, Ernest, 13, 14, 36
Bukovina, Northern, 120, 137
Bulgaria, 154, 160, 196-197, 200, 202
Bureau of Public Information (Sweden), 216
Burgin, Dr. Leslie, 13, 14, 36
Butler, Harold, 24

C

Cabinet, in England, 11; in Germany, 77; in Norway, 206; See also War Cabinet

Carol, King, 190, 191

Catholic Church, in Germany, 115-118

Cavagnari, Admiral, 157

Cavallero, General, 157, 158

Central Council of Trade Unions (U.S.S.R.), 133

Chamber of Deputies (France), 180, 182, 187

Chamberlain, Neville, 1, 2, 11, 12, 13, 15, 17-21, 23, 28, 31, 33, 36, 38, 43, 46, 47, 55, 66, 89, 106, 156

Charter of Labor (Italy), 163

Churchill, Winston, 11, 14, 15, 17, 19, 20, 22, 30, 31, 33, 34, 36, 40, 44, 106

Cianetti, 159

Ciano, Count Galeazzo, 148, 149, 159, 160, 197

Civil defense and evacuation, 8-11, 16, 24-25, 67-69

Civil Defense Act (1939) (England), 8

Civil Service, in England, 22-23, 47-48; in Germany, 80, 95-97; in Norway, 210

Civilian Advice Bureaus (England), 24

Clausewitz, 74, 97

Clemenceau, Georges, 171, 172, 173, 174, 187

Codreanu, 190

Commission of Soviet Control, 132

Committee of Imperial Defense (England), 2, 12

Communists, in England, 27, 31, 35, 39, 41; in France, 173, 174; in Norway, 206; in Sweden, 216

Communist Party of the U.S.S.R., 137, 138; congresses, 122, 123; influence in army, 129-130; influence in industry, 130; leading role, 126-127, 129; membership, 127-128, 131; purges, 128

Concordat of 1933, 117

Congress of Soviets, 125

Conscientious objectors, in England, 3, 6; See also Pacifists

Conscription, Military, in England, 2-4, 6, 69; in Germany, 114; in the U.S.S.R., 143

Conservative Party and Conservatives (England), 17, 20, 21, 26, 27, 34, 36, 38

Conservative Party (Sweden), 214

Constitution of 1814 (Norway), 205

Constitution of 1918 (No. 1) (U.S.S.R.), 126

Constitution of 1936 (U.S.S.R.), 125, 126, 127, 143

Constitutional Acts of 1940 (France), 178, 180, 182

Constitutional Law of 1875 (France), 182

Constitutional Law of 1940 (France), 180, 182

Consultative Committee (England), 66

Coördination of Defense, Minister for, (England), 11, 17

Corsica, 153

Council of Ministers (France), 183

Council of People's Commissars (U.S.S.R.), 132

Criminal Law Commission (Germany), 110

Croats, 165, 199, 200, 201, 202

Croix de Feu (France), 173

Cvetkovich, Dragisha, 199

Czechoslovakia, 102, 197

D

Daily Worker, (London), Suppression of, 7

Daladier, Edouard, 89, 156, 174, 180

Dalmatia, 202

Dalton, Hugh, 21

Danzig, 81, 82, 90

Dardanelles, 161, 193, 194, 195
Darlan, Admiral, 178, 183
De Vecchi, General, 157
"Decree Laws" (France), 186
Defense of the Realm Act (England), 5
Defense Acts (England), 4, 6-8, 15, 29, 35
Defense Regulations (England), 13, 15, 25, 32
Denmark, 150
Department of National Economy (Sweden), 215
Dicey, 7
Dobruja, 196
Doriot, Jacques, 177
Doumergue, Gaston, 186
Duca, Premier, 192
Duff Cooper, Alfred, 21
Duma (Estonia), 138
Duncan, Sir Andrew Rae, 20, 21, 48

E

Economic Council (U.S.S.R.), 132
Economic Policy Committee (England), 15
Economic Warfare, Creation of Ministry of (England), 19
Eden, Anthony, 19, 21
Egypt, 155
Elections, in England, 26-27; in U.S.S.R., 124-126, 129, 141-142; in France, 178, 180-181; in Sweden, 213-214
Eliot, T. S., 41
Emergency Committees (England), 9
Emergency Powers (Defense) Act, 1939 (England), 4, 5, 7, 8, 63, 71
Emergency Powers (Defense) Act, 1940 (England), 6, 7, 64
Emergency Powers (Defense) (No. 2) Act, 1940 (England), 6, 7, 35
Enabling Act (1933) (Germany), 77
Engels, Friedrich, 122

England, armed forces, 2-4; civil defense and evacuation, 8-11, 16, 24-25, 67-68; civil service, 22-23, 47-48; direction of military activities, 11-12; education, 67-70; government and labor, 63-67; growth of monopoly, 59; industrial conscription, 6, 15, 16; military conscription, 6, 69; ministerial changes, 18-22; Parliament, 25-40; production and supply, 16, 58-63; public finance, 49-53; regional and local organization, 9, 23-25, 70-73; social services, 53-58; War Cabinet, 16-18
English Commercial Corporation, Ltd., 62
Esthonia, annexation to U.S.S.R., 138; church, 140; collective farming, 141; new codes, 141; socialization, 138-140
Ethiopia, 49, 145, 146, 148, 149
Evacuation, See Civil Defense and Evacuation
Exchange Equalization Fund (England), 51

F

Factory Acts (England), change in administration of, 65
Farinacci, Roberto, 148, 161, 165, 166
Fascist Party (Italy), 165; relationship to army, 156
Fascists, in England, 5-6, 27, 39; in France, 172, 173, 174, 187; in Norway, 206, 208-211; in Roumania, 190-192; in Yugoslavia, 202
Faulhaber, Cardinal, 115
Feeding the People in War-Time, Sir John Orr and David Lubbock, 44
Finland, war with U.S.S.R., 120, 130, 151, 214, 216, 217
Fisher Act (England), 40
Fisher, H. A. L., 67
Fisher, Sir Warren, 22, 24
Flandin, Pierre, 183

Food, Creation of Ministry of (England), 18, 59-60
Food Policy Committee (England), 15
Food supply, in England, 18, 59-60; in Italy, 163; See also Rationing
Four-Year Plan (Germany), 76, 77, 108
France, causes of defeat, 171-175; elections, 180-181, 182; invasion by Germany, 151; Pétain régime, 175-187
France and the French, Sisley Huddleston, 179
Frank, 107
Fritsch, General von, 158
Frick, Dr. Wilhelm, 76, 79, 95
Funk, Dr. Walther, 76, 79, 86, 87

G

Gamelin, Marshal Maurice, 180
Gaue (Germany), 81-82, 105
Gayda, Virginio, 151
General Confederation of Employers (France), 184
General Confederation of Workers (France), 184
General Economic Council (Germany), 86-87
George II, King, 202
German-Italian military alliance, 147, 149, 152
German-Soviet Non-aggression Pact (1939), 103, 173
Germany, Church and State relations, 115-119; civil service, 80, 95-97; coördination of military and civilian branches of the government, 75-78; economic management, 83-88; growth of monopoly, 87-88; labor, 108-115; law, 104-108; morale, 88-93, 94-95; National Socialist Party, 93-99; Nazi revolution and the war, 118-119; regional organization, 78-83; trends in Nazi theory, 102-108

Gestapo (Germany), 119, 169
Gilmour, Sir John, 14
Goebbels, Dr. Joseph, 75, 91, 102, 108
Göring, Hermann, 75-78, 86, 87, 92
Gooch, G. P., 183, 186
Grand Council of Fascism (Italy), 163
Grandeur and Misery of Victory, Georges Clemenceau, 171
Grasset, Bernard, 176
Graziani, Marshal, 158, 159
Greece, 196; invasion of, 153-154, 155, 157, 160, 162, 164, 165, 166, 195, 197, 202-203
Greenwood, Arthur, 15, 17, 20, 40
Günther, Christian, 214, 217, 218

H

Haakon, King, 207, 208
Halifax, Lord, 17, 20
Hansson, Per Albin, 214, 217
Hatay Republic, 193
Haushofer, Karl, 101
Hayek, Professor F. A., 44
Hess, Rudolf, 75, 76, 86, 117
Himmler, Heinrich, 117, 169
Hitler, Adolf, 33, 74-77, 87, 88, 89, 91, 94, 98, 99, 101-105, 114, 117, 119, 147, 148, 150, 151, 171, 175, 177, 179, 189, 190, 194, 200-202
Hitler Youth, 92, 94
Hoare, Sir Samuel, 21, 36
Holland, 106, 117, 150
Home Security, Creation of Ministry of (England), 18
Hore-Belisha, Leslie, 20, 36
Hours of work, in England, 16; in Germany, 112, 114; in U.S.S.R., 133; See also Labor; Wages
House of Commons, 7, 16, 22, 26, 27, 28-32, 32-40 passim; secret sessions of, 30, 35
House of Lords, 22, 27, 28
Housing, in England, 56; in Germany, 115

How to Pay for the War, J. M.
  Keynes, 44
Howard, Roy, 124
Huber, E. R., 104
Huddleston, Sisley, 179
Hungary, 190, 202

I

Iceland, 212
Import Executive (England), 16
Independent Labor Party (England), 31, 35, 39
India, 40
Information, Creation of Ministry of (England), 19
Inonu, President Ismet, 195
International Law, Nazi view of, 105-108
Ireland, 2, 40
Iron Guard (Roumania), 190, 191, 192
Italy, campaigns in Greece and Africa, 153-155; change in personnel, 156-160; defeats by British, 158-159; entry into war, 151; growth of terrorism, 164-170; period of non-belligerency, 146-151; social and economic effects of war, 160-164; weakness of, 148-149

J

Japan, hostilities with U.S.S.R., 120
Jews, attacks on in Italy, 165, 166, attacks on in Roumania, 191
Jibuti, 153
Jibuti—Addis Ababa Railroad, 153
Joseph-Barthélemy, 183, 184

K

Keitel, Field-Marshal Wilhelm, 77
Keynes, J. M., 44
King in Council (England), 5, 6
Kircher, Dr. Rudolf, 89
Kirov, Sergei, 122, 123
Korizis, Alexander, 203
Körner, 87

Krupp, 193
Kvaternik, General Sladko, 202

L

Labor, in England, 6, 16, 63-67; in France, 63; in Germany, 63, 83, 84, 108-115; in Italy, 163; in Norway, 205, 211; in U.S.S.R., 133-135; *See also* Hours of work; Standard of living; Wages
Labor courts (Germany), 110
Labor front (Germany), 93, 108, 114
Labor Party and Laborites (England), 14, 17, 19, 20, 26, 27, 30-34, 36, 38, 39, 41
Labor party (Norway), 205, 206
Labor service (Germany), 92
Labor trustees (Germany), 109, 112
Lagarde, de, 101
Lammers, Dr., 77, 96
Landfried, Dr., 89
Latvia, annexation to U.S.S.R., 138; church, 140; collective farming, 142; new codes, 141; socialization, 138-140
Laval, Pierre, 177, 178, 183
Layton, Sir Walter, 44
Lederer, Emil, 119
Lees-Smith, H. B., 31
Lenin, V. I., 122
Levi, General, 165
Ley, Dr. Robert, 74, 83, 93, 111, 114
Liberal Party and Liberals (England), 19, 20, 21, 26, 27, 30, 31, 32, 36, 39
Libya, 159
Lithuania, annexation to U.S.S.R., 138; church, 140; collective farming, 142; new codes, 141; socialization, 138-140
Lloyd George, David, 11, 34, 36, 40, 75
Lloyd, Lord, 21, 36
London Passenger Transport Board, 61

Lord President's Committee (England), 15, 16
Low countries, invasion of, 151, 154; See also, Belgium; Holland
Lubbock, David, 44
Luther, Martin, 117

M

Manchukuo, hostilities with U.S. S.R., 120
Margesson, Capt. H. D., 21-22
Markovitch, 200
Martet, Jean. 187
Marx, Karl, 122
Marxian theory, evolution of in U.S.S.R., 122-124
Matchek, Dr. Vladimir, 199, 202
Matteoti, 164
Metaxas, Premier John, 202, 203
Military and Air Forces (Prolongation of Service) Act (1939) (England), 4
Military Service Act (1939) (England), 2, 3
Minister Council for National Defense (Germany), 75-78, 84-87, 95, 96, 111
Ministerial Committee on Military Coördination (England), 11
Ministry of Supply Act (1939) (England), 18
Monopoly, growth of, in England, 59; in Germany, 87-88
Morize, André, 173, 174
Morrison, Herbert, 9, 14, 15, 21, 48
Mosley, Sir Oswald, 5
Munich Conference (1938), 39, 102
Municipal Act (1935) (Germany), 80
Murry, J. Middleton, 41
Mussolini, Benito, 49, 145-147, 150-153, 159, 160, 166, 197, 198, 201, 203

N

Nasjonal Samling party (Norway), 206, 209, 210

National Arbitration Tribunal (England), 66
National Assembly (France), 176
National Assembly (Turkey), 195
National Assembly of Western Ukraine, 141
National Assembly of Western White Russia, 141
National Council (France), 181, 182
National Council of Social Service (England), 24
National Institution for Employment Exchanges and Unemployment Insurance (Germany), 109
National Labor Law (Germany), 109
National Peace Council (England), 41
National Registration Act (1939) (England), 4
National Service (Armed Forces) Act (1939) (England), 2, 3, 6
National Socialist Motor Corps (Germany), 94
National Socialist Party of Germany, 74, 81, 86, 92, 116-119; loss of prestige during war, 93-99
National Socialist Welfare Organization (Germany), 93-94
National Union, Government of (Sweden), 214
Naumann, 101
New Zealand, 51
Nice, 153
Niemöller, Pastor, 115
Norway, government before invasion, 205-206; invasion by Germany, 33, 106, 150, 151, 154, 205, 206-208, 216; Quisling government and its policies, 208-211
Norwegian Expedition (Franco-British), 12, 14, 20, 33, 35, 156
Norwegian Supreme Court, 208, 209
Nygaardsvold, Premier, 205, 207, 208

INDEX 247

O

Old Age and Widows Pensions Act
(1940) (England), 55
Orr, Sir John, 44
Osservatore Romano, growth of
circulation, 167-168
Ostmark Act (Germany), 82

P

Pacifists, in England, 27; *See also*
Conscientious objectors
Parliament, 7, 8, 11, 12, 25-40, 49, 55
Paul, Prince, 200, 202
Pavelitch, Dr. Ante, 202
Pavolini, 159
People's Commissariat of Justice of
the U.S.S.R., Orders of, 133
People's Convention (England), 41
People's Party (Sweden), 214
Perth, Lord, 197
Pétain, Marshal Henri Philippe, 175,
176, 178, 181-184
Peter, King, 200
Poland, 106, 124, 126, 142, 158; inva-
sion and occupation by Germany,
74, 78, 80, 90, 91, 96, 102, 105, 117,
147, 201; portion annexed to U.S.
S.R., 137; socialization in Soviet
portion, 141, 142
Pope Pius XII, 116, 117, 150
Popular front (France), 173
Posen, 80, 81, 82
Prasca, General, 157
Prices, in England, 45-46; in Ger-
many, 85-86, 113; in Italy, 161
Production and Supply, in England,
16, 58-63; in Germany, 83-88; in
Italy, 160-164; in U.S.S.R., 131-
137; *See also* Food supply; Labor
Production Council (England), 15
Production Executive (England), 16
Prolongation of Parliament Act
(England), 27
Protestants, in Germany, 115-118
Public Assistance Committees (Eng-
land), 71

Public Finance, in England, 49-53;
in Germany, 85
Public Services, in England, 58-63.

Q

Quisling, Major Vidkun, 206, 208-
211

R

Ramsay, Captain Archibald, 6
Rationing, in England, 19, 46; in
Germany, 83-85; in Italy, 161; *See
also* Food supply
Regional Commissioners (England),
4, 9, 24-25
Regional and Local Organization, in
England, 9, 23-25, 70-73; in France,
178, 181; in Germany, 78-83
Reichstag (Germany), 75, 94
Reith, Sir John (Lord), 36, 40
Representation of the People Act
(England), 40
Reserve and Auxiliary Forces Act
(1939) (England), 4
Reynaud, Paul, 174, 180
Ricci, 159
Riksdag (Sweden), 212-215
Riom trials, 179-180
Ripert, Professor, 180
Roumania, 196, 202; occupation by
German army, 153, 154, 160, 190-
192, 200
Royal Marines Act (1939) (Eng-
land), 4

S

Salter, Sir Arthur, 44
Sandler, Rickard, 214
Savoy, 153
Sayers, Dorothy, 41
Schacht, Dr. Hjalmar, 83
Schmitt, Carl, 104
Schoenerer, 101
Science in War, 44
Seim (Latvia and Lithuania), 138
Select Committee of the House of

Commons on National Expenditures, 16
Senate (France), 180, 182
Serbs, 199, 200, 201
Seyss-Inquart, Dr., 82
Shipping, Creation of Ministry of (England), 14, 62
Shop troops (Germany), 111
Sieburg, Friedrich, 176
Simon, Sir John, 21, 36, 50
Simovitch, General Dushan, 200, 201
Simplification Decree (Germany), 78, 79
Sinclair, Sir Archibald, 20, 31
Skoda, 193
Slovenes, 165, 200, 202
Social Democratic Party (Sweden), 214
Social services, in England, 53-58; in Germany, 86, 112, 115
Soddu, General, 157
Soviet of Nationalities (U.S.S.R.), 125
Soviet of the Union (U.S.S.R.), 125
Soviet Union (U.S.S.R.), addition of territory, 120; agriculture, 136-137; changing political theory, 122-124; Communist Party, 126-131; drive for production, 131-137; franchise and elections, 124-126; labor, 132-136; relations with Turkey, 193-195; Soviet institutions in new territories, 137-142
Spain, civil war in, 39, 145, 146, 148, 149
Squadristi (Italy), 168
Stalin, J. V., 122-125, 128
Stamp, Lord Josiah, 13-14
Standard of living, in England, 15-16, 56-57, 63-64; in Italy, 160-163; See also Hours of work; Labor; Wages
Stanley, Oliver, 20
State Employment Exchanges (Germany), 109-110

State of the Masses, Emil Lederer, 119
Statsraad (cabinet) (Norway), 206
Statutory Committee of Experts (Germany), 109
Storm Troops (Germany), 94
Storting (Parliament) (Norway), 206, 207, 210
Sudeten districts, 80, 81
Sudeten Gau Act (Germany), 81, 82
Superior Fascist Corporative Council (Albania), 198
Supply, Creation of Ministry of (England), 13, 18, 60-61
Supreme Court of Justice (France), 184
Supreme Court of the U.S.S.R., Orders of, 134
Supreme Soviet of the U.S.S.R., 125, 141
Sweden, 211; attempts to retain neutrality and independence, 216-219; continuation of Parliamentary government, 212-216; press and public information, 215-216

T

Tassinari, Giuseppe, 163
Taxes in England, 6, 45, 50-51; in Germany, 85; in Italy, 145, 163
Todt, Dr., 96
Trades Union Congress, General Council of (England), 66
Transylvania, 190, 191
Treachery Act (1940) (England), 6
Treasury (England), 47, 51
Trianon, Treaty of, 202
Tripartite Pact, See Anti-Comintern Pact
Tunisia, 153
Turkey, struggle for friendship of, 192-195

U

Ukraine, 120, 141
Unemployment Assistance (Emer-

gency Powers) Act (England), 55
Unemployment Assistance Board (England), 54, 55, 57, 71
United States, British Expenditure in, 51, 52; recognizes Pétain Government, 177
Utashi (Yugoslavia), 202

V

Vatican, 117, 167, 177
Versailles, Treaty of, 99, 102, 172
Vichy Government, *See* France; Pétain
Vickers, 193
Victor Emmanuel, King, 198
Vidovdan Constitution (Yugoslavia), 199

W

Wages, in England, 15, 45, 63-65; in Germany, 85-86, 108, 113, 114; in Italy, 161; in U.S.S.R., 133; *See also* Hours of work; Labor; Standard of living

Walz, G. A., 105
War Agricultural Executive Committees (England), 72
War Cabinet (England), 11, 16-18, 20, 48
War Damages Bill (England), 29
War Economy Ordinance (Germany), 84-85
West Prussia, 80
Weygand, General Maxime, 177
White Russia, 120, 141
Wilson, Sir Horace, 23
Woman's Labor Service (Germany), 92
Wood, Sir Kingsley, 18, 21, 50
Woolton (Lord), 21, 48
World War (I), 1, 5, 11, 16-17, 38, 67, 84, 143, 146, 157, 162, 171, 179, 198

Y

Yugoslavia, 199-202; invasion of, 197, 201-202, 203

Z

Zog, King, 197, 198